The Plant-Based Diet for Beginners

600 Easy, Delicious and Healthy Whole Food Recipes for Smart People on a Budget (21-Day Meal Plan to Reset & Energize Your Body)

Shoast Bentrin

Table of contents

Introduction

Diets have been dominating conversations and resolutions these days. With overeating, one of the greatest problems of first world countries, and because of social pressures surrounding youth to look skinny and beautiful; different diets have popped up each with their unique approaches. Unlike diet fads that promise a quick fix to lose weight, a plant-based diet increases overall wellness and helps to maintain a healthy body.

Are you interested to know more about the amazing plant-based diet?

Or, are you someone who is already implementing this fantastic diet but want to know more?

We have got you covered.

Read on to know more about plant-based diet and get started with its cooking.

Chapter 1: Understanding the Plant-Based Diet

What is Plant-Based Diet?

This diet means to mostly consume plant-derived food products such as greens, grains, fruits, and nuts. The individual can choose the level of restrictions on meat and other products. Being a vegan is not the only way to become someone who eats a plant-based diet. There are several types:

- Flexitarian

Those that follow this diet do not completely cut off any type of food. They can eat dairy, meat, and seafood. It's according to the person's needs

- Pescatarian

As the name suggests, in this diet along with plants, seafood and eggs can be eaten without hesitation.

- Vegetarian

Those that eat eggs and other dairy products with plant-based foods. They cannot eat fish or any meat.

- Vegan

They are strict plant-based food eaters who eat nothing in their diet but plant-derived foods.

Plants can provide high nutrients filled with protein and fat and lots of fiber but it lacks a few minerals and vitamins. To compensate for them, store-bought supplements need to be added to the diet.

Benefits of Plant-Based Diet

There are many benefits to follow this diet mainly overall increase in wellness and being less sick. The concept has been around for a long time that increasing consumption of plant-derived foods makes the person more active and healthier. These people also seem to be happier and less irritated which makes life easier and far more relaxing. There are other advantages which comes with the diet. Some of them are listed below:

- There's no need to count calories in this diet. It can be a tedious and time-wasting task that a busy person cannot afford. This diet simply allows some food and restricts the rest. A calorie doesn't tell much about the food, what nutrients are in it or is it healthy or not.
- It is a good way to lose weight. A recent 2018 control experiment showed that people that follow a vegan diet rather than those who eat meat, were more likely to lose weight. The study followed obese participants following there normal and some following vegan diets and the result was that dieters almost lost 15 pounds in 4 months.
- Plant-based foods are full of carbs and fiber which fills up the stomach quickly making you feel less hungry. You will consume less of the foods that will be no good for you like sodas or candies. Cravings will not hit you as hard as if you were hungry.
- There is a higher quantity of water in plant-based food which increases body metabolism and reduces appetite. Water has many benefits, being hydrated makes you have better hair, skin and makes you look fresh.

- Eating mostly plant-based foods increases mortality by preventing life long diseases. A recent 2019 done by the American Heart Association showed that plant-eaters were less likely to develop heart diseases. It is also linked with lowering the chances of stroke, diabetes type 2, hypertension, and obesity.
- It also has shown to increase insulin sensitivity in diabetic patients. In the 2009 study, over tens of thousands of participants were approached and the percentage of vegans developing diabetes was found to be 2.9% less than others. A review published in 2018 stated that diabetes is improved when following any diet that increases plant content.
- By following this diet, you will not only help yourself in becoming better but also push the environment to progress in the right direction. A lot of pollutants come from Barnes and poultry farms. Making meat puts high stress on our planet and by consuming less of it, you are leaving less of a carbon footprint. Also, by this diet, you are discouraging the use of meat as well.
- It doesn't require any sort of investment and a person can begin it as soon as they decide to. Plant-based products are everywhere and even in a normal diet, take a big portion of it. Some dieting programs and fads take a lot of money from people giving only temporary results but this diet has shown to reduce the most amount of weight.

For some people starting this diet can be hard but if you want to reach your weight loss goals or become generally more fit than this diet is suited for you.

How do You Start a Plant-Based Diet?

There are a few lifestyle changes one needs to do to start a plant-based diet. Going in too strongly will cause tension to build up only to be blown when a craving hit. Some may find it very difficult to follow but you only need to keep a few points in mind to achieve success.

- Increase greens in your diet. A variety of vegetables are present for choosing to offer different flavors and textures for soothing your tongue. Pick vegetables regularly for meal bases and a replacement for unhealthy snacks. The crunchiness and flavors of some veggies might decrease the likelihood of eating junk food.
- Most healthy diets don't just forbid the consumption of fats but instead tells you to replace bad fats which are derived from animals with good ones derived from plants. Seeds and olive oil are a good source of healthy fats which do not increase the body cholesterol levels.
- Cut down meat, especially red meat as much as you can. You can still consume it if you are following a more lenient diet but it is discouraged. Replace your meat with seafood or tofu which can be a good substitute for it.
- Rather than putting desserts on the table, you should place fruits or fruit dishes. They are a healthier option with the same hints of sugar to satisfy the sweet tooth. Some people crave sugar more, they can slowly cut off sugar from their diet by switching it for sweet fruits instead.
- Replace everyday cow's milk for plant-derived milk such as soy, almond, rice or coconut. Milk is an important part of a diet that is impractical to fully remove from the diet.
- Stay away from foods that have a lot of sugar like a Pepsi or are high in fat like french fries. Also do not buy processed food because they are riddled with salt and sugar, which are enemies to your body.
- Be aware that not every nutrient is being provided fully and arrange a replacement for that. Vit B12 is present in some cereal and in nutritional yeast. Iron is also less consumed so eat a healthy dose of cabbage, spinach or kidney beans to make up for it.

What to Eat and Avoid on a Plant-Based Diet?

You can eat:

- All vegetables, including greens like spinach, kale, chards, collards, asparagus, broccoli, cauliflower, bell peppers, tomatoes, onion, etc
- All fruits, including berries, avocado, apple, banana, watermelon, grapes, oranges, etc
- Plant-based alternates to meat like tofu and tempeh
- Plant-based milk and dairy products including coconut milk, almond milk, peanut butter, almond butter, cashew yogurt, etc
- All whole-grains, including brown rice, amaranth, quinoa, barley, all beans, whole wheat pasta, whole-grain bread, etc
- All nuts, including cashews, almonds, walnuts, macadamia nuts, etc
- All seeds like chia seeds, flaxseed, hempseeds, etc
- Lentils
- Millets
- Flax eggs
- Honey, maple syrup, coconut sugar, stevia, Splenda, erythritol, etc
- Unsweetened coffee and tea

You can not eat:

- Meat including beef, pork, and poultry
- Seafood including fish and shrimps
- Processed animal products like hot dogs, sausages
- Dairy items like butter, eggs, whole milk, yogurt, etc
- Sweetened drinks like soda, fruit juices, sweetened tea and coffee
- Fried food and fast foods
- White bread and white pasta

Chapter 2: Breakfast

Hot Pink Smoothie

Preparation time: 5 minutes; Cooking time: 0 minute; Servings: 1
Ingredients:

- 1 clementine, peeled, segmented
- 1/2 frozen banana
- 1 small beet, peeled, chopped
- 1/8 teaspoon sea salt
- 1/2 cup raspberries
- 1 tablespoon chia seeds
- 1/4 teaspoon vanilla extract, unsweetened
- 2 tablespoons almond butter
- 1 cup almond milk, unsweetened

Method:
1. Place all the ingredients in the order in a food processor or blender and then pulse for 2 to 3 minutes at high speed until smooth.
2. Pour the smoothie into a glass and then serve.

Nutrition Value:
   Calories: 278 Cal; Fat: 5.6 g; Carbs: 37.2 g; Protein: 6.2 g; Fiber: 13.2 g

Maca Caramel Frap

Preparation time: 5 minutes; Cooking time: 0 minute; Servings: 4
Ingredients:

- 1/2 of frozen banana, sliced
- 1/4 cup cashews, soaked for 4 hours
- 2 Medjool dates, pitted
- 1 teaspoon maca powder
- 1/8 teaspoon sea salt
- 1/2 teaspoon vanilla extract, unsweetened
- 1/4 cup almond milk, unsweetened
- 1/4 cup cold coffee, brewed

Method:
1. Place all the ingredients in the order in a food processor or blender and then pulse for 2 to 3 minutes at high speed until smooth.
2. Pour the smoothie into a glass and then serve.

Nutrition Value:
   Calories: 450 Cal; Fat: 170 g; Carbs: 64 g; Protein: 7 g; Fiber: 0 g

Peanut Butter Vanilla Green Shake

Preparation time: 5 minutes; Cooking time: 0 minute; Servings: 1
Ingredients:

- 1 teaspoon flax seeds
- 1 frozen banana
- 1 cup baby spinach
- 1/8 teaspoon sea salt
- 1/2 teaspoon ground cinnamon
- 1/4 teaspoon vanilla extract, unsweetened
- 2 tablespoons peanut butter, unsweetened
- 1/4 cup ice
- 1 cup coconut milk, unsweetened

Method:
1. Place all the ingredients in the order in a food processor or blender and then pulse for 2 to 3 minutes at high speed until smooth.
2. Pour the smoothie into a glass and then serve.

Nutrition Value:
   Calories: 298 Cal; Fat: 11 g; Carbs: 32 g; Protein: 24 g; Fiber: 8 g

Green Colada

Preparation time: 5 minutes; Cooking time: 0 minute; Servings: 1

Ingredients:

- 1/2 cup frozen pineapple chunks
- 1/2 banana
- 1/2 teaspoon spirulina powder
- 1/4 teaspoon vanilla extract, unsweetened
- 1 cup of coconut milk

Method:

1. Place all the ingredients in the order in a food processor or blender and then pulse for 2 to 3 minutes at high speed until smooth.
2. Pour the smoothie into a glass and then serve.

Nutrition Value:

Calories: 127 Cal; Fat: 3 g; Carbs: 25 g; Protein: 3 g; Fiber: 4 g

Chocolate Oat Smoothie

Preparation time: 5 minutes; Cooking time: 0 minute; Servings: 1

Ingredients:

- ¼ cup rolled oats
- 1 ½ tablespoon cocoa powder, unsweetened
- 1 teaspoon flax seeds
- 1 large frozen banana
- 1/8 teaspoon sea salt
- 1/8 teaspoon cinnamon
- ¼ teaspoon vanilla extract, unsweetened
- 2 tablespoons almond butter
- 1 cup coconut milk, unsweetened

Method:

1. Place all the ingredients in the order in a food processor or blender and then pulse for 2 to 3 minutes at high speed until smooth.
2. Pour the smoothie into a glass and then serve.

Nutrition Value:

Calories: 262 Cal; Fat: 7.3 g; Carbs: 50.4 g; Protein: 8.1 g; Fiber: 9.6 g

Peach Crumble Shake

Preparation time: 5 minutes; Cooking time: 0 minute; Servings: 1

Ingredients:

- 1 tablespoon chia seeds
- ¼ cup rolled oats
- 2 peaches, pitted, sliced
- ¾ teaspoon ground cinnamon
- 1 Medjool date, pitted
- ½ teaspoon vanilla extract, unsweetened
- 2 tablespoons lemon juice
- ½ cup of water
- 1 tablespoon coconut butter
- 1 cup coconut milk, unsweetened

Method:

1. Place all the ingredients in the order in a food processor or blender and then pulse for 2 to 3 minutes at high speed until smooth.
2. Pour the smoothie into a glass and then serve.

Nutrition Value:

Calories: 270 Cal; Fat: 4 g; Carbs: 28 g; Protein: 25 g; Fiber: 3 g

Wild Ginger Green Smoothie

Preparation time: 5 minutes; Cooking time: 0 minute; Servings: 1

Ingredients:

- 1/2 cup pineapple chunks, frozen
- 1/2 cup chopped kale
- 1/2 frozen banana
- 1 tablespoon lime juice

- 2 inches ginger, peeled, chopped
- 1/2 cup coconut milk, unsweetened
- 1/2 cup coconut water

Method:
1. Place all the ingredients in the order in a food processor or blender and then pulse for 2 to 3 minutes at high speed until smooth.
2. Pour the smoothie into a glass and then serve.

Nutrition Value:
Calories: 331 Cal; Fat: 14 g; Carbs: 40 g; Protein: 16 g; Fiber: 9 g

Berry Beet Velvet Smoothie

Preparation time: 5 minutes; Cooking time: 0 minute; Servings: 1

Ingredients:
- 1/2 of frozen banana
- 1 cup mixed red berries
- 1 Medjool date, pitted
- 1 small beet, peeled, chopped
- 1 tablespoon cacao powder
- 1 teaspoon chia seeds
- 1/4 teaspoon vanilla extract, unsweetened
- 1/2 teaspoon lemon juice
- 2 teaspoons coconut butter
- 1 cup coconut milk, unsweetened

Method:
1. Place all the ingredients in the order in a food processor or blender and then pulse for 2 to 3 minutes at high speed until smooth.
2. Pour the smoothie into a glass and then serve.

Nutrition Value:
Calories: 234 Cal; Fat: 5 g; Carbs: 42 g; Protein: 11 g; Fiber: 7 g

Spiced Strawberry Smoothie

Preparation time: 5 minutes; Cooking time: 0 minute; Servings: 1

Ingredients:
- 1 tablespoon goji berries, soaked
- 1 cup strawberries
- 1/8 teaspoon sea salt
- 1 frozen banana
- 1 Medjool date, pitted
- 1 scoop vanilla-flavored whey protein
- 2 tablespoons lemon juice
- ¼ teaspoon ground ginger
- ½ teaspoon ground cinnamon
- 1 tablespoon almond butter
- 1 cup almond milk, unsweetened

Method:
1. Place all the ingredients in the order in a food processor or blender and then pulse for 2 to 3 minutes at high speed until smooth.
2. Pour the smoothie into a glass and then serve.

Nutrition Value:
Calories: 182 Cal; Fat: 1.3 g; Carbs: 34 g; Protein: 6.4 g; Fiber: 0.7 g

Banana Bread Shake with Walnut Milk

Preparation time: 5 minutes; Cooking time: 0 minute; Servings: 2

Ingredients:
- 2 cups sliced frozen bananas
- 3 cups walnut milk
- 1/8 teaspoon grated nutmeg
- 1 tablespoon maple syrup
- 1 teaspoon ground cinnamon
- 1/2 teaspoon vanilla extract, unsweetened
- 2 tablespoons cacao nibs

Method:

1. Place all the ingredients in the order in a food processor or blender and then pulse for 2 to 3 minutes at high speed until smooth.
2. Pour the smoothie into two glasses and then serve.

Nutrition Value:
Calories: 339.8 Cal; Fat: 19 g; Carbs: 39 g; Protein: 4.3 g; Fiber: 1 g

Double Chocolate Hazelnut Espresso Shake

Preparation time: 5 minutes; Cooking time: 0 minute; Servings: 1
Ingredients:
- 1 frozen banana, sliced
- 1/4 cup roasted hazelnuts
- 4 Medjool dates, pitted, soaked
- 2 tablespoons cacao nibs, unsweetened
- 1 1/2 tablespoons cacao powder, unsweetened
- 1/8 teaspoon sea salt
- 1 teaspoon vanilla extract, unsweetened
- 1 cup almond milk, unsweetened
- 1/2 cup ice
- 4 ounces espresso, chilled

Method:
1. Place all the ingredients in the order in a food processor or blender and then pulse for 2 to 3 minutes at high speed until smooth.
2. Pour the smoothie into a glass and then serve.

Nutrition Value:
Calories: 210 Cal; Fat: 5 g; Carbs: 27 g; Protein: 16.8 g; Fiber: 0.2 g

Strawberry, Banana and Coconut Shake

Preparation time: 5 minutes; Cooking time: 0 minute; Servings: 1
Ingredients:
- 1 tablespoon coconut flakes
- 1 1/2 cups frozen banana slices
- 8 strawberries, sliced
- 1/2 cup coconut milk, unsweetened
- 1/4 cup strawberries for topping

Method:
1. Place all the ingredients in the order in a food processor or blender, except for topping and then pulse for 2 to 3 minutes at high speed until smooth.
2. Pour the smoothie into a glass and then serve.

Nutrition Value:
Calories: 335 Cal; Fat: 5 g; Carbs: 75 g; Protein: 4 g; Fiber: 9 g

Tropical Vibes Green Smoothie

Preparation time: 5 minutes; Cooking time: 0 minute; Servings: 1
Ingredients:
- 2 stalks of kale, ripped
- 1 frozen banana
- 1 mango, peeled, pitted, chopped
- 1/8 teaspoon sea salt
- 1/4 cup of coconut yogurt
- ½ teaspoon vanilla extract, unsweetened
- 1 tablespoon ginger juice
- ½ cup of orange juice
- ½ cup of coconut water

Method:
1. Place all the ingredients in the order in a food processor or blender and then pulse for 2 to 3 minutes at high speed until smooth.
2. Pour the smoothie into a glass and then serve.

Nutrition Value:
Calories: 197.5 Cal; Fat: 1.3 g; Carbs: 30 g; Protein: 16.3 g; Fiber: 4.8 g

Peanut Butter and Mocha Smoothie

Preparation time: 5 minutes; Cooking time: 0 minute; Servings: 1
Ingredients:

- 1 frozen banana, chopped
- 1 scoop of chocolate protein powder
- 2 tablespoons rolled oats
- 1/8 teaspoon sea salt
- ¼ teaspoon vanilla extract, unsweetened
- 1 teaspoon cocoa powder, unsweetened
- 2 tablespoons peanut butter
- 1 shot of espresso
- ½ cup almond milk, unsweetened

Method:

1. Place all the ingredients in the order in a food processor or blender and then pulse for 2 to 3 minutes at high speed until smooth.
2. Pour the smoothie into a glass and then serve.

Nutrition Value:

Calories: 380 Cal; Fat: 14 g; Carbs: 29 g; Protein: 38 g; Fiber: 4 g

Tahini Shake with Cinnamon and Lime

Preparation time: 5 minutes; Cooking time: 0 minute; Servings: 1
Ingredients:

- 1 frozen banana
- 2 tablespoons tahini
- 1/8 teaspoon sea salt
- ¾ teaspoon ground cinnamon
- ¼ teaspoon vanilla extract, unsweetened
- 2 teaspoons lime juice
- 1 cup almond milk, unsweetened

Method:

1. Place all the ingredients in the order in a food processor or blender and then pulse for 2 to 3 minutes at high speed until smooth.
2. Pour the smoothie into a glass and then serve.

Nutrition Value:

Calories: 225 Cal; Fat: 15 g; Carbs: 22 g; Protein: 6 g; Fiber: 8 g

Ginger and Greens Smoothie

Preparation time: 5 minutes; Cooking time: 0 minute; Servings: 1
Ingredients:

- 1 frozen banana
- 2 cups baby spinach
- 2-inch piece of ginger, peeled, chopped
- ¼ teaspoon cinnamon
- ¼ teaspoon vanilla extract, unsweetened
- 1/8 teaspoon salt
- 1 scoop vanilla protein powder
- 1/8 teaspoon cayenne pepper
- 2 tablespoons lemon juice
- 1 cup of orange juice

Method:

1. Place all the ingredients in the order in a food processor or blender and then pulse for 2 to 3 minutes at high speed until smooth.
2. Pour the smoothie into a glass and then serve.

Nutrition Value:

Calories: 320 Cal; Fat: 7 g; Carbs: 64 g; Protein: 10 g; Fiber: 12 g

Beet and Blood Orange Smoothie

Preparation time: 5 minutes; Cooking time: 0 minute; Servings: 1
Ingredients:

- 1 small blood orange, peeled, segmented
- 1 medium beet, peeled, diced
- ½ of frozen banana
- ⅛ teaspoon ground nutmeg
- ¼ teaspoon of sea salt
- ¼ teaspoon ground cardamom
- 2 tablespoons lemon juice
- ½ teaspoon ground cinnamon
- 1 tablespoon almond butter
- 1 cup of coconut milk, unsweetened

Method:
1. Place all the ingredients in the order in a food processor or blender and then pulse for 2 to 3 minutes at high speed until smooth.
2. Pour the smoothie into a glass and then serve.

Nutrition Value:
Calories: 204 Cal; Fat: 8 g; Carbs: 22 g; Protein: 11 g; Fiber: 8 g

Sweet Potato Smoothie

Preparation time: 5 minutes; Cooking time: 0 minute; Servings: 1
Ingredients:
- 1/2 cup frozen zucchini pieces
- 1 cup cubed cooked sweet potato, frozen
- 1/2 frozen banana
- 1/2 teaspoon sea salt
- 1/2 teaspoon cinnamon
- 1 scoop of vanilla protein powder
- 1/4 teaspoon nutmeg
- 1 tablespoon almond butter
- 1 1/2 cups almond milk, unsweetened

Method:
1. Place all the ingredients in the order in a food processor or blender and then pulse for 2 to 3 minutes at high speed until smooth.
2. Pour the smoothie into a glass and then serve.

Nutrition Value:
Calories: 235 Cal; Fat: 9.2 g; Carbs: 24 g; Protein: 14.6 g; Fiber: 2.4 g

Strawberry and Raspberry Smoothie

Preparation time: 5 minutes; Cooking time: 0 minute; Servings: 1
Ingredients:
- 1 cup frozen raspberries
- 3 Medjool dates, pitted
- 1 cup spinach
- 1 cup of frozen strawberries
- 1 scoop of vanilla protein powder
- 2 tablespoons almond butter
- 1 3/4 cups almond milk

Method:
1. Place all the ingredients in the order in a food processor or blender and then pulse for 2 to 3 minutes at high speed until smooth.
2. Pour the smoothie into a glass and then serve.

Nutrition Value:
Calories: 128 Cal; Fat: 2.6 g; Carbs: 20.1 g; Protein: 8.3 g; Fiber: 1.7 g

Chocolate Cherry Smoothie

Preparation time: 5 minutes; Cooking time: 0 minute; Servings: 1
Ingredients:
- 1 1/2 cups frozen cherries, pitted
- 1 cup spinach

- 1/2 small frozen banana
- 2 tablespoon cacao powder, unsweetened
- 1 tablespoon chia seeds
- 1 scoop of vanilla protein powder
- 1 teaspoon spirulina
- 1 1/2 cups almond milk, unsweetened

Method:
1. Place all the ingredients in the order in a food processor or blender and then pulse for 2 to 3 minutes at high speed until smooth.
2. Pour the smoothie into a glass and then serve.

Nutrition Value:
Calories: 284.6 Cal; Fat: 6.1 g; Carbs: 54.4 g; Protein: 12.5 g; Fiber: 11 g

Chocolate Banana Smoothie

Preparation time: 5 minutes; Cooking time: 0 minute; Servings: 1
Ingredients:
- 1 cup spinach
- 1 frozen banana
- 1 tablespoon chia seeds
- 2 tablespoon cacao powder, unsweetened
- 1 tablespoon ground flax seeds
- 1/2 teaspoon sea salt
- 1 teaspoon maca powder
- 1 scoop of vanilla protein powder
- 1 1/2 cups almond milk, unsweetened

Method:
1. Place all the ingredients in the order in a food processor or blender and then pulse for 2 to 3 minutes at high speed until smooth.
2. Pour the smoothie into a glass and then serve.

Nutrition Value:
Calories: 285 Cal; Fat: 3 g; Carbs: 63.1 g; Protein: 2.1 g; Fiber: 1.3 g

Lemon and Blueberry Smoothie

Preparation time: 5 minutes; Cooking time: 0 minute; Servings: 1
Ingredients:
- 1 1/2 cups frozen blueberries
- 1/2 frozen banana
- 1 tablespoon chia seeds
- 3 tablespoon lemon juice
- 1 teaspoon lemon zest
- 1 1/2 teaspoon cinnamon
- 1 1/2 cups almond milk, unsweetened
- 1 scoop of vanilla protein powder

Method:
1. Place all the ingredients in the order in a food processor or blender and then pulse for 2 to 3 minutes at high speed until smooth.
2. Pour the smoothie into a glass and then serve.

Nutrition Value:
Calories: 317 Cal; Fat: 4 g; Carbs: 67 g; Protein: 6 g; Fiber: 9 g

Mixed Berry Smoothie

Preparation time: 5 minutes; Cooking time: 0 minute; Servings: 1
Ingredients:
- 1/2 cup frozen raspberries
- 1/2 cup frozen blueberries
- 1/2 cup frozen strawberries
- 1 cup spinach
- 1 scoop of vanilla protein powder
- 1/2 frozen banana
- 1 3/4 cups almond milk, unsweetened

Method:
1. Place all the ingredients in the order in a food processor or blender and then pulse for 2 to 3 minutes at high speed until smooth.

2. Pour the smoothie into a glass and then serve.
Nutrition Value:
    Calories: 100 Cal; Fat: 100 g; Carbs: 100 g; Protein: 100 g; Fiber: 100 g

Kale and Spinach Smoothie

Preparation time: 5 minutes; Cooking time: 0 minute; Servings: 1
Ingredients:
- 1 cup spinach
- 1 cup kale
- 1 frozen banana
- 3 small dates, pitted
- 1 1/4 cup almond milk, unsweetened
- 1 scoop of vanilla protein powder
- 1 teaspoon cinnamon

Method:
1. Place all the ingredients in the order in a food processor or blender and then pulse for 2 to 3 minutes at high speed until smooth.
2. Pour the smoothie into a glass and then serve.

Nutrition Value:
    Calories: 158 Cal; Fat: 3.4 g; Carbs: 33.4 g; Protein: 3.4 g; Fiber: 5.9 g

Mango and Pineapple Smoothie

Preparation time: 5 minutes; Cooking time: 0 minute; Servings: 1
Ingredients:
- 3/4 cup mango chunks, frozen
- 1 cup sliced cucumber
- 1 cup pineapple chunks, frozen
- 2 cups fresh spinach
- 1 scoop of vanilla protein powder
- 1 teaspoon moringa powder
- 1 teaspoon pure vanilla extract, unsweetened
- 1 2/3 cup almond milk, unsweetened

Method:
1. Place all the ingredients in the order in a food processor or blender and then pulse for 2 to 3 minutes at high speed until smooth.
2. Pour the smoothie into a glass and then serve.

Nutrition Value:
    Calories: 335 Cal; Fat: 11 g; Carbs: 50 g; Protein: 4 g; Fiber: 2 g

Beet and Orange Smoothie ✔

Preparation time: 5 minutes; Cooking time: 0 minute; Servings: 1
Ingredients:
- 1 cup chopped zucchini rounds, frozen
- 1 cup spinach
- 1 small peeled navel orange, frozen
- 1 small chopped beet
- 1 scoop of vanilla protein powder
- 1 cup almond milk, unsweetened

Method:
1. Place all the ingredients in the order in a food processor or blender and then pulse for 2 to 3 minutes at high speed until smooth.
2. Pour the smoothie into a glass and then serve.

Nutrition Value:
    Calories: 253 Cal; Fat: 5 g; Carbs: 44.6 g; Protein: 3 g; Fiber: 8 g

Peanut Butter and Pumpkin Smoothie

Preparation time: 5 minutes; Cooking time: 0 minute; Servings: 1
Ingredients:
- 1/2 cup peach slices, frozen
- 2 teaspoon ground ginger

- 1/2 frozen banana
- 1 teaspoon cinnamon
- 1 scoop of vanilla protein powder
- 4 tablespoon powdered peanut butter
- 5 drops liquid stevia
- 1 cup almond milk, unsweetened
- 1/2 cup pumpkin puree

Method:
1. Place all the ingredients in the order in a food processor or blender and then pulse for 2 to 3 minutes at high speed until smooth.
2. Pour the smoothie into a glass and then serve.

Nutrition Value:
Calories: 366 Cal; Fat: 7.8 g; Carbs: 47 g; Protein: 33 g; Fiber: 13 g

Peanut Butter and Coffee Smoothie

Preparation time: 5 minutes; Cooking time: 0 minute; Servings: 1
Ingredients:
- 2 small frozen banana
- 1/2 teaspoon ground turmeric
- 1 tablespoon chia seeds
- 1 scoop of chocolate protein powder
- 2 tablespoons Peanut Butter
- 1 cup strong coffee, brewed

Method:
1. Place all the ingredients in the order in a food processor or blender and then pulse for 2 to 3 minutes at high speed until smooth.
2. Pour the smoothie into a glass and then serve.

Nutrition Value:
Calories: 189 Cal; Fat: 7 g; Carbs: 24.5 g; Protein: 10.3 g; Fiber: 2.6 g

Blueberry and Sweet Potato Smoothie

Preparation time: 5 minutes; Cooking time: 0 minute; Servings: 1
Ingredients:
- 1 1/4 cup frozen blueberries
- 1/2 cup frozen sweet potato, cooked
- 1/8 teaspoon sea salt
- 1 tablespoon cacao powder
- 1 scoop of chocolate protein powder
- 1 cup almond milk

Method:
1. Place all the ingredients in the order in a food processor or blender and then pulse for 2 to 3 minutes at high speed until smooth.
2. Pour the smoothie into a glass and then serve.

Nutrition Value:
Calories: 150.7 Cal; Fat: 2.9 g; Carbs: 27 g; Protein: 7.4 g; Fiber: 4.5 g

Chocolate, Avocado, and Banana Smoothie

Preparation time: 5 minutes; Cooking time: 0 minute; Servings: 1
Ingredients:
- 1 medium frozen banana
- 2 small dates, pitted
- 1/2 cup steamed and frozen cauliflower florets
- 1/4 of a medium avocado
- 1 teaspoon cinnamon
- 1 tablespoon cacao powder
- 1/2 teaspoon sea salt
- 1 teaspoon maca
- 1/2 scoop of vanilla protein powder
- 2 tablespoon cacao nibs
- 1 tablespoon almond butter
- 1 cup almond milk

Method:
1. Place all the ingredients in the order in a food processor or blender and then pulse for 2 to 3 minutes at high speed until smooth.

2. Pour the smoothie into a glass and then serve.

Nutrition Value:
Calories: 100 Cal; Fat: 100 g; Carbs: 100 g; Protein: 100 g; Fiber: 100 g

Breakfast Sandwich

Preparation time: 5 minutes; Cooking time: 6 minutes; Servings: 4

Ingredients:
- ¼ of a medium avocado, sliced
- 1 vegan sausage patty
- 2 teaspoon olive oil
- 1 cup kale
- 1/8 teaspoon salt
- 1/8 teaspoon black pepper
- 1 Tablespoon pepitas
- 1 English muffin, halved, toasted

For the Sauce:
- 1 teaspoon jalapeno, chopped
- 1/8 teaspoon smoky paprika
- 1 tablespoon mayonnaise, vegan

Method:
1. Take a sauté pan, place it over medium heat, add oil and when hot, add the patty and cook for 2 minutes.
2. Then slip the patty, push it to one side of the pan, add kale and pepitas to the other side, season with black pepper and salt, and cook for 2 to 3 minutes until kale has softened.
3. When done, remove the pan from heat and prepare the sauce by whisking its ingredients until combined.
4. Assemble the sandwich and for this, spread mayonnaise on the inside of muffin, top with avocado slices and patty, and then top with kale and pepitas.
5. Serve straight away

Nutrition Value:
Calories: 207.3 Cal; Fat: 4.5 g; Carbs: 26.2 g; Protein: 15.5 g; Fiber: 8 g

Broccoli and Quinoa Breakfast Patties

Preparation time: 5 minutes; Cooking time: 6 minutes; Servings: 4

Ingredients:
- 1 cup cooked quinoa, cooked
- 1/2 cup shredded broccoli florets
- 1/2 cup shredded carrots
- 2 cloves of garlic, minced
- 2 teaspoon parsley
- 1 1/2 teaspoon onion powder
- 1 1/2 teaspoon garlic powder
- 1/3 teaspoon salt
- 1/4 teaspoon black pepper
- 1/2 cup bread crumbs, gluten-free
- 2 tablespoon coconut oil
- 2 flax eggs

Method:
1. Prepare patties and for this, place all the ingredients in a large bowl, except for oil and stir until well combined and then shape the mixture into patties.
2. Take a skillet pan, place it over medium heat, add oil and when hot, add prepared patties in it and cook for 3 minutes per side until golden brown and crispy.
3. Serve patties with vegan sour creams.

Nutrition Value:
Calories: 229.6Cal; Fat: 11.1 g; Carbs: 27.7g; Protein: 9.3g; Fiber: 6.6 g

Potato Skillet Breakfast

Preparation time: 5 minutes; Cooking time: 15 minutes; Servings: 5

Ingredients:
- 1 ½ cup cooked black beans
- 1 1/4 pounds potatoes, diced
- 12 ounces spinach, destemmed
- 1 1/4 pounds red potatoes, diced

- 2 small avocados, sliced, for topping
- 1 medium green bell pepper, diced
- 1 jalapeno, minced
- 1 large white onion, diced
- 1 medium red bell pepper, diced
- 3 cloves of garlic, minced
- 1/2 teaspoon red chili powder
- 1/4 teaspoon salt
- 1 teaspoon cumin
- 1 tablespoon canola oil

Method:
1. Switch on the oven, then set it to 425 degrees F and let it preheat.
2. Meanwhile, take a skillet pan, place it over medium heat, add oil and when hot, add potatoes, season with salt, chili powder, and cumin, stir until mixed and cook for 2 minutes.
3. Transfer pan into the oven and roast potatoes for 20 minutes until cooked, stirring halfway through.
4. Then add remaining onion, bell peppers, garlic, and jalapeno, continue roasting for another 15 minutes, stirring halfway, and remove the pan from heat.
5. Transfer pan over medium heat, cook for 5 to 10 minutes until potatoes are thoroughly cooked, then stir spinach and beans and cook for 3 minutes until spinach leaves have wilted.
6. When done, top the skillet with cilantro and avocado and then serve.

Nutrition Value:
Calories: 198.6 Cal; Fat: 7 g; Carbs: 32 g; Protein: 3.8 g; Fiber: 4.4 g

Scrambled Tofu Breakfast Tacos

Preparation time: 5 minutes; Cooking time: 10 minutes; Servings: 4
Ingredients:
- 12 ounces tofu, pressed, drained
- 1/2 cup grape tomatoes, quartered
- 1 medium red pepper, diced
- 1 medium avocado, sliced
- 1 clove of garlic, minced
- 1/4 teaspoon ground turmeric
- 1/4 teaspoon ground black pepper
- 1/4 teaspoon salt
- 1/4 teaspoon cumin
- 1 teaspoon olive oil
- 8 corn tortillas

Method:
1. Take a skillet pan, place it over medium heat, add oil and when hot, add pepper and garlic and cook for 2 minutes.
2. Then add tofu, crumble it, sprinkle with black pepper, salt, and all the spices, stir and cook for 5 minutes.
3. When done, distribute tofu between tortilla, top with tomato and avocado, and serve.

Nutrition Value:
Calories: 240 Cal; Fat: 8 g; Carbs: 26 g; Protein: 12 g; Fiber: 4 g

Peanut Butter and Banana Bread Granola

Preparation time: 10 minutes; Cooking time: 32 minutes; Servings: 6
Ingredients:
- 1/2 cup Quinoa
- 1/2 cup mashed banana
- 3 cup rolled oats, old-fashioned
- 1 cup banana chips, crushed
- 1 cup peanuts, salted
- 1 teaspoon. salt
- 1 teaspoon. cinnamon
- 1/4 cup brown sugar
- 1/4 cup honey
- 2 teaspoon. vanilla extract, unsweetened
- 1/3 cup peanut butter
- 6 tablespoon. unsalted butter

Method:

1. Switch on the oven, then set it to 325 degrees F and let it preheat.
2. Meanwhile, take two rimmed baking sheets, line them with parchment sheets, and set aside until required.
3. Place oats in a bowl, add quinoa, banana chips, cinnamon, salt, and sugar and stir until combined.
4. Take a small saucepan, place it over medium-low heat, add butter and honey and cook for 4 minutes until melted, stirring frequently.
5. Then remove the pan from heat, add banana and vanilla, stir until mixed, then spoon the mixture into the oat mixture and stir until incorporated.
6. Distribute granola evenly between two baking sheets, spread evenly, and then bake for 25 minutes until golden brown, rotating the sheets halfway.
7. When done, transfer baking sheets on wire racks, cool the granola, then break it into pieces and serve.
8. Serve straight away.

Nutrition Value:
Calories: 655 Cal; Fat: 36 g; Carbs: 70 g; Protein: 18 g; Fiber: 12 g

Sweet Potato Breakfast Hash

Preparation time: 5 minutes; Cooking time: 28 minutes; Servings: 4
Ingredients:

- 4 cups cubed sweet potatoes, peeled
- 1/2 teaspoon sea salt
- 1/2 teaspoon turmeric
- 1/2 teaspoon cumin
- 1 teaspoon smoked paprika
- 2 cups diced white onion
- 2 cloves of garlic, peeled, minced
- 1/4 cup chopped cilantro
- 1 tablespoon coconut oil
- ½ cup vegan guacamole, for serving
- 1 ½ cup pica de Gallo

Method:
1. Take a skillet pan, place it over medium heat, add oil and when it melts, add onion, potatoes, and garlic, season with salt, paprika, turmeric, and cumin, stir and cook for 25 minutes until potatoes are slightly caramelized.
2. Then remove the pan from heat, add cilantro and distribute evenly between serving plates.
3. Top the sweet potato hash with guacamole and pico de gallo and then serve.

Nutrition Value:
Calories: 211.3 Cal; Fat: 8 g; Carbs: 22.2 g; Protein: 12.5 g; Fiber: 3.5 g

Chickpea Flour Omelet

Preparation time: 5 minutes; Cooking time: 12 minutes; Servings: 1
Ingredients:

- 1/4 cup chickpea flour
- 1/2 teaspoon chopped chives
- ½ cup spinach, chopped
- 1/4 teaspoon turmeric
- 1/4 teaspoon garlic powder
- 1/8 teaspoon ground black pepper
- 1/2 teaspoon baking power
- 1 tablespoon nutritional yeast
- 1/2 teaspoon vegan egg
- 1/4 cup and 1 tablespoon water

Method:
1. Take a bowl, place all the ingredients in it, except for spinach, whisk until combined and let it stand for 5 minutes.
2. Then take a skillet pan, place it over low heat, grease it with oil and when hot, pour in prepared and cook for 3 minutes until edges are dry.
3. Then top half of the omelet with spinach, fold with the other half and continue cooking for 2 minutes.

4. Slide omelet to a plate and serve with ketchup.
Nutrition Value:
Calories: 150 Cal; Fat: 2 g; Carbs: 24.4 g; Protein: 10.2 g; Fiber: 5.8 g

Chocolate Chip, Strawberry and Oat Waffles

Preparation time: 10 minutes; Cooking time: 25 minutes; Servings: 6
Ingredients:
- 6 tablespoons chocolate chips, semi-sweet
- ½ cup chopped strawberries
- Powdered sugar as needed for topping

Dry Ingredients:
- 1/4 cup oats
- 1 1/2 tablespoon ground flaxseeds
- 1 1/2 cup whole wheat pastry flour
- 2 1/2 tablespoon cocoa powder
- 1/4 teaspoon salt
- 2 teaspoons baking powder

Wet Ingredients:
- 1/3 cup mashed bananas
- 2 tablespoon maple syrup
- 2 tablespoon coconut oil
- 1/2 teaspoon vanilla extract, unsweetened
- 1/4 cup applesauce, unsweetened
- 1 3/4 cup almond milk, unsweetened

Method:
1. Take a medium bowl, place all the dry ingredients in it, and whisk until mixed.
2. Take a large bowl, place all the wet ingredients in it, whisk until combined, and then whisk in dry ingredients mixture in four batches until incorporated, don't overmix.
3. Let the batter stand at room temperature for 5 minutes and in the meantime, switch on the waffle iron and let it preheat until hot.
4. Then ladle one-sixth of the batter in it and cook until golden brown and firm.
5. Cook remaining waffles in the same manner and when done, top them with chocolate chips and berries, sprinkle with sugar and then serve.

Nutrition Value:
Calories: 261 Cal; Fat: 10 g; Carbs: 41 g; Protein: 6 g; Fiber: 6 g

Vegetarian Breakfast Casserole

Preparation time: 10 minutes; Cooking time: 35 minutes; Servings: 4
Ingredients:
- 5 medium potatoes, about 22 ounces, boiled
- 10 ounces silken tofu
- 5 ounces tempeh, cubed
- 1 tablespoon chives, cut into rings
- 1 medium white onion, peeled chopped
- ¾ teaspoon ground black pepper
- 1 ½ teaspoon salt
- 1 teaspoon turmeric
- 2 1/2 teaspoons paprika powder
- 1 1/2 tablespoons olive oil
- 1 tablespoon corn starch
- 1 teaspoon soy sauce
- 1 tablespoon barbecue sauce
- 1/2 teaspoon liquid smoke
- 1/2 cup vegan cheese

Method:
1. Switch on the oven, then set it to 350 degrees F and let it preheat.
2. Meanwhile, peel the boiled potatoes, then cut them into cubes and set aside until required.
3. Prepare tempeh and for this, take a skillet pan, place it over medium heat, add half of the oil, and when hot, add half of the onion and cook for 1 minute.

4. Then add tempeh pieces, season with 1 teaspoon paprika, add soy sauce, liquid smoke and BBQ sauce, season with salt and black pepper and cook tempeh for 5 minutes, set aside until required.
5. Take a large skillet pan, place it over medium heat, add remaining oil and onion and cook for 2 minutes until beginning to soften.
6. Then add potatoes, season with ½ teaspoon paprika, salt, and black pepper to taste and cook for 5 minutes until crispy, set aside until required.
7. Take a medium bowl, place tofu in it, then add remaining ingredients and whisk until smooth.
8. Take a casserole dish, place potatoes and tempeh in it, top with tofu mixture, sprinkle some more cheese, and bake for 20 minutes until done.
9. Serve straight away.

Nutrition Value:
Calories: 212 Cal; Fat: 7 g; Carbs: 28 g; Protein: 11 g; Fiber: 5 g

Scrambled Eggs with Aquafaba

Preparation time: 5 minutes; Cooking time: 15 minutes; Servings: 2

Ingredients:
- 6 ounces tofu, firm, pressed, drained
- 1/2 cup aquafaba
- 1 1/2 tablespoons olive oil
- 1 tablespoon nutritional yeast
- 1/4 teaspoon black salt
- 1/8 teaspoon ground turmeric
- 1/4 teaspoon ground black pepper

Method:
1. Take a food processor, add tofu, yeast, black pepper, salt, and turmeric, then pour in aquafaba and olive oil and pulse for 1 minute until smooth.
2. Take a skillet pan, place it over medium heat, and when hot, add tofu mixture and cook for 1 minute.
3. Cover the pan, continue cooking for 3 minutes, then uncover the pan and pull the mixture across the pan with a wooden spoon until soft forms.
4. Continue cooking for 10 minutes until resembles soft scrambled eggs, folding tofu mixture gently and heat over medium heat, then remove the pan from heat and season with salt and black pepper to taste.
5. Serve straight away

Nutrition Value:
Calories: 208 Cal; Fat: 5.1 g; Carbs: 31.3 g; Protein: 8.3 g; Fiber: 10.4 g

Chickpea and Zucchini Scramble

Preparation time: 5 minutes; Cooking time: 20 minutes; Servings: 2

Ingredients:
- 1/2 cup diced zucchini
- 1/4 cup chopped onions
- ¼ teaspoon ground black pepper
- 1 tablespoon thyme, chopped
- ½ teaspoon salt
- 1/2 cup chickpea flour
- 1 teaspoon olive oil
- 1/2 cup vegetable broth

Method:
1. Take a medium bowl, add chickpea flour and then whisk in broth until smooth.
2. Take a medium skillet pan, place it over medium-high heat, add oil and when hot, add onion and cook for 5 minutes.
3. Add zucchini, continue cooking for 5 minutes until vegetables begin to brown, and then season vegetables with black pepper, salt, and thyme and stir until mixed.

4. Then stir in chickpea flour mixture and cook for 5 to 10 minutes until cooked and mixture is no longer wet
5. Serve straight away

Nutrition Value:
Calories: 231 Cal; Fat: 4 g; Carbs: 40 g; Protein: 12 g; Fiber: 11 g

Sweet Potato and Apple Latkes

Preparation time: 5 minutes; Cooking time: 15 minutes; Servings: 4
Ingredients:
- 1 large sweet potato, peeled, grated
- 1/2 of medium white onion, diced
- 1 apple, peeled, cored, grated
- 2 tablespoons spelt flour
- 1 tablespoon arrowroot powder
- ½ teaspoon cracked black pepper
- 1 teaspoon salt
- 1 teaspoon turmeric
- 1 tablespoon olive oil and more for frying
- Tahini lemon drizzle, for serving

Method:
1. Wrap grated potato and apple in a cheesecloth, then squeeze moisture as much as possible and then place in a bowl.
2. Add remaining ingredients and then stir until combined.
3. Take a skillet pan, place it over medium-high heat, add oil and when hot, drop in prepared batter, shape them into a round patty and cook for 4 minutes per side until crispy and brown.
4. Serve latkes with Tahini lemon drizzle.

Nutrition Value:
Calories: 174.4 Cal; Fat: 9.5 g; Carbs: 18.5 g; Protein: 4.5 g; Fiber: 2.6 g

Breakfast Tacos

Preparation time: 15 minutes; Cooking time: 0 minute; Servings: 4
Ingredients:
For The Filling:
- 12 ounces of cooked black bean and tofu scramble

For the Mango Pineapple Salsa:
- 1/3 cup diced tomatoes
- 1 medium shallot, peeled, diced
- ½ cup diced mango
- 1 jalapeno, deseeded, diced
- 2 teaspoon minced garlic
- ½ cup diced pineapple
- 1 tablespoon cilantro
- ¼ teaspoon cracked black pepper
- ¼ teaspoon salt
- 2 tablespoons lime juice

For The Tacos:
- 1 avocado, pitted, diced
- 4 small tortillas, warmed
- Chopped cilantro for garnish

Method:
1. Prepare salsa and for this, place all its ingredients in a bowl and stir until mixed.
2. Then prepare tofu scramble, distribute it evenly between tortillas and top evenly with prepared salsa and avocado.
3. Garnish with cilantro and serve.

Nutrition Value:
Calories: 283.6 Cal; Fat: 3.3 g; Carbs: 50.7 g; Protein: 13 g; Fiber: 8.1 g

Enchilada Breakfast Casserole

Preparation time: 10 minutes; Cooking time: 25 minutes; Servings: 8

Ingredients:

- 15 ounces cooked corn
- 1 batch of vegan breakfast eggs
- 15 ounces cooked pinto beans
- 3 medium zucchini, sliced into rounds
- 10 ounces of vegan cheddar cheese, shredded
- 24 ounces red enchilada sauce
- 12 corn tortillas, cut into wedges
- Shredded lettuce for serving
- Vegan sour cream for serving

Method:

1. Take a skillet pan, grease it with oil and press the vegan breakfast eggs into the bottom of the pan in an even layer.
2. Spread with 1/3 of enchilada sauce, then sprinkle with half of the cheese and cover with half of the tortilla wedges.
3. Cover the wedges with 1/3 of the sauce, then layer with beans, corn, and zucchini, cover with remaining tortilla wedges, and spread the remaining sauce on top.
4. Cover the pan with lid, place it over medium heat and cook for 25 minutes until cheese had melted, zucchini is tender, and sauce is bubbling.
5. When done, let the casserole stand for 10 minutes, top with lettuce and sour cream, then cut the casserole into wedges, and serve.

Nutrition Value:

Calories: 197.8 Cal; Fat: 8.9 g; Carbs: 15 g; Protein: 12 g; Fiber: 1.5 g

Fig Oatmeal Bake

Preparation time: 5 minutes; Cooking time: 15 minutes; Servings: 4
Ingredients:

- 2 fresh figs, sliced
- 5 dried figs, chopped
- 4 tablespoons chopped walnuts
- 1 ½ cups oats
- 1 teaspoon cinnamon
- 2 tablespoons agave syrup
- 1 teaspoon baking powder
- 2 tablespoons unsalted butter, melted
- 3 tablespoons flaxseed egg
- ¾ cup of coconut milk

Method:

1. Switch on the oven, then set it to 350 degrees F and let it preheat.
2. Meanwhile, take a bowl, place all the ingredients in it, except for fresh figs and stir until combined.
3. Take an 8-inch square pan, line it with parchment sheet, spoon in the prepared mixture, top with fig slices, and bake for 30 minutes until cooked and set.
4. Serve straight away

Nutrition Value:

Calories: 372.8 Cal; Fat: 9.2 g; Carbs: 65.6 g; Protein: 11.6 g; Fiber: 11.1 g

Vegan Breakfast Sandwich

Preparation time: 15 minutes; Cooking time: 8 minutes; Servings: 3
Ingredients:

- 1 cup of spinach
- 6 slices of pickle
- 14 oz tofu, extra-firm, pressed
- 2 medium tomatoes, sliced
- 1/2 teaspoon garlic powder
- ¼ teaspoon ground black pepper
- 1/2 teaspoon black salt
- 1 teaspoon turmeric
- 1 tablespoon coconut oil
- 2 tablespoons vegan mayo
- 3 slices of vegan cheese
- 6 slices of gluten-free bread, toasted

Method:

1. Cut tofu into six slices, and then season its one side with garlic, black pepper, salt, and turmeric.
2. Take a skillet pan, place it over medium heat, add oil and when hot, add seasoned tofu slices in it, season side down, and cook for 3 minutes until crispy and light brown.
3. Then flip the tofu slices and continue cooking for 3 minutes until browned and crispy.
4. When done, transfer tofu slices on a baking sheet, in the form of a set of two slices side by side, then top each set with a cheese slice and broil for 3 minutes until cheese has melted.
5. Spread mayonnaise on both sides of slices, top with two slices of tofu, cheese on the side, top with spinach, tomatoes, pickles, and then close the sandwich.
6. Cut the sandwich into half and then serve.

Nutrition Value:
Calories: 364 Cal; Fat: 12 g; Carbs: 51 g; Protein: 16 g; Fiber: 3 g

Vegan Fried Egg

Preparation time: 5 minutes; Cooking time: 8 minutes; Servings: 4
Ingredients:
- 1 block of firm tofu, firm, pressed, drained
- ½ teaspoon ground black pepper
- ½ teaspoon salt
- 1 tablespoon vegan butter
- 1 cup vegan toast dipping sauce

Method:
1. Cut tofu into four slices, and then shape them into a rough circle by using a cookie cutter.
2. Take a frying pan, place it over medium heat, add butter and when it melts, add prepared tofu slices in a single layer and cook for 3 minutes per side until light brown.
3. Transfer tofu to serving dishes, make a small hole in the middle of tofu by using a small cookie cutter and fill the hole with dipping sauce.
4. Garnish eggs with black pepper and sauce and then serve.

Nutrition Value:
Calories: 86 Cal; Fat: 9 g; Carbs: 0.5 g; Protein: 2 g; Fiber: 0 g

Sweet Crepes

Preparation time: 5 minutes; Cooking time: 8 minutes; Servings: 5
Ingredients:
- 1 cup of water
- 1 banana
- 1/2 cup oat flour
- 1/2 cup brown rice flour
- 1 teaspoon baking powder
- 1 tablespoon coconut sugar
- 1/8 teaspoon salt

Method:
1. Take a blender, place all the ingredients in it except for sugar and salt and pulse for 1 minute until smooth.
2. Take a skillet pan, place it over medium-high heat, grease it with oil and when hot, pour in ¼ cup of batter, spread it as thin as possible, and cook for 2 to 3 minutes per side until golden brown.
3. Cook remaining crepes in the same manner, then sprinkle with sugar and salt and serve.

Nutrition Value:
Calories: 160.1 Cal; Fat: 4.3 g; Carbs: 22 g; Protein: 8.3 g; Fiber: 0.6 g

Spinach Artichoke Quiche

Preparation time: 10 minutes; Cooking time: 55 minutes; Servings: 4
Ingredients:
- 14 oz tofu, soft
- 14 oz of artichokes, chopped

- 2 cups spinach
- ½ of a large onion, peeled, chopped
- 1 lemon, juiced
- 1 teaspoon minced garlic
- ¼ teaspoon salt
- ¼ teaspoon ground black pepper
- 1 teaspoon dried basil
- ½ teaspoon turmeric
- 1 tablespoon coconut oil
- 1 teaspoon Dijon mustard
- ½ cup nutritional yeast
- 2 large tortillas, cut into half

Method:
1. Switch on the oven, then set it to 350 degrees F and let it preheat.
2. Take a pie plate, grease it with oil, place tortilla to cover the bottom and sides of the plate and bake for 10 to 15 minutes until baked.
3. Meanwhile, take a large pan, place it over medium heat, add oil and when hot, add onion and cook for 5 minutes.
4. Then add garlic, cook for 1 minute until fragrant, stir in spinach and cook for 4 minutes until the spinach has wilted, set aside when done.
5. Place tofu in a food processor, add all the spices, yeast, and lemon juice and pulse for 2 minutes until smooth.
6. Then add cooked onion mixture and artichokes, blend for 15 to 25 times until combined, and then pour the mixture over crust in the pie plate.
7. Bake quiche for 45 minutes until done, then cut it into wedges and serve.

Nutrition Value:
Calories: 100.3 Cal; Fat: 4.7 g; Carbs: 5 g; Protein: 9.3 g; Fiber: 0.7 g

Tofu Scramble

Preparation time: 5 minutes; Cooking time: 18 minutes; Servings: 4
Ingredients:
For the Spice Mix:
- 1 teaspoon black salt
- 1/4 teaspoon garlic powder
- 1 teaspoon red chili powder
- 1 teaspoon ground cumin
- 3/4 teaspoons turmeric
- 2 tablespoons nutritional yeast

For the Tofu Scramble:
- 2 cups cooked black beans
- 16 ounces tofu, firm, pressed, drained
- 1 chopped red pepper
- 1 1/2 cups sliced button mushrooms
- 1/2 of white onion, chopped
- 1 teaspoon minced garlic
- 1 tablespoon olive oil

Method:
1. Take a skillet pan, place it over medium-high heat, add oil and when hot, add onion, pepper, mushrooms, and garlic and cook for 8 minutes until golden.
2. Meanwhile, prepare the spice mix and for this, place all its ingredients in a bowl and stir until combined.
3. When vegetables have cooked, add tofu in it, crumble it, then add black beans, sprinkle with prepared spice mix, stir and cook for 8 minutes until hot.
4. Serve straight away

Nutrition Value:
Calories: 175 Cal; Fat: 9 g; Carbs: 10 g; Protein: 14 g; Fiber: 3 g

Pumpkin Muffins

Preparation time: 15 minutes; Cooking time: 30 minutes; Servings: 9
Ingredients:
- 2 Tablespoon mashed ripe banana
- 1.5 flax eggs
- 1 teaspoon vanilla extract, unsweetened

- 1/4 cup maple syrup
- 1/4 cup olive oil
- 2/3 cup coconut sugar
- 3/4 cup pumpkin puree
- 1 1/4 teaspoon pumpkin pie spice
- 1/4 teaspoon sea salt
- 1/2 teaspoon ground cinnamon
- 2 teaspoon baking soda
- 1/2 cup water
- 1/2 cup almond meal
- 1 cup gluten-free flour blend
- 3/4 cup rolled oats
- For the Crumble:
- 2 Tablespoon chopped pecans
- 3 1/2 Tablespoon gluten-free flour blend
- 3 Tablespoon coconut sugar
- 1/8 teaspoon cinnamon
- 1/8 teaspoon pumpkin pie spice
- 1 1/4 Tablespoon coconut oil

Method:
1. Switch on the oven, then set it to 350 degrees F and let it preheat.
2. Meanwhile, prepare the muffin batter and for this, place the first seven ingredients in a bowl and whisk until combined.
3. Then whisk in the next five ingredients until mixed and gradually beat in remaining ingredients until incorporated and smooth batter comes together.
4. Prepare crumble, and for this, place all of its ingredients in a bowl and stir until combined.
5. Distribute the batter evenly between ten muffin tins lined with muffin liners, top with prepared crumble, and then bake for 30 minutes until muffins are set and the tops are golden brown.
6. When done, let muffin cool for 5 minutes, then take them out to cool completely and serve.

Nutrition Value:
Calories: 329 Cal; Fat: 12.7 g; Carbs: 52.6 g; Protein: 4.6 g; Fiber: 5 g

Tomato and Asparagus Quiche

Preparation time: 40 minutes; Cooking time: 35 minutes; Servings: 12
Ingredients:
For the Dough:
- 2 cups whole wheat flour
- 1/2 teaspoon salt

For the Filling:
- 14 oz silken tofu
- 6 cherry tomatoes, halved
- 2 green onions, cut into rings
- 10 sun-dried tomatoes, in oil, chopped
- 7 oz green asparagus, diced
- 3/4 cup vegan margarine
- 1/3 cup water

- 1 1/2 tablespoons herbs de Provence
- 1 tablespoon cornstarch
- 1 teaspoon turmeric
- 3 tablespoons olive oil

Method:
1. Switch on the oven, then set it to 350 degrees F and let it preheat.
2. Pre the dough and for this, take a bowl, place all the ingredients for it, beat until incorporated, then knead for 5 minutes until smooth and refrigerate the dough for 30 minutes.
3. Meanwhile, take a skillet pan, place it over medium heat, add 1 tablespoon oil and when hot, add green onion and cook for 2 minutes, set aside until required.
4. Place a pot half full wit salty water over medium heat, bring it to boil, then add asparagus and boil for 3 minutes until tender, drain and set aside until required.
5. Take a medium bowl, add tofu along with herbs de Provence, starch, turmeric, and oil, whisk until smooth and then fold in tomatoes, green onion, and asparagus until mixed.

6. Divide the prepared dough into twelve sections, take a muffin tray, line it twelve cups with baking cups, and then press a dough ball at the bottom of each cup and all the way up.
7. Fill the cups with prepared tofu mixture, top with tomatoes, and bake for 35 minutes until cooked.
8. Serve straight away.

Nutrition Value:

Calories: 206 Cal; Fat: 14 g; Carbs: 16 g; Protein: 4 g; Fiber: 2 g

Simple Vegan Breakfast Hash

Preparation time: 10 minutes; Cooking time: 25 minutes; Servings: 4

Ingredients:

For the Potatoes:
- 1 large sweet potato, peeled, diced
- 3 medium potatoes, peeled, diced
- 1 tablespoon onion powder
- 2 teaspoons sea salt
- 1 tablespoon garlic powder
- 1 teaspoon ground black pepper
- 1 teaspoon dried thyme
- 1/4 cup olive oil

For the Skillet Mixture:
- 1 medium onion, peeled, diced
- 5 cloves of garlic, peeled, minced
- ¼ teaspoon of sea salt
- ¼ teaspoon ground black pepper
- 1 teaspoon olive oil

Method:
1. Switch on the oven, then set it to 450 degrees F and let it preheat.
2. Meanwhile, take a casserole dish, add all the ingredients for the potatoes, toss until coated, and then cook for 20 minutes until crispy, stirring halfway.
3. Meanwhile, take a skillet pan, place it over medium heat, add oil and when hot, add onion and garlic, season with salt and black pepper and cook for 5 minutes until browned.
4. When potatoes have roasted, add garlic and cooked onion mixture, stir until combined, and serve.

Nutrition Value:

Calories: 212 Cal; Fat: 10 g; Carbs: 28 g; Protein: 3 g; Fiber: 4 g

Chickpeas on Toast

Preparation time: 5 minutes; Cooking time: 15 minutes; Servings: 6

Ingredients:
- 14-oz cooked chickpeas
- 1 cup baby spinach
- 1/2 cup chopped white onion
- 1 cup crushed tomatoes
- ½ teaspoon minced garlic
- ¼ teaspoon ground black pepper
- 1/2 teaspoon brown sugar
- 1 teaspoon smoked paprika powder
- 1/3 teaspoon sea salt
- 1 tablespoon olive oil
- 6 slices of gluten-free bread, toasted

Method:
1. Take a frying pan, place it over medium heat, add oil and when hot, add onion and cook for 2 minutes.
2. Then stir in garlic, cook for 30 seconds until fragrant, stir in paprika and continue cooking for 10 seconds.
3. Add tomatoes, stir, bring the mixture to simmer, season with black pepper, sugar, and salt and then stir in chickpeas.
4. Sir, in spinach, cook for 2 minutes until leaves have wilted, then remove the pan from heat and taste to adjust seasoning.

5. Serve cooked chickpeas on toasted bread.

Nutrition Value:
    Calories: 305 Cal; Fat: 7.6 g; Carbs: 45 g; Protein: 13 g; Fiber: 8 g

Blueberry Muffins

Preparation time: 5 minutes; Cooking time: 15 minutes; Servings: 12
Ingredients:

- 2 cups fresh blueberries
- 2 cups all-purpose flour
- 2½ teaspoons baking powder
- ½ teaspoon salt
- ¼ teaspoon baking soda
- ½ cup and 2tablespoon. sugar
- zest of 1 lemon
- 1 teaspoon apple cider vinegar
- ¼ cup and 2 tablespoons. canola oil
- 1 cup of soy milk
- 1 teaspoon vanilla extract, unsweetened

Method:
1. Switch on the oven, then set it to 450 degrees F and let it preheat.
2. Meanwhile, take a small bowl, add vinegar and milk, whisk until combined, and let it stand to curdle.
3. Take a large bowl, add flour, salt, baking powder, and soda, and stir until mixed.
4. Whisk in sugar, lemon zest, oil, and vanilla into soy milk mixture, then gradually whisk in flour mixture until incorporated and fold in berries until combined.
5. Take a twelve cups muffin tray, grease them with oil, distribute the prepared batter in them and bake for 25 minutes until done and the tops are browned.
6. Let muffins cool for 5 minutes, then cool them completely and serve.

Nutrition Value:
    Calories: 160 Cal; Fat: 5 g; Carbs: 25 g; Protein: 2 g; Fiber: 2 g

Ultimate Breakfast Sandwich

Preparation time: 40 minutes; Cooking time: 10 minutes; Servings: 4
Ingredients:
For the Tofu:

- 12 ounces tofu, extra-firm, pressed, drain
- 1/2 teaspoon garlic powder
- 1 teaspoon liquid smoke
- 2 tablespoons nutritional yeast
- 1 teaspoon Sriracha sauce
- 2 tablespoons soy sauce
- 2 tablespoons olive oil
- 2 tablespoons water

For the Vegan Breakfast Sandwich:

- 1 large tomato, sliced
- 4 English muffins, halved, toasted
- 1 avocado, mashed

Method:
1. Prepare tofu, and for this, cut tofu into four slices and set aside.
2. Stir together remaining ingredients of tofu, pour the mixture into a bag, then add tofu pieces, toss until coated and marinate for 30 minutes.
3. Take a skillet pan, place it over medium-high heat, add tofu slices along with the marinade and cook for 5 minutes per side.
4. Prepare sandwich and for this, spread mashed avocado on the inner of the muffin, top with a slice of tofu, layer with a tomato slice and then serve.

Nutrition Value:
    Calories: 277 Cal; Fat: 9.1 g; Carbs: 33.1 g; Protein: 16.1 g; Fiber: 3.6 g

Waffles with Fruits

Preparation time: 10 minutes; Cooking time: 20 minutes; Servings: 4
Ingredients:

- 1 1/4 cup all-purpose flour
- 2 teaspoon baking powder
- 3 tablespoon sugar
- 1/4 teaspoon salt
- 2 teaspoon vanilla extract, unsweetened
- 2 tablespoon coconut oil
- 1 1/4 cup soy milk
- Sliced fruits, for topping
- Vegan whipping cream, for topping

Method:
1. Switch on the waffle maker and let it preheat.
2. Meanwhile, place flour in a bowl, stir in salt, baking powder, and sugar and whisk in whisk in remaining ingredients, except for topping, until incorporated.
3. Ladle the batter into the waffle maker and cook until firm and brown.
4. When done, top waffles with fruits and whipped cream and serve.

Nutrition Value:
Calories: 277 Cal; Fat: 8.3 g; Carbs: 42.5 g; Protein: 6.2 g; Fiber: 1.5 g

Chickpea Omelet

Preparation time: 5 minutes; Cooking time: 10 minutes; Servings: 1
Ingredients:

- 3 Tablespoon chickpea flour
- 1 small white onion, peeled, diced
- ½ teaspoon black salt
- 2 tablespoons chopped the dill
- 2 tablespoons chopped basil
- 1/8 teaspoon ground black pepper
- 2 Tablespoon olive oil
- 8 Tablespoon water

Method:
1. Take a bowl, add flour in it along with salt and black pepper, stir until mixed, and then whisk in water until creamy.
2. Take a skillet pan, place it over medium heat, add 1 tablespoon oil and when hot, add onion and cook for 4 minutes until cooked.
3. Add onion to omelet mixture and then stir until combined.
4. Add remaining oil into the pan, pour in prepared batter, spread evenly, and cook for 3 minutes per side until cooked.
5. Serve omelet with bread.

Nutrition Value:
Calories: 150 Cal; Fat: 2 g; Carbs: 24.4 g; Protein: 10.2 g; Fiber: 5.8 g

Scrambled Tofu Breakfast Burrito

Preparation time: 15 minutes; Cooking time: 20 minutes; Servings: 4
Ingredients:
For the Tofu:

- 12-ounce tofu, extra-firm, pressed
- 1/4 cup minced parsley
- 1 ½ teaspoon minced garlic
- 1 teaspoon nutritional yeast
- 1/4 teaspoon sea salt
- 1/2 teaspoon red chili powder
- 1/2 teaspoon cumin
- 1 teaspoon olive oil
- 1 Tablespoon hummus

For the Vegetables:

- 5 baby potatoes, chopped
- 1 medium red bell pepper, sliced
- 2 cups chopped kale
- 1/2 teaspoon ground cumin
- 1/8 teaspoon sea salt
- 1/2 teaspoon red chili powder

- 1 teaspoon oil

The Rest
- 4 large tortillas
- 1 medium avocado, chopped
- Cilantro as needed
- Salsa as needed

Method:
1. Switch on the oven, then set it to 400 degrees F and let it preheat.
2. Take a baking sheet, add potato and bell pepper, drizzle with oil, season with all the spices, toss until coated and bake for 15 minutes until tender and nicely browned.
3. Then add kale to the potatoes, cook for 5 minutes, and set aside until required.
4. In the meantime, take a skillet pan, place it over medium heat, add oil and when hot add tofu, crumble it well and cook for 10 minutes until lightly browned.
5. In the meantime, take a small bowl, add hummus and remaining ingredients for the tofu and stir until combined.
6. Add hummus mixture into tofu, stir and cook for 3 minutes, set aside until required.
7. Assemble the burritos and for this, distribute roasted vegetables on the tortilla, top with tofu, avocado, cilantro, and salsa, roll and then serve.

Nutrition Value:
Calories: 441 Cal; Fat: 19.6 g; Carbs: 53.5 g; Protein: 16.5 g; Fiber: 8 g

Pancake

Preparation time: 10 minutes; Cooking time: 18 minutes; Servings: 4
Ingredients:
Dry Ingredients:
- 1 cup buckwheat flour
- 1/8 teaspoon salt
- ½ teaspoon gluten-free baking powder
- ½ teaspoon baking soda

Wet Ingredients:
- 1 tablespoon almond butter
- 2 tablespoon maple syrup
- 1 tablespoon lime juice
- 1 cup coconut milk, unsweetened

Method:
1. Take a medium bowl, add all the dry ingredients and stir until mixed.
2. Take another bowl, place all the wet ingredients, whisk until combined, and then gradually whisk in dry ingredients mixture until smooth and incorporated.
3. Take a frying pan, place it over medium heat, add 2 teaspoons oil and when hot, drop in batter and cook for 3 minutes per side until cooked and lightly browned.
4. Serve pancakes and fruits and maple syrup.

Nutrition Value:
Calories: 148 Cal; Fat: 8.2 g; Carbs: 15 g; Protein: 4.6 g; Fiber: 1.7 g

Chapter 3: Soups and Stews

Cream of Mushroom Soup

Preparation time: 5 minutes; Cooking time: 12 minutes; Servings: 6
Ingredients:
- 1 medium white onion, peeled, chopped
- 16 ounces button mushrooms, sliced
- 1 ½ teaspoon minced garlic
- 1/4 cup all-purpose flour
- 1/2 teaspoon ground black pepper
- 1 teaspoon dried thyme
- 1/4 teaspoon nutmeg
- 1/2 teaspoon salt
- 2 tablespoons vegan butter
- 4 cups vegetable broth
- 1 1/2 cups coconut milk, unsweetened

Method:
1. Take a large pot, place it over medium-high heat, add butter and when it melts, add onions and garlic, stir in garlic and cook for 5 minutes until softened and nicely brown.
2. Then sprinkle flour over vegetables, continue cooking for 1 minute, then add remaining ingredients, stir until mixed and simmer for 5 minutes until thickened.
3. Serve straight away

Nutrition Value:
Calories: 120 Cal; Fat: 7 g; Carbs: 10 g; Protein: 2 g; Fiber: 6 g

Cauliflower and Horseradish Soup

Preparation time: 5 minutes; Cooking time: 20 minutes; Servings: 4
Ingredients:
- 2 medium potatoes, peeled, chopped
- 1 medium cauliflower, florets and stalk chopped
- 1 medium white onion, peeled, chopped
- 1 teaspoon minced garlic
- 2/3 teaspoon salt
- 1/3 teaspoon ground black pepper
- 4 teaspoons horseradish sauce
- 1 teaspoon dried thyme
- 3 cups vegetable broth
- 1 cup coconut milk, unsweetened

Method:
1. Place all the vegetables in a large pan, place it over medium-high heat, add thyme, pour in broth and milk and bring the mixture to boil.
2. Then switch heat to medium level, simmer the soup for 15 minutes and remove the pan from heat.
3. Puree the soup by using an immersion blender until smooth, season with salt and black pepper, and serve straight away.

Nutrition Value:
Calories: 160 Cal; Fat: 2.6 g; Carbs: 31 g; Protein: 6 g; Fiber: 6 g

Curry Lentil Soup

Preparation time: 5 minutes; Cooking time: 40 minutes; Servings: 6
Ingredients:
- 1 cup brown lentils
- 1 medium white onion, peeled, chopped
- 28 ounces diced tomatoes
- 1 ½ teaspoon minced garlic
- 1 inch of ginger, grated
- 3 cups vegetable broth
- 1/2 teaspoon salt
- 2 tablespoons curry powder
- 1 teaspoon cumin
- 1/2 teaspoon cayenne
- 1 tablespoon olive oil

- 1 1/2 cups coconut milk, unsweetened
- ¼ cup chopped cilantro

Method:
1. Take a soup pot, place it over medium-high heat, add oil and when hot, add onion, stir in garlic and ginger and cook for 5 minutes until golden brown.
2. Then add all the ingredients except for milk and cilantro, stir until mixed and simmer for 25 minutes until lentils have cooked.
3. When done, stir in milk, cook for 5 minutes until thoroughly heated and then garnish the soup with cilantro.
4. Serve straight away

Nutrition Value:

Calories: 269 Cal; Fat: 15 g; Carbs: 26 g; Protein: 10 g; Fiber: 10 g

Chickpea Noodle Soup

Preparation time: 5 minutes; Cooking time: 18 minutes; Servings: 6
Ingredients:
- 1 cup cooked chickpeas
- 8 ounces rotini noodles, whole-wheat
- 4 celery stalks, sliced
- 2 medium white onions, peeled, chopped
- 4 medium carrots, peeled, sliced
- 2 teaspoons minced garlic
- 8 sprigs of thyme
- 1 teaspoon salt
- 1/3 teaspoon ground black pepper
- 1 bay leaf
- 2 tablespoons olive oil
- 2 quarts of vegetable broth
- ¼ cup chopped fresh parsley

Method:
1. Take a large pot, place it over medium heat, add oil and when hot, add all the vegetables, stir in garlic, thyme and bay leaf and cook for 5 minutes until vegetables are golden and sauté.
2. Then pour in broth stir and bring the mixture to boil.
3. Add chickpeas and noodles into boiling soup, continue cooking for 8 minutes until noodles are tender, and then season soup with salt and black pepper.
4. Garnish with parsley and serve straight away

Nutrition Value:

Calories: 260 Cal; Fat: 5 g; Carbs: 44 g; Protein: 7 g; Fiber: 4 g

Mexican Lentil Soup

Preparation time: 5 minutes; Cooking time: 45 minutes; Servings: 6
Ingredients:
- 2 cups green lentils
- 1 medium red bell pepper, cored, diced
- 1 medium white onion, peeled, diced
- 2 cups diced tomatoes
- 8 ounces diced green chilies
- 2 celery stalks, diced
- 2 medium carrots, peeled, diced
- 1 ½ teaspoon minced garlic
- 1/2 teaspoon salt
- 1 tablespoon cumin
- 1/4 teaspoon smoked paprika
- 1 teaspoon oregano
- 1/8 teaspoon hot sauce
- 2 tablespoons olive oil
- 8 cups vegetable broth
- ¼ cup cilantro, for garnish
- 1 avocado, peeled, pitted, diced, for garnish

Method:
1. Take a large pot over medium heat, add oil and when hot, add all the vegetables, reserving tomatoes and chilies, and cook for 5 minutes until softened.
2. Then add garlic, stir in oregano, cumin, and paprika, and continue cooking for 1 minute.

3. Add lentils, tomatoes and green chilies, season with salt, pour in the broth and simmer the soup for 40 minutes until cooked.
4. When done, ladle soup into bowls, top with avocado and cilantro and serve straight away

Nutrition Value:

Calories: 235 Cal; Fat: 9 g; Carbs: 32 g; Protein: 9 g; Fiber: 10 g

Corn and Potato Chowder

Preparation time: 5 minutes; Cooking time: 35 minutes; Servings: 4

Ingredients:

- 2 ears of corn
- 10 ounces tofu, extra-firm, drained cubed
- 1 1/2 cups frozen corn kernels
- 1/4 medium onion, peeled, chopped
- 3 medium potatoes, peeled, cubed
- 1/4 medium red bell pepper, cored, chopped
- ¼ cup cilantro, chopped
- 2/3 teaspoon salt
- 1/4 cup coconut cream
- 7 cups of vegetable broth

Method:

1. Prepare the ears of corn and for this, remove their skin and husk, then cut each corn into four pieces and place them in a large pot.
2. Place the pot over medium-high heat, add cilantro, onion and bell pepper, pour in the broth, bring the mixture to boil, then switch heat to medium level and cook for 20 minutes until corn pieces are tender.
3. Add potatoes, cook for 8 minutes until fork tender, then add tofu and kernels, simmer for 5 minutes and taste to adjust seasoning.
4. Remove pot from heat, stir in cream until combined and serve straight away

Nutrition Value:

Calories: 159 Cal; Fat: 2.4 g; Carbs: 29 g; Protein: 6.6 g; Fiber: 2.2 g

Cauliflower Soup

Preparation time: 10 minutes; Cooking time: 40 minutes; Servings: 2

Ingredients:

- 1 small head of cauliflower, cut into florets
- 4 tablespoons pomegranate seeds
- 2 sprigs of thyme and more for garnishing
- 1 teaspoon minced garlic
- 2/3 teaspoon salt
- 1/3 teaspoon ground black pepper
- 1 tablespoon olive oil
- 1 1/2 cups vegetable stock
- 1/2 cup coconut milk, unsweetened

Method:

1. Take a pot, place it over medium heat, add oil and when hot, add garlic and cook for 1 minute until fragrant.
2. Add florets, thyme, pour in the stock and bring the mixture to boil.
3. Switch heat to the medium low level, simmer the soup for 30 minutes until florets are tender, then remove the pot from heat, discard the thyme and puree using an immersion blender until smooth.
4. Stir milk into the soup, season with salt and black pepper, then garnish with pomegranate seeds and thyme sprigs and serve.

Nutrition Value:

Calories: 184 Cal; Fat: 11 g; Carbs: 17 g; Protein: 3 g; Fiber: 3 g

Red Pepper and Tomato Soup

Preparation time: 10 minutes; Cooking time: 40 minutes; Servings: 4

Ingredients:
- 2 carrots, peeled, chopped
- 1 1/4 pounds red bell peppers, deseeded, sliced into quarters
- 1/2 of medium red onion, peeled, sliced into thin wedges
- 16 ounces small tomatoes, halved
- 1 tablespoon chopped basil
- 1/2 teaspoon salt
- 2 cups vegetable broth

Method:
1. Switch on the oven, then set it to 450 degrees F and let it preheat.
2. Then place all the vegetables in a single on a baking sheet lined with foil and roast for 40 minutes until the skins of peppers are slightly charred.
3. When done, remove the baking sheet from the oven, let them cool for 10 minutes, then peel the peppers and transfer all the vegetables into a blender.
4. Add basil and salt to the vegetables, pour in the broth, and puree the vegetables until smooth.
5. Serve straight away.

Nutrition Value:
Calories: 77.4 Cal; Fat: 1.8 g; Carbs: 14.4 g; Protein: 3.3 g; Fiber: 3.3 g

Asparagus Soup

Preparation time: 10 minutes; Cooking time: 20 minutes; Servings: 4
Ingredients:
- 1/2 head of medium cauliflower, cut into florets
- 1 medium white onion, peeled, sliced
- 2 pounds asparagus, ends trimmed, chopped
- 2 teaspoons minced garlic
- ½ teaspoon ground black pepper
- 1/2 cup nutritional yeast
- ½ teaspoon salt
- 1 lemon, juiced
- 1 tablespoon olive oil
- 6 cups vegetable broth

Method:
1. Take a large stockpot, place it over medium-high heat, add oil and when hot, add onions and garlic, and cook for 7 minutes until onions are translucent.
2. Then add cauliflower florets and asparagus, pour in vegetable broth, bring to boil, then switch heat to medium level and simmer for 10 minutes until vegetables are tender.
3. Puree soup by using an immersion blender, then return it over medium heat, season with salt and black pepper, stir in lemon juice and yeast and serve straight away.

Nutrition Value:
Calories: 133 Cal; Fat: 4 g; Carbs: 20 g; Protein: 8 g; Fiber: 6 g

Wonton Soup

Preparation time: 15 minutes; Cooking time: 10 minutes; Servings: 4
Ingredients:
For the Soup:
- 4 cups vegetable broth

For the Wontons Filling:
- 1 cup chopped mushrooms
- 1/4 cup walnuts, chopped
- 1 green onion, chopped
- 1/2 inch of ginger, grated
- ½ teaspoon minced garlic
- 2 green onions, chopped

- 1 tablespoon rice vinegar
- 2 teaspoons soy sauce
- 1 teaspoon brown sugar
- 20 Vegan Wonton Wrappers

Method:

1. Prepare wonton filling and for this, take a bowl, place all the ingredients in it, except for wrapper and toss until well combined.
2. Place a wonton wrapper on working space, place 1 teaspoon of prepared filling in the middle, then brush some water at the edges, fold over to shape like a half-moon, and seal the wrappers by pinching the edges.
3. Take a large pot, place it over medium-high heat, add broth, and bring it to boil.
4. Then drop prepared wontons in it, one at a time, and boil for 5 minutes.
5. When cooked, garnish the soup with green onions and serve.

Nutrition Value:
Calories: 196.9 Cal; Fat: 4 g; Carbs: 31 g; Protein: 6.6 g; Fiber: 2.4 g

Butternut Squash and Coconut Milk Soup

Preparation time: 10 minutes; Cooking time: 35 minutes; Servings: 6
Ingredients:
- 1 cup diced parsnips
- 2 cups diced sweet potato
- 1 large sweet onion, peeled, diced
- 1 ½ cups diced carrots
- 4 cups diced butternut squash
- 2 teaspoons minced garlic
- 1/4 teaspoon ground ginger
- ¼ teaspoon ground black pepper
- ½ teaspoon of sea salt
- 1/4 teaspoon ground allspice
- 1 teaspoon poultry seasoning
- 1 teaspoon pumpkin pie spice
- 1/4 teaspoon ground cinnamon
- 32 ounces vegetable stock
- 14 ounces coconut milk, unsweetened

Method:
1. Take a large Dutch oven, place it over medium heat, add onions, drizzle with 2 tablespoons water and cook for 5 minutes until softened, drizzling with more 2 tablespoons at a time if required.
2. Then stir in garlic, cook for another minute, switch heat to the high level, add remaining ingredients, reserving milk, salt, and black pepper, and bring the soup to boil.
3. Then switch heat to medium-low level and simmer for 20 minutes until vegetables are tender.
4. When done, puree soup by using an immersion blender, then stir in coconut milk, season with salt and black pepper and cook for 3 minutes until warm.
5. Serve straight away.

Nutrition Value:
Calories: 188.4 Cal; Fat: 7.7 g; Carbs: 29.3 g; Protein: 3.7 g; Fiber: 8.2 g

Broccoli Cheese Soup

Preparation time: 10 minutes; Cooking time: 15 minutes; Servings: 4
Ingredients:
- 1 medium potato, peeled, diced
- 2 ribs celery, diced
- 1 medium white onion, peeled, diced
- 2 medium yellow summer squash, diced
- 1 medium carrot, peeled, diced
- 6 cups chopped broccoli florets
- 1 teaspoon minced garlic
- 1 bay leaf
- 1/3 teaspoon ground black pepper
- ¼ cup nutritional yeast
- 1 tablespoon lemon juice
- 2 tablespoons apple cider vinegar
- ½ cup cashews
- 3 cups of water

Method:
1. Take a large pot, place it over medium-high heat, add all the vegetables in it, except for florets, add bay leaf, pour in water and bring the mixture to boil.

2. Then switch heat to medium-low and simmer for 10 minutes until vegetables are tender.
3. Meanwhile, place broccoli florets in another pot, place it over medium-low heat and cook for 4 minutes or more until broccoli has steamed.
4. When done, remove broccoli from the pot, reserve 1 cup of its liquid, and set aside until required.
5. When vegetables have cooked, remove the bay leaf, add remaining ingredients in it, reserving broccoli and its liquid, and then puree the soup by using an immersion blender until smooth.
6. Then add steamed broccoli along with its liquid, stir well and serve straight away.

Nutrition Value:
Calories: 223.5 Cal; Fat: 12 g; Carbs: 19 g; Protein: 10.6 g; Fiber: 1.7 g

Potato and Kale Soup

Preparation time: 5 minutes; Cooking time: 15 minutes; Servings: 2
Ingredients:
- 1 small white onion, peeled, chopped
- 2 ½ cups cubed potatoes
- 2 cups leek, cut into rings
- 1/2 cup chopped carrots
- 1/2 cup chopped celery
- ½ teaspoon minced garlic
- 2/3 teaspoon salt
- 1/3 teaspoon ground black pepper
- 1 tablespoon olive oil
- 3 1/2 cups vegetable broth
- 1 cup kale, cut into stripes
- Croutons, for serving

Method:
1. Take a large pot, place it over medium heat, add oil and when hot, add onion and cook for 2 minutes until sauté.
2. Stir in garlic, cook for another minute, then add all the vegetables and continue cooking for 3 minutes.
3. Pour in broth, cook for 15 minutes, then add kale and cook for 2 minutes until tender.
4. Season soup with salt and black pepper, puree by using an immersion blender until smooth, then top with croutons and serve.

Nutrition Value:
Calories: 337 Cal; Fat: 7 g; Carbs: 62 g; Protein: 10 g; Fiber: 8 g

Vegan Pho

Preparation time: 5 minutes; Cooking time: 15 minutes; Servings: 6
Ingredients:
- 1 package of wide rice noodles, cooked
- 1 medium white onion, peeled, quartered
- 2 teaspoons minced garlic
- 1 inch of ginger, sliced into coins
- 8 cups vegetable broth
- 3 whole cloves
- 2 tablespoons soy sauce
- 3 whole star anise
- 1 cinnamon stick
- 3 cups of water

For Toppings:
- Basil as needed for topping
- Chopped green onions as needed for topping
- Ming beans as needed for topping
- Hot sauce as needed for topping
- Lime wedges for serving

Method:
1. Take a large pot, place it over medium-high heat, add all the ingredients for soup in it, except for soy sauce and broth, and bring it to boil.
2. Then switch heat to medium-low level, simmer the soup for 30 minutes and then stir in soy sauce.

3. When done, distribute cooked noodles into bowls, top with soup, then top with toppings and serve.

Nutrition Value:
Calories: 31 Cal; Fat: 0 g; Carbs: 7 g; Protein: 0 g; Fiber: 2 g

Roasted Cauliflower Soup

Preparation time: 10 minutes; Cooking time: 60 minutes; Servings: 4
Ingredients:

- 1 medium head of cauliflower, cut into florets
- 1 small white onion, peeled, diced
- 1 medium carrot, peeled, diced
- 1 stalk of celery, diced
- 1 head of garlic, top off
- 2/3 teaspoon salt
- 1/3 teaspoon ground black pepper
- 1 teaspoon smoked paprika
- 2 tablespoons nutritional yeast
- 1 teaspoon hot smoked paprika
- 4 tablespoons olive oil
- 12 ounces coconut milk, unsweetened
- 4 cups vegetable broth
- ½ cup chopped parsley

Method:
1. Switch on the oven, then set it to 400 degrees F and let it preheat.
2. Place top off garlic on a piece of foil, drizzle with 1 tablespoon oil, and then wrap.
3. Place cauliflower florets in a bowl, drizzle with 2 tablespoons oil, season with salt and black pepper, and toss until well coated.
4. Take a baking sheet, spread cauliflower florets in it in a single layer, add wrapped garlic and bake for 30 minutes until roasted.
5. Then place a large pot over medium-high heat, add remaining oil and when hot, add onions and cook for 3 minutes.
6. Then add celery and carrot, continue cooking for 3 minutes, season with salt and paprika, pour in broth, and bring it to a boil.
7. Add roasted garlic and florets, bring the mixture to boil, then switch heat to medium-low level and simmer for 15 minutes.
8. Puree the soup by using an immersion blender, stir in milk and yeast until mixed and simmer for 3 minutes until hot.
9. Garnish soup with parsley and then serve.

Nutrition Value:
Calories: 102.2 Cal; Fat: 6.3 g; Carbs: 11 g; Protein: 2.7 g; Fiber: 4.6 g

Curried Apple and Sweet Potato Soup

Preparation time: 10 minutes; Cooking time: 38 minutes; Servings: 6
Ingredients:

- 2 cups diced sweet apples
- 1/2 of medium white onion, peeled chopped
- 4 cups diced sweet potatoes
- 1 teaspoon minced garlic
- 1 tablespoon grated ginger
- 1/4 teaspoon nutmeg
- 1 teaspoon curry powder
- 2/3 teaspoon salt
- 1/3 teaspoon ground black pepper
- 1/2 teaspoon cinnamon
- 1 tablespoon olive oil
- 2 cups apple cider
- 1 cup vegetable stock
- 1 cup coconut milk, unsweetened

For Garnish:

- 1/2 cup baked apple chips
- 1/4 cup toasted pumpkin seeds
- 1/4 cup coconut milk, unsweetened

Method:

1. Take a large pot, place it over medium-high heat and when hot, add oil and onion and cook 5 minutes until translucent.
2. Add garlic and ginger, stir in all the spices, then add sweet potatoes and cook for 4 minutes until sauté.
3. Switch heat to medium-low level, add apples, pour in milk, stock, and cider coconut and simmer 25 minutes until vegetables are softened.
4. Puree the soup by using an immersion blender, season with salt and black pepper, and distribute into bowls.
5. Top with garnishing and then serve.

Nutrition Value:
Calories: 170 Cal; Fat: 8.4 g; Carbs: 22 g; Protein: 3.1 g; Fiber: 5 g

Ramen Noodle Soup

Preparation time: 10 minutes; Cooking time: 20 minutes; Servings: 2
Ingredients:
For The Mushrooms and Tofu:
- 2 cups sliced shiitake mushrooms
- 6 ounces tofu, extra-firm, drained, sliced
- 1 tablespoon olive oil
- 1 tablespoon soy sauce

For the Noodle Soup:
- 2 packs of dried ramen noodles
- 1 medium carrot, peeled, grated
- 1 inch of ginger, grated
- 1 teaspoon minced garlic
- ¾ cup baby spinach leaves
- 1 tablespoon olive oil
- 6 cups vegetable broth

For Garnish:
- Sesame seeds as needed
- Soy sauce as needed
- Sriracha sauce as needed

Method:
1. Prepare mushrooms and tofu and for this, place tofu pieces in a plastic bag, add soy sauce, seal the bag and turn it upside until tofu is coated.
2. Take a skillet pan, place it over medium heat, add oil and when hot, add tofu slices and cook for 5 to 10 minutes until crispy and browned on all sides, flipping frequently and when done, set aside until required.
3. Add mushrooms into the pan, cook for 8 minutes until golden, pour soy sauce from tofu pieces in it, and stir until coated.
4. Meanwhile, prepare noodle soup and for this, take a soup pot, place it over medium-high heat, add oil and when hot, add garlic and ginger and cook for 1 minute until fragrant.
5. Then pour in the broth, bring the mixture to boil, add noodles and cook until tender.
6. Then stir spinach into the noodle soup, remove the pot from heat and distribute evenly between bowls.
7. Add mushrooms and tofu along with garnishing and then serve.

Nutrition Value:
Calories: 647 Cal; Fat: 12 g; Carbs: 106 g; Protein: 28 g; Fiber: 6 g

Lasagna Soup

Preparation time: 5 minutes; Cooking time: 5 hours and 12 minutes; Servings: 6
Ingredients:
For the Lasagna Soup:
- 3/4 cup dried brown lentils
- 1 medium white onion, peeled, diced
- 3 cups chopped spinach leaves
- 14 ounces crushed tomatoes

- 14 ounces diced tomatoes
- 1 ½ teaspoon minced garlic
- 1 teaspoon dried basil

For the Vegan Pesto Ricotta:
- 1/4 pound tofu, extra firm, drained
- 1 cup cashews, soaked, drained
- 2/3 teaspoon salt
- 1/3 teaspoon ground black pepper

- 1 teaspoon dried oregano
- 8 lasagna noodles, broken into pieces
- 4 1/2 cups vegetable broth

- 4 tablespoons pesto, vegan
- 1 tablespoon lemon juice
- 1/4 cup almond milk

Method:
1. Prepare the lasagna soup and for this, switch on the slow cooker, add lentils, onion, and garlic in it, stir in basil and oregano, pour in broth, and stir until mixed.
2. Shut the slow cooker with lid and cook for 2 hours at a high heat setting.
3. Meanwhile, prepare the pesto ricotta, and for this, place cashews in a blender, add milk and pulse until smooth.
4. Then tofu, pulse until mixture resembles ricotta cheese, then tip it in a bowl and stir in remaining ingredients until combined, set aside until required.
5. Then stir in all the tomatoes, continue cooking for 3 hours at high heat setting, add noodles and spinach, stir until mixed and cook for 12 minutes until spinach leaves have wilted.
6. When done, season the soup with salt and black pepper and then serve with prepared pesto ricotta.

Nutrition Value:
Calories: 450 Cal; Fat: 16.8 g; Carbs: 55.2 g; Protein: 22.6 g; Fiber: 13.2 g

Hot and Sour Soup

Preparation time: 5 minutes; Cooking time: 20 minutes; Servings: 4
Ingredients:
- 2 tablespoons dried wood ears
- 3.5 ounces bamboo shoots, sliced into thin strips
- 1 medium carrot, peeled, sliced into thin strips
- 5 dried shiitake mushrooms
- 1 tablespoon grated ginger
- 1 teaspoon minced garlic
- 1 teaspoon ground black pepper
- 1 teaspoon salt
- 1/4 cup soy sauce

- 1 teaspoon sugar
- 1/2 cup rice vinegar
- 4 cups vegetable stock
- 1 1/2 cup water, boiling
- 7.5 ounces tofu, extra-firm, drained
- 1 tablespoon green onion tops, chopped
- ¼ cup water, at room temperature
- 2 tablespoons cornstarch
- 1 teaspoon sesame oil

Method:
1. Take a small bowl, place wood ears in it, then pour in boiling water until covered and let stand for 30 minutes.
2. Meanwhile, take another bowl, place mushrooms in it, pour in 1 ½ cup water and let the mushrooms stand for 30 minutes.
3. After 30 minutes, drain the wood ears, rinse well and cut into slices, remove and discard the hard bits.
4. Similarly, drain the mushrooms, reserving their soaking liquid and slice the mushrooms, removing and discarding their stems.
5. Take a large pot, place it over medium-high heat, add all the ingredients including reserved mushroom liquid, leave the last five ingredients, stir well and bring the mixture to boil.

6. Then switch heat to medium level and simmer the soup for 10 minutes until cooked.
7. Meanwhile, place cornstarch in a bowl, add water at room temperature, and stir well until smooth.
8. Cut tofu into 1-inch pieces, add into the simmering soup along with cornstarch mixture, and continue to simmer the soup until it reaches to desired thickness.
9. Drizzle with sesame oil, distribute soup into bowls, garnish with green onions and serve.

Nutrition Value:

Calories: 152 Cal; Fat: 2 g; Carbs: 35 g; Protein: 4 g; Fiber: 8 g

Potato and Corn Chowder

Preparation time: 5 minutes; Cooking time: 16 minutes; Servings: 6
Ingredients:

- 1 tablespoon olive oil
- 2 medium carrots, peeled, chopped
- 2 ribs celery, chopped
- 1 medium white onion, peeled, chopped
- 1 ½ teaspoon minced garlic
- 1/4 cup all-purpose flour
- 1 teaspoon dried thyme
- 4 cups chopped white potatoes
- 2 cups vegetable broth
- 2 cups almond milk, unsweetened
- 3 tablespoons nutritional yeast
- 1 cup frozen corn kernels
- 1 teaspoon salt
- 1/4 teaspoon ground black pepper

Method:

1. Take a large pot, place it over medium-high heat, add oil and when hot, add onion, carrots, celery, and garlic and cook for 5 minutes until golden brown.
2. Then sprinkle with flour and thyme, stir until coated, cook for 1 minute until the flour has browned, then add yeast, potatoes, milk, and broth and stir until mixed.
3. Bring the mixture to simmer, cook for 8 minutes until tender, then add corn and season the soup with salt and black pepper.
4. Serve straight away.

Nutrition Value:

Calories: 126 Cal; Fat: 3 g; Carbs: 18 g; Protein: 6 g; Fiber: 3 g

Thai Coconut Soup

Preparation time: 10 minutes; Cooking time: 15 minutes; Servings: 12
Ingredients:

- 2 mangos, peeled, cut into bite-size pieces
- 1/2 cup green lentils, cooked
- 2 sweet potatoes, peeled, cubed
- 1/2 cup quinoa, cooked
- 1 green bell pepper, cored, cut into strips
- ½ teaspoon chopped basil
- ½ teaspoon chopped rosemary
- 2 tablespoons red curry paste
- 1/4 cup mixed nut
- 2 teaspoons orange zest
- 30 ounces coconut milk, unsweetened

Method:

1. Take a large saucepan, place it over medium-high heat, add sweet potatoes, pour in the milk and bring the mixture to boil.
2. Then switch heat to medium-low level, add remaining ingredients, except for quinoa and lentils, stir and cook for 15 minutes until vegetables have softened.
3. Then stir in quinoa and lentils, cook for 3 minutes until hot, and then serve.

Nutrition Value:

Calories: 232 Cal; Fat: 19.8 g; Carbs: 10.2 g; Protein: 7.8 g; Fiber: 0.8 g

Spanish Chickpea and Sweet Potato Stew

Preparation time: 5 minutes; Cooking time: 35 minutes; Servings: 4

Ingredients:

- 14 ounces cooked chickpeas
- 1 small sweet potato, peeled, cut into ½-inch cubes
- 1 medium red onion, sliced
- 3 ounces baby spinach
- 14 ounces crushed tomatoes
- 2 teaspoons minced garlic
- 1 teaspoon salt
- 1 1/2 teaspoons ground cumin
- 2 teaspoons harissa paste
- 2 teaspoons maple syrup
- ½ teaspoon ground black pepper
- 2 teaspoons sugar
- 1 tablespoon olive oil
- 1/2 cup vegetable stock
- 2 tablespoons chopped parsley
- 1 ounce slivered almonds, toasted
- Brown rice, cooked, for serving

Method:

1. Take a large saucepan, place it over low heat, add oil and when hot, add onion and garlic and cook for 5 minutes.
2. Then add sweet potatoes, season with cumin, stir in harissa paste and cook for 2 minutes until toasted.
3. Switch heat to medium-low level, add tomatoes and chickpeas, pour in vegetable stock, stir in maple syrup and sugar and simmer for 25 minutes until potatoes have softened, stirring every 10 minutes.
4. Then add spinach, cook for 1 minute until its leaves have wilted, and season with salt and black pepper.
5. When done, distribute cooked rice between bowls, top with stew, garnish with parsley and almonds and serve.

Nutrition Value:

Calories: 348 Cal; Fat: 16.5 g; Carbs: 41.2 g; Protein: 7.2 g; Fiber: 5.3 g

Pomegranate and Walnut Stew

Preparation time: 10 minutes; Cooking time: 55 minutes; Servings: 6

Ingredients:

- 1 head of cauliflower, cut into florets
- 1 medium white onion, peeled, diced
- 1 1/2 cups California walnuts, toasted
- 1 cup yellow split peas
- 1 1/2 tablespoons honey
- ¼ teaspoon salt
- ½ teaspoon turmeric
- ½ teaspoon cinnamon
- 2 tablespoons olive oil, separated
- 4 cups pomegranate juice
- 2 tablespoons chopped parsley
- 2 tablespoons chopped walnuts, for garnishing

Method:

1. Take a medium saute pan, place it over medium heat, add walnuts, cook for 5 minutes until toasted and then cool for 5 minutes.
2. Transfer walnuts to the food processor, pulse for 2 minutes until ground, and set aside until required.
3. Take a large saute pan, place it over medium heat, add 1 tablespoon oil and when hot, add onion and cook for 5 minutes until softened.
4. Switch heat to medium-low heat, then add lentils and walnuts, stir in cinnamon, salt, and turmeric, pour in honey and pomegranate, stir until mixed and simmer the mixture for 40 minutes until the sauce has reduced by half and lentils have softened.
5. Meanwhile, place cauliflower florets in a food processor and then pulse for 2 minutes until mixture resembles rice.

6. Take a medium to saute pan, place it over medium heat, add remaining oil and when hot, add cauliflower rice, cook for 5 minutes until softened, and then season with salt.
7. Serve cooked pomegranate and walnut sauce with cooked cauliflower rice and garnish with walnuts and parsley.

Nutrition Value:
Calories: 439 Cal; Fat: 25 g; Carbs: 67 g; Protein: 21 g; Fiber: 3 g

Sweet Potato, Kale and Peanut Stew

Preparation time: 10 minutes; Cooking time: 45 minutes; Servings: 3
Ingredients:

- 1/4 cup red lentils
- 2 medium sweet potatoes, peeled, cubed
- 1 medium white onion, peeled, diced
- 1 cup kale, chopped
- 2 tomatoes, diced
- 1/4 cup chopped green onion
- 1 teaspoon minced garlic
- 1 inch of ginger, grated
- 2 tablespoons toasted peanuts
- ¼ teaspoon ground black pepper
- 1 teaspoon ground cumin
- 1/2 teaspoon turmeric
- 1/8 teaspoon cayenne pepper
- 1 tablespoon peanut butter
- 1 1/2 cups vegetable broth
- 2 teaspoons coconut oil

Method:
1. Take a medium pot, place it medium heat, add oil and when it melts, add onions and cook for 5 minutes.
2. Then stir in ginger and garlic, cook for 2 minutes until fragrant, add lentils and potatoes along with all the spices, and stir until mixed.
3. Stir in tomatoes, pour in the broth, bring the mixture to boil, then switch heat to the low level and simmer for 30 minutes until cooked.
4. Then stir in peanut butter until incorporated and then puree by using an immersion blender until half-pureed.
5. Return stew over low heat, stir in kale, cook for 5 minutes until its leaves wilts, and then season with black pepper and salt.
6. Garnish the stew with peanuts and green onions and then serve.

Nutrition Value:
Calories: 401 Cal; Fat: 6.7 g; Carbs: 77.3 g; Protein: 10.8 g; Fiber: 16 g

Vegetarian Irish Stew

Preparation time: 5 minutes; Cooking time: 38 minutes; Servings: 6
Ingredients:

- 1 cup textured vegetable protein, chunks
- ½ cup split red lentils
- 2 medium onions, peeled, sliced
- 1 cup sliced parsnip
- 2 cups sliced mushrooms
- 1 cup diced celery,
- 1/4 cup flour
- 4 cups vegetable stock
- 1 cup rutabaga
- 1 bay leaf
- ½ cup fresh parsley
- 1 teaspoon sugar
- ¼ teaspoon ground black pepper
- 1/4 cup soy sauce
- ¼ teaspoon thyme
- 2 teaspoons marmite
- ¼ teaspoon rosemary
- 2/3 teaspoon salt
- ¼ teaspoon marjoram

Method:
1. Take a large soup pot, place it over medium heat, add oil and when it gets hot, add onions and cook for 5 minutes until softened.

2. Then switch heat to the low level, sprinkle with flour, stir well, add remaining ingredients, stir until combined and simmer for 30 minutes until vegetables have cooked.
3. When done, season the stew with salt and black pepper and then serve.

Nutrition Value:
Calories: 117.4 Cal; Fat: 4 g; Carbs: 22.8 g; Protein: 6.5 g; Fiber: 7.3 g

White Bean and Cabbage Stew

Preparation time: 5 minutes; Cooking time: 8 hours; Servings: 4
Ingredients:

- 3 cups cooked great northern beans
- 1.5 pounds potatoes, peeled, cut in large dice
- 1 large white onion, peeled, chopped
- ½ head of cabbage, chopped
- 3 ribs celery, chopped
- 4 medium carrots, peeled, sliced
- 14.5 ounces diced tomatoes
- 1/3 cup pearled barley
- 1 teaspoon minced garlic
- ½ teaspoon ground black pepper
- 1 bay leaf
- 1 teaspoon dried thyme
- ½ teaspoon crushed rosemary
- 1 teaspoon salt
- ½ teaspoon caraway seeds
- 1 tablespoon chopped parsley
- 8 cups vegetable broth

Method:
1. Switch on the slow cooker, then add all the ingredients except for salt, parsley, tomatoes, and beans and stir until mixed.
2. Shut the slow cooker with lid, and cook for 7 hours at low heat setting until cooked.
3. Then stir in remaining ingredients, stir until combined and continue cooking for 1 hour.
4. Serve straight away

Nutrition Value:
Calories: 150 Cal; Fat: 0.7 g; Carbs: 27 g; Protein: 7 g; Fiber: 9.4 g

Spinach and Cannellini Bean Stew

Preparation time: 10 minutes; Cooking time: 15 minutes; Servings: 6
Ingredients:

- 28 ounces cooked cannellini beans
- 24 ounces tomato passata
- 17 ounces spinach chopped
- ¼ teaspoon ground black pepper
- 2/3 teaspoon salt
- 1 ¼ teaspoon curry powder
- 1 cup cashew butter
- ¼ teaspoon cardamom
- 2 tablespoons olive oil
- 1 teaspoon salt
- ¼ cup cashews
- 2 tablespoons chopped basil
- 2 tablespoons chopped parsley

Method:
1. Take a large saucepan, place it over medium heat, add 1 tablespoon oil and when hot, add spinach and cook for 3 minutes until fried.
2. Then stir in butter and tomato passata until well mixed, bring the mixture to a near boil, add beans and season with ¼ teaspoon curry powder, black pepper, and salt.
3. Take a small saucepan, place it over medium heat, add remaining oil, stir in cashew, stir in salt and curry powder and cook for 4 minutes until roasted, set aside until required.
4. Transfer cooked stew into a bowl, top with roasted cashews, basil, and parsley, and then serve.

Nutrition Value:
Calories: 242 Cal; Fat: 10.2 g; Carbs: 31 g; Protein: 11 g; Fiber: 8.5 g

Fennel and Chickpeas Provençal

Preparation time: 10 minutes; Cooking time: 50 minutes; Servings: 4

Ingredients:

- 15 ounces cooked chickpeas
- 3 fennel bulbs, sliced
- 1 medium onion, peeled, sliced
- 15 ounces diced tomatoes
- 10 black olives, pitted, cured
- 10 Kalamata olives, pitted
- 1 ½ teaspoon minced garlic
- 1 teaspoon salt
- 1/8 teaspoon ground black pepper
- 1 teaspoon Herbes de Provence
- 1/2 teaspoon red pepper flakes
- 2 tablespoons olive oil
- 1/2 cup water
- 2 tablespoons chopped parsley

Method:

1. Take a saucepan, place it over medium-high heat, add oil and when hot, add onion, fennel, and garlic and cook for 20 minutes until softened.
2. Then add remaining ingredients except for olives and chickpeas, bring the mixture to boil, switch heat to medium-low level and simmer for 15 minutes.
3. Then add remaining ingredients, cook for 10 minutes until hot, garnish stew with parsley and serve.

Nutrition Value:

Calories: 395 Cal; Fat: 13 g; Carbs: 56 g; Protein: 16 g; Fiber: 13 g

Cabbage Stew

Preparation time: 10 minutes; Cooking time: 50 minutes; Servings: 6

Ingredients:

- 12 ounces cooked Cannellini beans
- 8 ounces smoked tofu, firm, sliced
- 1 medium cabbage, chopped
- 1 large white onion, peeled, julienned
- 2 ½ teaspoon minced garlic
- 1 tablespoon sweet paprika
- 5 tablespoons tomato paste
- 3 teaspoons smoked paprika
- 1/3 teaspoon ground black pepper
- 2 teaspoons dried thyme
- 2/3 teaspoon salt
- ½ tsp ground coriander
- 3 bay leaves
- 4 tablespoons olive oil
- 1 cup vegetable broth

Method:

1. Take a large saucepan, place it over medium heat, add 3 tablespoons oil and when hot, add onion and garlic and cook for 3 minutes or until saute.
2. Add cabbage, pour in water, simmer for 10 minutes or until softened, then stir in all the spices and continue cooking for 30 minutes.
3. Add beans and tomato paste, pour in water, stir until mixed and cook for 15 minutes until thoroughly cooked.
4. Take a separate skillet pan, add 1 tablespoon oil and when hot, add tofu slices and cook for 5 minutes until golden brown on both sides.
5. Serve cooked cabbage stew with fried tofu.

Nutrition Value:

Calories: 182 Cal; Fat: 8.3 g; Carbs: 27 g; Protein: 5.5 g; Fiber: 9.4 g

Kimchi Stew

Preparation time: 10 minutes; Cooking time: 25 minutes; Servings: 4

Ingredients:

- 1 pound tofu, extra-firm, pressed, cut into 1-inch pieces
- 4 cups napa cabbage kimchi, vegan, chopped
- 1 small white onion, peeled, diced

- 2 cups sliced shiitake mushroom caps
- 1 ½ teaspoon minced garlic
- 2 tablespoons soy sauce
- 2 tablespoons olive oil, divided
- 4 cups vegetable broth
- 2 tablespoons chopped scallions

Method:
1. Take a large pot, place it over medium heat, add 1 tablespoon oil and when hot, add tofu pieces in a single layer and cook for 10 minutes until browned on all sides.
2. When cooked, transfer tofu pieces to a plate, add remaining oil to the pot and when hot, add onion and cook for 5 minutes until soft.
3. Stir in garlic, cook for 1 minute until fragrant, stir in kimchi, continue cooking for 2 minutes, then add mushrooms and pour in broth.
4. Switch heat to medium-high level, bring the mixture to boil, then switch heat to medium-low level and simmer for 10 minutes until mushrooms are softened.
5. Stir in tofu, taste to adjust seasoning, and garnish with scallions.
6. Serve straight away.

Nutrition Value:
Calories: 153 Cal; Fat: 8.2 g; Carbs: 25 g; Protein: 8.4 g; Fiber: 2.6 g

African Peanut Lentil Soup

Preparation time: 10 minutes; Cooking time: 25 minutes; Servings: 3
Ingredients:
- 1/2 cup red lentils
- 1/2 medium white onion, sliced
- 2 medium tomatoes, chopped
- 1/2 cup baby spinach
- 1/2 cup sliced zucchini
- 1/2 cup sliced sweet potatoes
- ½ cup sliced potatoes
- ½ cup broccoli florets
- 2 teaspoons minced garlic
- 1 inch of ginger, grated
- 1 tablespoon tomato paste
- 1/4 teaspoon ground black pepper
- 1 teaspoon salt
- 1 ½ teaspoon ground cumin
- 2 teaspoons ground coriander
- 2 tablespoons peanuts
- 1 teaspoon Harissa Spice Blend
- 1 tablespoon sambal oelek
- 1/4 cup almond butter
- 1 teaspoon olive oil
- 1 teaspoon lemon juice
- 2 ½ cups vegetable stock

Method:
1. Take a large saucepan, place it over medium heat, add oil and when hot, add onion and cook for 5 minutes until translucent.
2. Meanwhile, place tomatoes in a blender, add garlic, ginger and sambal oelek along with all the spices and pulse until pureed.
3. Pour this mixture into the onions, cook for 5 minutes, then add remaining ingredients except for spinach, peanuts and lemon juice and simmer for 15 minutes.
4. Taste to adjust the seasoning, stir in spinach, and cook for 5 minutes until cooked.
5. Ladle soup into bowls, garnish with lime juice and peanuts and serve.

Nutrition Value:
Calories: 411 Cal; Fat: 17 g; Carbs: 50 g; Protein: 20 g; Fiber: 18 g

Spicy Bean Stew

Preparation time: 5 minutes; Cooking time: 50 minutes; Servings: 4
Ingredients:
- 7 ounces cooked black eye beans
- 14 ounces chopped tomatoes
- 2 medium carrots, peeled, diced
- 7 ounces cooked kidney beans
- 1 leek, diced
- ½ a chili, chopped
- 1 teaspoon minced garlic
- 1/3 teaspoon ground black pepper

- 2/3 teaspoon salt
- 1 teaspoon red chili powder
- 1 lemon, juiced
- 3 tablespoons white wine
- 1 tablespoon olive oil
- 1 2/3 cups vegetable stock

Method:
1. Take a large saucepan, place it over medium-high heat, add oil and when hot, add leeks and cook for 8 minutes or until softened.
2. Then add carrots, continue cooking for 4 minutes, stir in chili and garlic, pour in the wine, and continue cooking for 2 minutes.
3. Add tomatoes, stir in lemon juice, pour in the stock and bring the mixture to boil.
4. Switch heat to medium level, simmer for 35 minutes until stew has thickened, then add both beans along with remaining ingredients and cook for 5 minutes until hot.
5. Serve straight away.

Nutrition Value:
Calories: 114 Cal; Fat: 1.6 g; Carbs: 19 g; Protein: 6 g; Fiber: 8.4 g

Eggplant, Onion and Tomato Stew

Preparation time: 5 minutes; Cooking time: 5 minutes; Servings: 4
Ingredients:
- 3 1/2 cups cubed eggplant
- 1 cup diced white onion
- 2 cups diced tomatoes
- 1 teaspoon ground cumin
- 1/8 teaspoon ground cayenne pepper
- 1 teaspoon salt
- 1 cup tomato sauce
- 1/2 cup water

Method:
1. Switch on the instant pot, place all the ingredients in it, stir until mixed, and seal the pot.
2. Press the 'manual' button and cook for 5 minutes at high-pressure setting until cooked.
3. When done, do quick pressure release, open the instant pot, and stir the stew.
4. Serve straight away.

Nutrition Value:
Calories: 88 Cal; Fat: 1 g; Carbs: 21 g; Protein: 3 g; Fiber: 6 g

White Bean Stew

Preparation time: 5 minutes; Cooking time: 10 hours and 10 minutes; Servings: 10
Ingredients:
- 2 cups chopped spinach
- 28 ounces diced tomatoes
- 2 pounds white beans, dried
- 2 cups chopped chard
- 2 large carrots, peeled, diced
- 2 cups chopped kale
- 3 large celery stalks, diced
- 1 medium white onion, peeled, diced
- 1 ½ teaspoon minced garlic
- 2 tablespoons salt
- 1 teaspoon dried rosemary
- ½ teaspoon Ground black pepper, to taste
- 1 teaspoon dried thyme
- 1 teaspoon dried oregano
- 1 bay leaf
- 10 cups water

Method:
1. Switch on the slow cooker, add all the ingredients in it, except for kale, chard, and spinach and stir until combined.
2. Shut the cooker with lid and cook for 10 hours at a low heat setting until thoroughly cooked.
3. When done, stir in kale, chard, and spinach, and cook for 10 minutes until leaves wilt.
4. Serve straight away.

Nutrition Value:

Calories: 109 Cal; Fat: 2.4 g; Carbs: 17.8 g; Protein: 5.3 g; Fiber: 6 g

Brussel Sprouts Stew

Preparation time: 10 minutes; Cooking time: 55 minutes; Servings: 4
Ingredients:
- 35 ounces Brussels sprouts
- 5 medium potato, peeled, chopped
- 1 medium onion, peeled, chopped
- 2 carrot, peeled, cubed
- 2 teaspoons smoked paprika
- 1/8 teaspoon ground black pepper
- 1/8 teaspoon salt
- 3 tablespoons caraway seeds
- 1/2 teaspoon red chili powder
- 1 tablespoon nutmeg
- 1 tablespoon olive oil
- 4 ½ cups hot vegetable stock

Method:
1. Take a large pot, place it over medium-high heat, add oil and when hot, add onion and cook for 1 minute.
2. Then add carrot and potato, cook for 2 minutes, then add Brussel sprouts and cook for 5 minutes.
3. Stir in all the spices, pour in vegetable stock, bring the mixture to boil, switch heat to medium-low and simmer for 45 minutes until cooked and stew reach to desired thickness.
4. Serve straight away.

Nutrition Value:
Calories: 156 Cal; Fat: 3 g; Carbs: 22 g; Protein: 12 g; Fiber: 5.1100 g

Vegetarian Gumbo

Preparation time: 10 minutes; Cooking time: 45 minutes; Servings: 4
Ingredients:
- 1 1/2 cups diced zucchini
- 16-ounces cooked red beans
- 4 cups sliced okra
- 1 1/2 cups diced green pepper
- 1 1/2 cups chopped white onion
- 1 1/2 cups diced red bell pepper
- 8 cremini mushrooms, quartered
- 1 cup sliced celery
- 3 teaspoons minced garlic
- 1 medium tomato, chopped
- 1 teaspoon red pepper flakes
- 1 teaspoon dried thyme
- 3 tablespoons all-purpose flour
- 1 tablespoon smoked paprika
- 1 teaspoon dried oregano
- 1/4 teaspoon nutmeg
- 1 teaspoon soy sauce
- 1 1/2 teaspoons liquid smoke
- 2 tablespoons mustard
- 1 tablespoon apple cider vinegar
- 1 tablespoon Worcestershire sauce, vegetarian
- 1/2 teaspoon hot sauce
- 3 tablespoons olive oil
- 4 cups vegetable stock
- 1/2 cups sliced green onion
- 4 cups cooked jasmine rice

Method:
1. Take a Dutch oven, place it over medium heat, add oil and flour and cook for 5 minutes until fragrant.
2. Switch heat to the medium low level, and continue cooking for 20 minutes until roux becomes dark brown, whisking constantly.
3. Meanwhile, place the tomato in a food processor, add garlic and onion along with remaining ingredients, except for stock, zucchini, celery, mushroom, green and red bell pepper, and pulse for 2 minutes until smooth.
4. Pour the mixture into the pan, return pan over medium-high heat, stir until mixed, and cook for 5 minutes until all the liquid has evaporated.

5. Stir in stock, bring it to simmer, then add remaining vegetables and simmer for 20 minutes until tender.
6. Garnish gumbo with green onions and serve with rice.

Nutrition Value:
Calories: 160 Cal; Fat: 7.3 g; Carbs: 20 g; Protein: 7 g; Fiber: 5.7 g

Black Bean and Quinoa Stew

Preparation time: 10 minutes; Cooking time: 6 hours; Servings: 6
Ingredients:

- 1 pound black beans, dried, soaked overnight
- 3/4 cup quinoa, uncooked
- 1 medium red bell pepper, cored, chopped
- 1 medium red onion, peeled, diced
- 1 medium green bell pepper, cored, chopped
- 28-ounce diced tomatoes
- 2 dried chipotle peppers
- 1 ½ teaspoon minced garlic
- 2/3 teaspoon sea salt
- 2 teaspoons red chili powder
- 1/3 teaspoon ground black pepper
- 1 teaspoon coriander powder
- 1 dried cinnamon stick
- 1/4 cup cilantro
- 7 cups of water

Method:
1. Switch on the slow cooker, add all the ingredients in it, except for salt, and stir until mixed.
2. Shut the cooker with lid and cook for 6 hours at a high heat setting until cooked.
3. When done, stir salt into the stew until mixed, remove cinnamon sticks and serve.

Nutrition Value:
Calories: 308 Cal; Fat: 2 g; Carbs: 70 g; Protein: 23 g; Fiber: 32 g

Root Vegetable Stew

Preparation time: 10 minutes; Cooking time: 8 hours and 10 minutes; Servings: 6
Ingredients:

- 2 cups chopped kale
- 1 large white onion, peeled, chopped
- 1 pound parsnips, peeled, chopped
- 1 pound potatoes, peeled, chopped
- 2 celery ribs, chopped
- 1 pound butternut squash, peeled, deseeded, chopped
- 1 pound carrots, peeled, chopped
- 3 teaspoons minced garlic
- 1 pound sweet potatoes, peeled, chopped
- 1 bay leaf
- 1 teaspoon ground black pepper
- 1/2 teaspoon sea salt
- 1 tablespoon chopped sage
- 3 cups vegetable broth

Method:
1. Switch on the slow cooker, add all the ingredients in it, except for the kale, and stir until mixed.
2. Shut the cooker with lid and cook for 8 hours at a low heat setting until cooked.
3. When done, add kale into the stew, stir until mixed, and cook for 10 minutes until leaves have wilted.
4. Serve straight away.

Nutrition Value:
Calories: 120 Cal; Fat: 1 g; Carbs: 28 g; Protein: 4 g; Fiber: 6 g

Portobello Mushroom Stew

Preparation time: 10 minutes; Cooking time: 8 hours; Servings: 4
Ingredients:

- 8 cups vegetable broth
- 1 cup dried wild mushrooms
- 1 cup dried chickpeas
- 3 cups chopped potato
- 2 cups chopped carrots
- 1 cup corn kernels
- 2 cups diced white onions
- 1 tablespoon minced parsley
- 3 cups chopped zucchini
- 1 tablespoon minced rosemary
- 1 1/2 teaspoon ground black pepper
- 1 teaspoon dried sage
- 2/3 teaspoon salt
- 1 teaspoon dried oregano
- 3 tablespoons soy sauce
- 1 1/2 teaspoons liquid smoke
- 8 ounces tomato paste

Method:
1. Switch on the slow cooker, add all the ingredients in it, and stir until mixed.
2. Shut the cooker with lid and cook for 10 hours at a high heat setting until cooked.
3. Serve straight away.

Nutrition Value:
Calories: 447 Cal; Fat: 36 g; Carbs: 24 g; Protein: 11 g; Fiber: 2 g

Chapter 4: Salads

Chopped Kale Power Salad

Preparation time: 10 minutes; Cooking time: 40 minutes; Servings: 4
Ingredients:
For the Salad:

- 15 ounces cooked chickpeas
- 8 cups chopped kale
- 6 cups diced sweet potatoes
- 1 large avocado, pitted, diced
- 1/4 cup chopped red onion
- 2 teaspoons and 1 tablespoon olive oil, divided
- 1/4 teaspoon ground black pepper
- 3/4 teaspoons salt, divided
- 1/3 cup chopped almonds
- 1/2 of a large lemon, juiced
- 1/3 cup dried cranberries

For the Lemon Tahini Dressing:

- 1/2 cup tahini
- 1/4 teaspoon salt
- 1 lemon juiced
- 6 tablespoons warm water

Method:
1. Place diced sweet potatoes on a sheet pan, drizzle with 2 teaspoon oil, season with ¼ teaspoon black pepper and ½ teaspoon salt and bake for 40 minutes at 375 degrees F until roasted, tossing halfway.
2. Meanwhile, place chopped kale in a bowl, drizzle with lemon juice and remaining oil, season with remaining salt, toss until combined, and massage the leaves for 1 minute.
3. Prepare the dressing and for this, place all of its ingredients in a bowl and whisk until combined.
4. Top kale salad with sweet potatoes, drizzle with tahini dressing, and serve.

Nutrition Value:
Calories: 82 Cal; Fat: 2 g; Carbs: 15 g; Protein: 2 g; Fiber: 1 g

Greens Salad with Black Eyed Peas

Preparation time: 5 minutes; Cooking time: 6 minutes; Servings: 3
Ingredients:

- 2 cups cooked black-eyed peas, cooked
- 1/2 cup cooked quinoa
- 3 cups chopped purple cabbage
- 5 cups chopped kale
- 1/2 of a shallot, peeled, chopped
- 1 1/2 cup shredded carrot
- 1 teaspoon minced garlic
- 1/2 teaspoon sea salt
- 1/3 teaspoon ground black pepper
- 1 tablespoon apple cider vinegar and more as needed
- 1 tablespoon lemon juice
- 2 tablespoons olive oil

Method:
1. Sauté garlic, shallot, and cabbage in 1 tablespoon for 2 minutes over medium heat, then add remaining oil along with kale, season with salt, and cook for 4 minutes until kale has wilted.
2. Transfer the vegetables to a bowl, add remaining ingredients and toss until combined.
3. Serve straight away

Nutrition Value:
Calories: 166 Cal; Fat: 5.3 g; Carbs: 28.6 g; Protein: 4.2 g; Fiber: 6.7 g

Pear, Pomegranate and Roasted Butternut Squash Salad

Preparation time: 10 minutes; Cooking time: 10 minutes; Servings: 3

Ingredients:

- 1 medium butternut squash, peeled, cut into noodles
- 5 ounces of arugula
- 1 large pear, spiralized

For the Vinaigrette:

- ½ teaspoon minced garlic
- 1 teaspoon white sesame seeds
- ¼ teaspoon ground black pepper
- 1 tablespoon maple syrup

- ¾ cup pomegranate seeds
- 2/3 teaspoon salt
- 1/3 teaspoon ground black pepper
- 3/4 cup chopped walnuts

- 1 tablespoon olive oil
- 1 tablespoon soy sauce
- 1 tablespoon sesame oil
- 2 tablespoons apple cider vinegar

Method:

1. Place butternut squash noodles on a baking sheet, spray with oil, season with salt and black pepper and roast for 10 minutes at 400 degrees F until cooked.
2. Meanwhile, prepare the vinaigrette and for this, place all its ingredients in a bowl and whisk until combined.
3. When done, place pear, walnuts, and arugula in a large bowl, then add squash, drizzle with vinaigrette and toss until combined.
4. Serve straight away.

Nutrition Value:

Calories: 423 Cal; Fat: 29 g; Carbs: 38 g; Protein: 8 g; Fiber: 6 g

Cranberry and Quinoa Salad

Preparation time: 15 minutes; Cooking time: 0 minute; Servings: 6

Ingredients:

- 2 cups cooked quinoa
- 1/4 cup chopped red onion
- 1/2 cup shredded carrots
- 1/2 cup dried cranberries
- 1/2 cup diced green bell pepper
- 4 tablespoons chopped cilantro
- 1 ½ teaspoon curry powder
- 2/3 teaspoon salt

- 1/3 teaspoon ground black pepper
- 1/8 teaspoon cumin
- 1/3 cup toasted sliced almonds
- 4 tablespoons pepitas
- Olive oil as needed for drizzling
- 1 lime, juiced
- Lime, sliced into wedges

Method:

1. Place all the ingredients in a large bowl, toss until well combined and let the salad refrigerate for 15 minutes.
2. Serve straight away.

Nutrition Value:

Calories: 199 Cal; Fat: 6 g; Carbs: 30 g; Protein: 6 g; Fiber: 4 g

Black Bean Taco Salad

Preparation time: 10 minutes; Cooking time: 30 minutes; Servings: 4

Ingredients:

For the Black Beans:

- 1 1/2 cups cooked black beans
- 1/2 teaspoon garlic powder
- 1/2 teaspoon salt
- 1/2 teaspoon cayenne

- 1/2 teaspoon smoked paprika
- 2 teaspoons red chili powder
- 1 teaspoon cumin
- 1/4 cup water

For the Roasted Chickpeas:

- 1 1/2 cups cooked chickpeas
- 1/2 teaspoon salt
- 1 teaspoon red chili powder

For the Salad:
- 1 medium red bell pepper, cored, diced
- 1 medium head of green leaf lettuce

For the Dressing:
- 1 ½ cup vegan Cumin Ranch Dressing

- 1/4 teaspoon cinnamon
- 1 teaspoon cumin

- 1 cup fresh corn kernels
- 2 chopped tomatoes
- 1 avocado, pitted, diced

Method:
1. Season chickpeas with salt, cinnamon, chili powder, and cumin, spread them in an even layer on a baking sheet and bake for 30 minutes at 400 degrees F until roasted, stirring halfway.
2. Meanwhile, prepare the black beans and for this, place them on a skillet pan, add remaining ingredients, stir until well mixed and cook for 5 minutes until warmed, set aside until required.
3. Assemble salad and for this, place all its ingredients in a bowl, toss until mixed, then add roasted chickpeas and black beans, drizzle with ranch dressing and serve.

Nutrition Value:
Calories: 332 Cal; Fat: 7 g; Carbs: 51 g; Protein: 16 g; Fiber: 17 g

Cucumber Salad with Tofu

Preparation time: 10 minutes; Cooking time: 10 minutes; Servings: 4

Ingredients:
- 2 large cucumbers, sliced
- ½ of medium green bell pepper, sliced into strips
- 14 ounces tofu, extra-firm, drained, cubed
- 3 green onions, chopped

- ½ of green chili pepper, deseeded, sliced into thin strips
- 3 large carrots, shaved into ribbons
- ¼ teaspoon salt
- 1/3 cup roasted almond slices
- 1/2 cup cilantro leaves and stem
- 1 tablespoon sesame oil

For the Dressing:
- 2 cloves of garlic, peeled
- 1-inch piece of ginger, grated
- ¼ teaspoon red pepper flakes
- 1 tablespoon soy sauce

- 2 tablespoons rice vinegar
- 1 teaspoon maple syrup
- 6 tablespoons sesame oil

Method:
1. Fry tofu cubes in hot sesame oil over medium heat for 10 minutes until browned and then set aside.
2. Meanwhile, sprinkle salt over cucumber slices, set aside for 10 minutes, then drain them, rinse them and pat dry with paper towels.
3. Prepare the dressing, and for this, place all its ingredients in a food processor and process for 2 minutes until smooth.
4. Place everything in a large bowl, toss until well coated, then top the salad with extra nuts and green onions and serve.

Nutrition Value:
Calories: 461 Cal; Fat: 40.5 g; Carbs: 14.2 g; Protein: 19.4 g; Fiber: 4.7 g

Roasted Vegetable and Quinoa Salad

Preparation time: 10 minutes; Cooking time: 25 minutes; Servings: 4

Ingredients:

For the Roasted Vegetables:
- 1 carrot, peeled, chopped
- 1 medium sweet potato, peeled, chopped
- 1 red bell pepper, cored, cubed
- 1 zucchini, peeled, cubed

For the Quinoa:
- 1/2 cup frozen peas
- 1 1/2 cup cooked quinoa

For the dressing:
- 1 teaspoon minced garlic
- 1/4 teaspoon salt
- 1/4 teaspoon cinnamon
- 1/2 teaspoon ground cumin

- 1 tablespoon dried mixed herbs
- 1 red onion, peeled, sliced
- 1 tablespoon olive oil
- 1/2 teaspoon salt
- ¼ teaspoon ground black pepper

- 1 cup chopped kale

- 3 tablespoons tahini
- 1/2 teaspoon brown rice syrup
- 2 tablespoons olive oil
- 3 tablespoons lemon juice

Method:
1. Place all the vegetables in a large baking dish, season with salt and black pepper, sprinkle with herbs, drizzle with oil, toss until mixed, and then bake them for 25 minutes at 392 degrees F until roasted.
2. Cook the quinoa in a saucepan, add kale and peas in the last three minutes, and when done, let it stand for 10 minutes.
3. Prepare the dressing, and for this, place all of its ingredients in a blender and pulse until smooth.
4. Place everything in a large bowl, drizzle with dressing and toss until mixed.
5. Serve straight away.

Nutrition Value:
Calories: 151 Cal; Fat: 4.7 g; Carbs: 23.7 g; Protein: 4.8 g; Fiber: 3.6 g

Kidney Beans, Quinoa, Vegetable and Salsa Bowl

Preparation time: 5 minutes; Cooking time: 20 minutes; Servings: 2

Ingredients:

For the Kidney Beans:
- 1 ½ cups cooked kidney beans
- 3/4 teaspoon salt
- 1 large tomato
- 3 cloves of garlic, peeled
- 1/2 teaspoon onion powder
- 1/2-inch piece of ginger
- 1/2 teaspoon paprika
- 1/2 teaspoon dried fenugreek leaves

- 1/3 teaspoon red chili powder
- 1/4 teaspoon turmeric
- 1 teaspoon coriander powder
- 1/2 teaspoon garam masala
- 1/2 teaspoon cumin powder
- 1 teaspoon lemon juice
- 1/2 cup water

For the Vegetables:
- Sliced roasted zucchini as needed
- Sliced roasted broccoli stems as needed

- Sliced radishes as needed
- Sliced lettuce as needed
- Mango salsa as needed

Method:
1. Prepare the beans, and for this, place all the ingredients, except the first two ones, in a blender, pulse until smooth, then add this mixture into a saucepan and cook for 7 minutes over medium heat until thickened.
2. Then stir in beans, season with salt, and cook for 12 minutes until beans are very tender.

3. When done, place beans in a large bowl, top with vegetables and salsa, toss until mixed and serve.

Nutrition Value:
Calories: 503 Cal; Fat: 2 g; Carbs: 94 g; Protein: 32 g; Fiber: 24 g

Lentil Fattoush Salad

Preparation time: 10 minutes; Cooking time: 7 minutes; Servings: 2
Ingredients:
For the Salad:
- 1/3 cup green lentils, cooked
- ¼ small cucumber, chopped
- 2 stalks of celery, chopped
- 1 small radish, peeled, sliced
- 4 cups arugula
- 1 carrot, chopped
- ¼ cup dates, chopped
- 1/3 teaspoon salt
- 2 teaspoons olive oil
- 1 pita pocket, whole-wheat, chopped
- 2 tablespoons toasted sunflower seeds

For the Vinaigrette:
- 1 tablespoon Dijon mustard
- 2 tablespoons balsamic vinegar
- 1 tablespoon maple syrup
- 2 tablespoons olive oil

Method:
1. Place pita pieces on a cookie sheet lined with parchment paper, drizzle with oil, and season with salt, toss until mixed, spread evenly, and bake for 7 minutes at 425 degrees F until golden, and when done, cool them.
2. Meanwhile, prepare the vinaigrette and for this, place all of its ingredients in a bowl and whisk until combined.
3. Add remaining ingredients in a bowl, add cooled pita chips, drizzle with vinaigrette and toss until mixed.
4. Serve straight away.

Nutrition Value:
Calories: 460 Cal; Fat: 24 g; Carbs: 52 g; Protein: 11 g; Fiber: 11 g

Rainbow Salad Bowl

Preparation time: 10 minutes; Cooking time: 0 minute; Servings: 4
Ingredients:
- 1 cup cooked quinoa
- 1 tablespoon hemp seeds
- 1 head of romaine lettuce, rib removed, leaves chopped
- 1/2 avocado, peeled, pitted, sliced
- ¼ of pickled red onion
- 1/2 cup diced cucumber
- ¼ cup pomegranate seeds
- ½ of lime, juiced
- 1/2 cup cilantro lime hummus

Method:
1. Place all the ingredients except for lime juice, hummus, and hemp seeds in a bowl and toss until mixed.
2. Place hummus in the middle, drizzle with lime juice, sprinkle with hemp seeds, and then serve.

Nutrition Value:
Calories: 42 Cal; Fat: 1 g; Carbs: 6 g; Protein: 3 g; Fiber: 2.8 g

Sweet Potato Salad

Preparation time: 10 minutes; Cooking time: 35 minutes; Servings: 4
Ingredients:

- 2 large sweet potatoes, peeled, 1 1/2-inch cubes
- 1/3 teaspoon ground black pepper
- 1/2 teaspoon salt

For the Dressing:
- 1 small bunch of chives, chopped
- 1 medium shallot, peeled, diced
- 2 spring onions, trimmed, diced

- 1/2 teaspoon paprika
- 1/2 teaspoon oregano
- 1/2 teaspoon cayenne pepper
- 1 tablespoon olive oil

- 1 tablespoon maple syrup
- 2 teaspoons olive oil
- 3 tablespoons red wine vinegar

Method:
1. Spread sweet potato cubes on a baking sheet, drizzle with oil, season with all the spices, toss until mixed, spread evenly, and then bake for 35 minutes at 390 degrees F until roasted.
2. Prepare the dressing and for this, place all of its ingredients in a bowl and stir until combined.
3. When sweet potatoes have roasted, let them cool for 10 minutes, then drizzle with salad dressing and serve straight away.

Nutrition Value:
Calories: 257 Cal; Fat: 6.1 g; Carbs: 48.8 g; Protein: 3.3 g; Fiber: 7.7 g

Lentil Salad with Spinach

Preparation time: 10 minutes; Cooking time: 0 minute; Servings: 4
Ingredients:
For the Salad:
- 2 small apples, cut into small pieces
- 3 cups cooked brown lentils
- ½ cup fresh spinach
- 1/2 cup walnuts, chopped

- 1 medium avocado, pitted, cut into slices
- 1 pomegranate, halved, seeded, rinsed

For the dressing:
- 1 clove of garlic, peeled
- ¼ teaspoon ground black pepper
- ¼ teaspoon salt
- 2 teaspoons orange zest

- 3 tablespoons tahini
- 2 tablespoons olive oil
- 4 tablespoons orange juice
- 6 tablespoons water

Method:
1. Prepare the dressing, and for this, place all of its ingredients in a food processor and pulse until smooth.
2. Prepare the salad and for this, place all its ingredients in a bowl, toss until mixed, then drizzle with prepared dressing and stir until combined.
3. Serve straight away.

Nutrition Value:
Calories: 310 Cal; Fat: 17.7 g; Carbs: 30.3 g; Protein: 11.2 g; Fiber: 11 g

Butternut Squash and Kale Salad

Preparation time: 10 minutes; Cooking time: 8 minutes; Servings: 4
Ingredients:
For the Salad:
- 6 cups butternut squash, spiralized
- 5 cups kale, chopped, steamed

- 1/3 cup pumpkin seeds
- 1/2 cup pomegranate seeds

For the Dressing:
- ½ teaspoon salt
- ½ teaspoon ground black pepper

- 1/2 teaspoon cinnamon
- 1 tablespoon maple syrup

- 1/2 teaspoon mustard
- 2 tablespoons apple cider vinegar
- 3 tablespoons olive oil

Method:
1. Place spiralized squash on a baking sheet, toss with olive oil and bake for 8 minutes at 400 degrees F until roasted.
2. When done, let squash cool for 10 minutes, then add it into a large bowl along with remaining ingredients for the salad and toss until mixed.
3. Prepare the dressing and for this, place all of its ingredients in a bowl and stir until combined.
4. Drizzle the dressing over the salad, toss until mixed, and then serve.

Nutrition Value:
Calories: 200 Cal; Fat: 5 g; Carbs: 48 g; Protein: 6 g; Fiber: 4 g

Grilled Corn Salad Bowl

Preparation time: 10 minutes; Cooking time: 0 minute; Servings: 4
Ingredients:
- ½ cup of beluga lentils, cooked
- 2 ears of fresh corn, grilled
- ½ cup pickled onions
- 1 medium avocado, peeled, sliced
- 1 green chili, chopped
- 2 cups arugula
- ¼ teaspoon ground black pepper
- 2/3 teaspoon salt
- 2 limes, juiced
- 4 tablespoons olive oil
- 10 basil leaves, chopped
- ¼ cup pine nuts, toasted

Method:
1. Place all the ingredients in the bowl, except for lime juice and oil, and stir until mixed.
2. Drizzle with lime juice and oil, toss until mixed and serve.

Nutrition Value:
Calories: 179 Cal; Fat: 6.3 g; Carbs: 30 g; Protein: 6.3 g; Fiber: 5.5 g

Nectarine and Arugula Salad

Preparation time: 5 minutes; Cooking time: 15 minutes; Servings: 8
Ingredients:
- 4 cups arugula
- 2 tablespoons pine nuts, toasted
- 4 cups torn lettuce
- 3 medium nectarines, sliced
- 2 tablespoons crumbled blue cheese

For the Dressing:
- 1/8 teaspoon salt
- 1 teaspoon Dijon mustard
- 1/8 teaspoon ground black pepper
- 2 teaspoons sugar
- 2 tablespoons raspberry vinegar
- 3 tablespoons olive oil

Method:
1. Prepare the dressing and for this, place all of its ingredients in a bowl and whisk until smooth.
2. Prepare the salad and for this, place all its ingredients in a bowl, toss until mixed, then drizzle with prepared dressing and stir until combined.
3. Serve straight away.

Nutrition Value:
Calories: 101 Cal; Fat: 7 g; Carbs: 9 g; Protein: 2 g; Fiber: 1 g

Roasted Butternut Squash Salad

Preparation time: 10 minutes; Cooking time: 30 minutes; Servings: 4
Ingredients:

For the Dressing:
- 1/8 teaspoon salt
- 2 tablespoons lime juice
- 1 tablespoon olive oil

- 1 teaspoon sriracha
- 1/2 teaspoon honey

For the Salad:
- 4 cups arugula
- 1 pound butternut squash, peeled, cubed
- 1 1/2 teaspoons olive oil
- 3/4 cups cooked black beans

- 1/4 teaspoon ground black pepper
- 1/4 teaspoon salt
- 1/2 teaspoon ground cumin
- 1/4 cup pepitas, toasted

Method:
1. Place squash cubes on a baking tray, drizzle with oil, season with salt, black pepper, and cumin, toss until coated and bake for 30 minutes until roasted.
2. Meanwhile, prepare the dressing and for this, place all of its ingredients in a bowl and whisk until smooth.
3. When squash is done, let it cool for 10 minutes, then place it in a bowl along with remaining ingredients of the salad, drizzle with dressing and toss until mixed.
4. Serve straight away.

Nutrition Value:
Calories: 219 Cal; Fat: 13 g; Carbs: 22.4 g; Protein: 7.2 g; Fiber: 7 g

Farro, Cannellini Bean, and Pesto Salad

Preparation time: 10 minutes; Cooking time: 15 minutes; Servings: 4
Ingredients:
For the Pesto:
- 1/2 of a lemon, juiced
- 2 cups parsley
- 4 cloves of garlic, peeled
- 1/3 cup brazil nuts

- 1 teaspoon salt
- 1/4 cup nutritional yeast
- 1/2 cup olive oil

For the Salad:
- 19 ounces white kidney beans, cooked
- 2 cups farro, cooked
- 2 cups spinach
- ¼ teaspoon ground black pepper

- ¼ teaspoon salt
- 1/3 cup prepared parsley pesto
- ½ of a lemon, juiced

Method:
1. Cook the farro until tender, add spinach in the last 5 minutes and cook until its leaves wilt.
2. Meanwhile, prepare the pesto, and for this, place all of its ingredients in a blender and pulse until smooth.
3. Transfer farro and spinach in a bowl, let it cool for 15 minutes, then add remaining ingredients for the salad, drizzle with pesto and toss until combined.
4. Serve straight away.

Nutrition Value:
Calories: 415 Cal; Fat: 8 g; Carbs: 60 g; Protein: 25 g; Fiber: 11 g

BBQ Chickpea Salad

Preparation time: 10 minutes; Cooking time: 10 minutes; Servings: 2
Ingredients:
- 2 cups cooked chickpeas
- 1 cup frozen corn kernel

- ¼ of medium red onion, sliced
- 1 cup cherry tomatoes, halved

- 6 cups chopped romaine lettuce
- 1 cup cucumber, sliced
- 6 Tablespoons Ranch Dressing
- 1/2 cup vegan BBQ sauce
- Lime wedges for garnish

Method:
1. Simmer chickpeas in the BBQ sauce for 10 minutes until chickpeas are glazed with it.
2. Then divide remaining ingredients between two bowls, top with chickpeas, drizzle with dressing and serve with lime wedges.

Nutrition Value:
Calories: 457 Cal; Fat: 25 g; Carbs: 57 g; Protein: 6 g; Fiber: 6 g

Chickpea and Kale Salad

Preparation time: 15 minutes; Cooking time: 0 minute; Servings: 4

Ingredients:
For the Dressing:
- 2 tablespoons olive oil
- ½ teaspoon ground black pepper
- 1 teaspoon salt
- 1/4 cup balsamic vinegar
- 2 tablespoons maple syrup

For the Salad:
- 30 ounces cooked chickpeas
- 1 1/2 bunch of kale, chopped
- 1 medium avocado, peeled, pitted, cubed
- 1/2 cup dried cranberries
- 1/2 teaspoon salt
- 1 cup diced red onion
- 1/2 cup chopped basil
- 1/2 cup almonds, roasted, salted, chopped

Method:
1. Prepare the dressing and for this, place all of its ingredients in a bowl and whisk until smooth.
2. Place kale in a bowl, season with ¼ teaspoon salt, massage it into the kale for 1 minute until soften and set aside until.
3. Place remaining ingredients in another bowl, toss until combined, then top the mixture over kale and drizzle with the dressing.
4. Top the salad with additional almonds and serve.

Nutrition Value:
Calories: 149 Cal; Fat: 8 g; Carbs: 16 g; Protein: 4 g; Fiber: 3 g

Butternut Squash Quinoa Salad

Preparation time: 10 minutes; Cooking time: 25 minutes; Servings: 4

Ingredients:
For the Salad:
- 1 cup quinoa, cooked
- 3 cups butternut squash, chopped
- 1/3 cup dried cranberries
- 1/3 cup chopped red onion
- 2/3 teaspoon salt
- 1/3 teaspoon ground black pepper
- 3 tablespoons toasted pumpkin seeds
- 1 tablespoon olive oil

For the Dressing:
- ½ teaspoon minced garlic
- 1/3 teaspoon salt
- 1/3 teaspoon ground black pepper
- 1 teaspoon honey
- 1/4 cup balsamic vinegar
- 1 teaspoon Dijon mustard
- 1/2 cup olive oil

Method:
1. Spread butternut squash on a baking sheet, drizzle with oil, season with black pepper and salt and bake for 25 minutes until roasted and tender.

2. Meanwhile, prepare the dressing and for this, place all of its ingredients in a bowl and whisk until smooth.
3. When done, let squash for 10 minutes, then place them in a bowl, add remaining ingredients for the salad in it, drizzle with dressing and toss until coated.
4. Refrigerate the salad for a minimum of 2 hours and then serve.

Nutrition Value:
Calories: 385 Cal; Fat: 25 g; Carbs: 38 g; Protein: 6.2 g; Fiber: 8 g

Simple Quinoa Salad

Preparation time: 10 minutes; Cooking time: 0 minute; Servings: 4
Ingredients:
- 1/2 cup quinoa, cooked
- 12 black olives
- 1/4 cup cooked corn
- 1/4 cup chopped carrots
- 1 avocado, pitted, sliced
- 12 cherry tomatoes, halved
- 1/3 teaspoon salt
- 1/3 teaspoon ground black pepper
- 2 tablespoons olive oil

Method:
1. Place all the ingredients in a bowl, and then stir until incorporated.
2. Taste the salad to adjust seasoning and serve straight away.

Nutrition Value:
Calories: 246 Cal; Fat: 16.2 g; Carbs: 23.3 g; Protein: 5.1 g; Fiber: 6.4 g

Cobb Salad

Preparation time: 10 minutes; Cooking time: 0 minute; Servings: 4
Ingredients:
For the Salad:
- 1/2 cup cooked red beans
- 1/2 cup cooked corn
- 1 medium head of romaine lettuce, shredded
- 1/2 cup chopped tempeh bacon
- 1/2 cup diced tomatoes
- 1/2 cup diced avocado
- 1/2 cup cashews, unsalted

For the Dressing:
- 1 teaspoon garlic powder
- 2 tablespoons lemon juice
- 3 tablespoons soy sauce
- 2 tablespoons cider vinegar
- 1/4 cup agave syrup
- 2 tablespoons Dijon mustard
- 1/4 cup olive oil
- 1/4 cup water

Method:
1. Prepare the dressing, and for this, place all of its ingredients in a food processor and pulse until smooth.
2. Place all the ingredients for the salad in a large dish, arrange each ingredient in a row, and then drizzle with prepared dressing.
3. Serve straight away.

Nutrition Value:
Calories: 279 Cal; Fat: 17.5 g; Carbs: 26.7 g; Protein: 8 g; Fiber: 5.1 g

Greek Salad

Preparation time: 10 minutes; Cooking time: 0 minute; Servings: 4
Ingredients:
- 40 black olives, pitted
- ½ of medium red onion, peeled, sliced
- 4 tomatoes, sliced
- 1 medium cucumber, peeled, sliced
- 1 medium green bell pepper, cored, sliced

- ¼ cup tofu Feta cheese
- 1 tablespoon chopped oregano
- 1/3 teaspoon ground black pepper
- 1/3 teaspoon salt
- 2 tablespoons olive oil

Method:
1. Place all the ingredients in a bowl, and then stir until incorporated.
2. Taste the salad to adjust seasoning and serve straight away.

Nutrition Value:
Calories: 79 Cal; Fat: 4.5 g; Carbs: 9.9 g; Protein: 1.6 g; Fiber: 2.1 g

Vegan Caesar Salad

Preparation time: 10 minutes; Cooking time: 30 minutes; Servings: 4

Ingredients:
- ½ cup chickpea croutons
- 10 ounces tofu, firmed, drain, dice
- 1 romaine lettuce, chopped
- 1 cup vegan Caesar dressing
- ¼ cup grated vegan Parmesan cheese

For the Dressing:
- ½ teaspoon garlic powder
- ½ teaspoon ground black pepper
- ½ teaspoon sweet paprika
- ½ teaspoon onion powder
- ½ teaspoon cumin
- ½ teaspoon dried thyme
- 3 tablespoons soy sauce
- 3 tablespoons water

Method:
1. Place tofu pieces on a baking sheet lined with baking paper and then bake for 30 minutes at 390 degrees F until golden brown on all sides, turning halfway.
2. Meanwhile, prepare the dressing and for this, place all of its ingredients in a bowl and whisk until smooth.
3. When tofu has roasted, let it cool for 5 minutes, then add to the bowl along with remaining ingredients for the salad, drizzle with prepared dressing and toss until combined.
4. Serve straight away.

Nutrition Value:
Calories: 469 Cal; Fat: 28 g; Carbs: 86.5 g; Protein: 38.5 g; Fiber: 29 g

Potato Salad with Vegan Ranch Dressing

Preparation time: 2 hours and 10 minutes; Cooking time: 0 minute; Servings: 2

Ingredients:
- 1/2 cup cooked corn kernels
- 14 ounces potatoes, peeled, steamed
- 12 green olives
- ½ of medium white onion, peeled, sliced
- 12 cherry tomatoes, halved
- Vegan Ranch Dressing as needed

Method:
1. Boil potatoes for 20 minutes until softened, then let cool for 10 minutes and dice them.
2. Place diced potatoes in a bowl along with remaining ingredients and toss until well combined.
3. Let the salad refrigerate f0r a minimum of 2 hours and then serve.

Nutrition Value:
Calories: 256 Cal; Fat: 3.5 g; Carbs: 51.4 g; Protein: 6.8 g; Fiber: 7.4 g

Vegan Chinese Salad

Preparation time: 10 minutes; Cooking time: 0 minute; Servings: 4

Ingredients:

For the Salad:
- 1 iceberg lettuce, chopped
- 1/4 cup soybean sprouts
- 2 carrots, peeled, julienned
- 1/4 cup agar, hydrated

For the Dressing:
- 1/4 teaspoon salt
- 1/4 cup coconut sugar
- 1 tablespoon olive oil
- 1/4 cup apple cider vinegar

Method:
1. Soak agar in water until hydrated, then drain it and place it in a bowl along with remaining ingredients for the salad.
2. Meanwhile, prepare the dressing and for this, place all of its ingredients in a food processor and pulse until smooth.
3. Drizzle the dressing over the salad, stir until well mixed and then serve.

Nutrition Value:
Calories: 114 Cal; Fat: 4 g; Carbs: 20.6 g; Protein: 1.5 g; Fiber: 2.6 g

Zucchini Noodles with Avocado Sauce

Preparation time: 10 minutes; Cooking time: 0 minute; Servings: 2

Ingredients:
- 1 zucchini, spiralized into noodles
- 12 slices of cherry tomatoes

For the Dressing:
- 1 medium avocado, pitted, sliced
- 1 1/4 cup basil
- 2 tablespoons lemon juice
- 4 tablespoons pine nuts
- 1/3 cup water

Method:
1. Prepare the dressing, and for this, place all of its ingredients in a food processor and pulse until smooth.
2. Prepare the salad and for this, place zucchini noodles and tomato in a salad bowl, drizzle with the dressing, and toss until well coated.
3. Serve straight away.

Nutrition Value:
Calories: 313 Cal; Fat: 26.8 g; Carbs: 18.7 g; Protein: 6.8 g; Fiber: 9.7 g

Heirloom Tomato Salad

Preparation time: 10 minutes; Cooking time: 0 minute; Servings: 6

Ingredients:
For the Salad:
- 1 pound heirloom tomatoes, cut into wedges
- ½ teaspoon salt
- ½ teaspoon ground black pepper
- ¼ cup basil leaves, for serving

For the Dressing:
- 2 cups grape tomatoes, halved
- ¼ teaspoon ground black pepper
- ½ teaspoon salt
- 2 tablespoons chopped chives
- 1 teaspoon honey
- 1/4 cup olive oil
- 2 tablespoons apple cider vinegar

Method:
1. Prepare the dressing for this, whisk together honey, vinegar, oil, salt, and black pepper until combined, then add chives and tomatoes and toss until combined.
2. Prepare the salad and for this, place tomatoes on a plate, season with salt and black pepper, drizzle with the dressing and top with basil.
3. Serve straight away.

Nutrition Value:
Calories: 105 Cal; Fat: 9.5 g; Carbs: 6 g; Protein: 1 g; Fiber: 1 g

Roasted Rhubarb Salad

Preparation time: 10 minutes; Cooking time: 5 minutes; Servings: 4
Ingredients:

- 8 cups mixed baby greens
- 2 cups chopped rhubarb
- ¼ cup chopped walnuts, toasted
- 2 tablespoons sugar
- ½ cup crumbled vegan goat cheese
- ¼ cup raisins

- For the Dressing:
- 1 tablespoon minced shallot
- 2 tablespoons balsamic vinegar
- ¼ teaspoon ground black pepper
- 1 tablespoon olive oil
- ¼ teaspoon salt

Method:

1. Place rhubarb in a bowl, sprinkle with sugar, let them stand for 10 minutes, then spread them in an even layer and bake for 5 minutes at 450 degrees F until softened.
2. Meanwhile, prepare the dressing and for this, place all of its ingredients in a bowl and whisk until smooth.
3. Then add mixed greens, toss until well coated, and then top with roasted rhubarb, nuts, raisins, and cheese.
4. Serve straight away.

Nutrition Value:
Calories: 197 Cal; Fat: 12 g; Carbs: 21 g; Protein: 5 g; Fiber: 3 g

Zucchini Salad

Preparation time: 10 minutes; Cooking time: 15 minutes; Servings: 4
Ingredients:

- 2 cups cubed zucchini
- 1 tablespoon chopped mint
- 1 small white onion, peeled, sliced
- ½ of a lemon, juiced
- 1 teaspoon minced garlic
- 2 tablespoons olive oil

- 1/8 teaspoon ground white pepper
- ¼ teaspoon salt
- 1/8 teaspoon ground turmeric
- 1/2 teaspoon ground cumin
- 7 saffron threads

Method:

1. Take a skillet pan, place it over medium heat, add oil and when hot, add onion and garlic, and cook for 4 minutes until softened.
2. Then add remaining ingredients, except for salt, black pepper, lime juice, and mint, stir until mixed and cook for 8 minutes until zucchini is tender-crisp.
3. When done, let the salad cool for 10 minutes, then season with salt and black pepper, drizzle with lemon juice, sprinkle with mint and serve.

Nutrition Value:
Calories: 93 Cal; Fat: 7.2 g; Carbs: 7.8 g; Protein: 1.6 g; Fiber: 1.9 g

Watermelon and Mint Salad

Preparation time: 5 minutes; Cooking time: 0 minute; Servings: 4
Ingredients:

- 5 cups watermelon, cubed
- 1 lemon, juiced
- 1 cucumber, deseeded, chopped
- ½ teaspoon ground black pepper

- 1 cup mint , chopped
- 1 tablespoon maple syrup
- 2 tablespoons olive oil

Method:

1. Take a large bowl and place cucumber and watermelon in it.
2. Whisk together lemon juice, oil, and maple syrup until combined and then drizzle it over salad.
3. Sprinkle mint on top, toss until just mixed and serve.

Nutrition Value:

Calories: 120 Cal; Fat: 5 g; Carbs: 18 g; Protein: 2 g; Fiber: 2 g

Beet, Mushroom and Avocado Salad

Preparation time: 15 minutes; Cooking time: 20 minutes; Servings: 4

Ingredients:

- 8 ounces cooked beets, chopped
- 4 medium portobello mushroom caps
- 5 ounces baby kale
- 2 medium avocados, pitted, sliced
- 1 small shallot, peeled, chopped
- ¾ teaspoon salt
- ¼ teaspoon ground black pepper
- 1/4 cup lemon juice
- 3 tablespoons olive oil
- 2 sheets of matzo, cut into bite-size pieces

Method:
1. Place mushroom caps on a baking sheet, spray them with oil, then season them with ½ teaspoon salt and bake for 20 minutes at 450 degrees F until tender.
2. Place shallots in a small bowl, add black pepper and remaining salt, pour in oil and lemon juice and whisk until combined.
3. Place kale and beets in a dish, drizzle with shallot mixture and toss until combined.
4. When mushrooms have roasted, let them cool for 10 minutes, then slice them and to the kale mixture along with remaining ingredients.
5. Toss until well combined and serve.

Nutrition Value:

Calories: 370 Cal; Fat: 26 g; Carbs: 32 g; Protein: 7 g; Fiber: 11 g

Summer Pesto Pasta

Preparation time: 10 minutes; Cooking time: 10 minutes; Servings: 4

Ingredients:

For the dressing:

- ½ of a lemon, juiced, zested
- 1/2 cup basil pesto
- ½ teaspoon salt
- ½ teaspoon ground black pepper

For the Salad:

- 2 ears of corn, shucked
- 1 small green bell pepper, cored, cut into sixths
- 1 medium yellow squash, peeled, ½-inch sliced
- 1 medium zucchini, peeled, ½-inch sliced
- 4 green onions, trimmed, chopped
- 2 cups grape tomatoes, halved
- ½ teaspoon salt
- ½ teaspoon ground black pepper
- 2 tablespoons olive oil
- 1/4 cup parsley, chopped
- 1 pound spaghetti, whole-grain, cooked

Method:
1. Prepare the dressing, and for this, place all of its ingredients in a bowl, whisk until combined, and set aside until required.
2. Take a large bowl, place corn in it, add green onion, zucchini, squash and bell pepper, season with salt and black pepper, drizzle with oil and toss until well coated.

3. Grill the onions for 2 minutes, grill the zucchini, squash, and bell pepper for 6 minutes until lightly charred and tender and frill the corn for 10 minutes until lightly charred, turning halfway.
4. Cut kernels from the bowl, chop the grilled vegetables, add them to a bowl and then add remaining ingredients for the salad.
5. Drizzle salad with prepared dressing, toss until well combined, and then serve straight away.

Nutrition Value:
Calories: 370 Cal; Fat: 12 g; Carbs: 54 g; Protein: 12 g; Fiber: 5 g

Tomato Basil Salad

Preparation time: 10 minutes; Cooking time: 0 minute; Servings: 4
Ingredients:

- 3 tablespoons chopped red onion
- 1 pound tomatoes, chopped
- 10 leaves of basil, cut into ribbons
- 1/4 teaspoon ground black pepper
- 1/2 teaspoon salt
- 2 tablespoons white balsamic vinegar

Method:
1. Take a large bowl, place all the ingredients in it, stir until well combined, and then let it sit for 5 minutes.
2. Refrigerate the salad for a minimum of 2 hours and then serve straight away.

Nutrition Value:
Calories: 26 Cal; Fat: 0 g; Carbs: 5 g; Protein: 1 g; Fiber: 1 g

Spiralized Zucchini and Carrot Salad

Preparation time: 10 minutes; Cooking time: 0 minute; Servings: 6
Ingredients:
For the Salad:

- 2 scallions, sliced
- 2 large zucchini. spiralized
- 1 red chile, sliced
- 1 large carrot, spiralized

For the Dressing:

- 1 1/2 teaspoon grated ginger
- 2 teaspoons brown sugar
- 1/4 cup lime juice
- 1 tablespoon soy sauce
- 2 tablespoons toasted peanut oil

For Toppings:

- 1/2 cup chopped peanuts, roasted
- 1/3 cup chopped cilantro

Method:
1. Prepare the dressing and for this, place all of its ingredients in a bowl and whisk until combined.
2. Take a large bowl, place all the ingredients for the salad in it, stir until mixed, then drizzle with the dressing and toss until coated.
3. Top the salad with nuts and cilantro and then serve straight away.

Nutrition Value:
Calories: 150 Cal; Fat: 11 g; Carbs: 11 g; Protein: 5 g; Fiber: 3 g

Sweet Potato and Cauliflower Salad

Preparation time: 10 minutes; Cooking time: 30 minutes; Servings: 8
Ingredients:
For the Salad:

- 1 1/2-pound small sweet potatoes, peeled, cut into ½-inch wedges
- 2/3 cup pomegranate seeds

- 1 small head of cauliflower, cut into florets
- 8 cups mixed lettuces

For the Dressing:
- 4 tablespoons olive oil, divided
- 1/2 teaspoon salt

- 1/2 teaspoon salt
- 1/4 teaspoon ground black pepper
- 3 tablespoons olive oil, divided

- 1/4 teaspoon ground black pepper
- 3 tablespoons apple cider vinegar

Method:
1. Take a baking sheet, place all the vegetables for the salad on it, drizzle with oil, season with salt and black pepper, toss until well coated, and then bake for 30 minutes at 425 degrees F until roasted.
2. Meanwhile, prepare the dressing and for this, place all of its ingredients in a bowl and whisk until combined.
3. When vegetables have roasted, let them cool for 10 minutes, then place them in a large bowl along with remaining ingredients for the salad, drizzle with the dressing and toss until coated.
4. Serve straight away.

Nutrition Value:
Calories: 330 Cal; Fat: 14 g; Carbs: 33 g; Protein: 9.8 g; Fiber: 18 g

Tropical Radicchio Slaw

Preparation time: 15 minutes; Cooking time: 8 minutes; Servings: 6
Ingredients:
- 2 medium heads of radicchio, quartered
- 1/4 cup chopped basil leaves
- 2 cups chopped pineapple

- 1/2 teaspoon ground black pepper
- 1/2 teaspoon salt
- 2 tablespoons olive oil
- 2 tablespoons orange juice

Method:
1. Brush radicchio with oil on both sides and then grill for 8 minutes until tender, turning halfway.
2. When grilled, let radicchio cool for 10 minutes, then slice them thinly and place them in a bowl.
3. Add remaining ingredients, toss until combined, and serve.

Nutrition Value:
Calories: 40 Cal; Fat: 2 g; Carbs: 5 g; Protein: 0 g; Fiber: 1 g

Fennel and Asparagus Salad

Preparation time: 10 minutes; Cooking time: 8 minutes; Servings: 4
Ingredients:
For the Salad:
- 1 cup sliced asparagus, trimmed
- 1 large leek, white part sliced in circles only
- 1 medium avocado, pitted, sliced

For the Dressing:
- 1 tablespoon thyme
- 2 tablespoons lemon juice
- ¾ teaspoon sea salt

- 2 cups thinly sliced fennel bulb, trimmed
- 3 tablespoons olive oil
- ¼ cup almonds, toasted

- ½ teaspoon ground black pepper
- 1 teaspoon ground coriander
- 3 tablespoons olive oil

Method:
1. Prepare the dressing and for this, place all of its ingredients in a bowl and whisk until combined.

2. Sauté leeks in oil for 6 minutes or until it wilts and turns golden brown, then season with some salt and let it cool.
3. Take a large bowl, place all the ingredients for the salad in it, except for almonds, drizzle with the salad dressing and toss until well coated.
4. Top the salad with the almonds and then serve.

Nutrition Value:
Calories: 273 Cal; Fat: 27 g; Carbs: 9.1 g; Protein: 3.3 g; Fiber: 4.6 g

Carrot Salad with Quinoa

Preparation time: 10 minutes; Cooking time: 0 minute; Servings: 6
Ingredients:
For the Salad:
- 1 cup quinoa, cooked
- 3 cups grated carrots
- 3 scallions, sliced
- 2 cups sliced celery
- 1 bunch of cilantros, chopped
- ½ teaspoon minced garlic

- ½ teaspoon salt
- ½ teaspoon allspice
- ¼ teaspoon ground black pepper
- 1 tablespoon apple cider vinegar
- ½ teaspoon cayenne pepper
- ½ cup chopped almonds, toasted

For the Vinaigrette:
- ½ teaspoon salt
- 2 tablespoons honey
- ½ teaspoon ground black pepper

- ¼ cup olive oil
- ¼ cup apple cider vinegar

Method:
1. Prepare the vinaigrette and for this, place all of its ingredients in a bowl and whisk until combined.
2. Prepare the salad and for this, place all of its ingredients in a bowl, drizzle with the vinaigrette, and toss until well combined.
3. Serve straight away.

Nutrition Value:
Calories: 272 Cal; Fat: 15.3 g; Carbs: 31.4 g; Protein: 6.5 g; Fiber: 5.2 g

Thai Noodle Salad

Preparation time: 10 minutes; Cooking time: 0 minute; Servings: 6
Ingredients:
For the Thai Peanut Sauce:
- 3 thin slices of ginger
- ½ teaspoon salt
- 3 tablespoon lime juice
- 1 clove of garlic, peeled
- 1 teaspoon cayenne pepper

- 2 tablespoons soy sauce
- ¼ cup peanut butter
- 3 tablespoons sesame oil
- ¼ cup of orange juice
- 3 tablespoons honey

For the Salad:
- 6 ounces brown rice noodles, cooked
- 4 cups mix of shredded cabbage, radish, and carrots
- 3 scallions, sliced

- 1 medium red bell pepper, peeled, sliced
- 1 tablespoon jalapeño, chopped
- ½ bunch of cilantro, chopped
- ½ cup roasted peanuts, crushed

Method:
1. Prepare the sauce, and for this, place all of its ingredients in a blender and pulse until smooth.

2. Take a large bowl, place all the ingredients for the salad in it, except for almonds, top with prepared sauce and toss until well coated.
3. Top the salad with almonds and then serve straight away.

Nutrition Value:
Calories: 286 Cal; Fat: 13 g; Carbs: 40 g; Protein: 3.8 g; Fiber: 2.6 g

Kohlrabi Slaw

Preparation time: 10 minutes; Cooking time: 0 minute; Servings: 4

Ingredients:

For the Citrus Dressing:
- 1/2 teaspoon salt
- 1/4 cup honey
- 1 tablespoon rice wine vinegar
- ¼ cup of orange juice
- 2 tablespoons lime juice
- 1/4 cup olive oil

For the Salad:
- 6 cups kohlrabi, trimmed, peeled, cut into matchsticks
- ½ of a jalapeno, minced
- 1 orange, juiced, zested
- ½ cup chopped cilantro
- 1 lime, juiced, zested
- 1/4 cup chopped scallion

Method:
1. Prepare the dressing and for this, place all of its ingredients in a small bowl and whisk until smooth.
2. Take a large bowl, place all the ingredients for the salad in it, top with prepared dressing and toss until well coated.
3. Top the salad with almonds and then serve straight away.

Nutrition Value:
Calories: 109.4 Cal; Fat: 4.8 g; Carbs: 10.8 g; Protein: 4.4 g; Fiber: 4.4 g

Cherry Tomato and Tofu Salad

Preparation time: 10 minutes; Cooking time: 0 minute; Servings: 2

Ingredients:

For the Salad:
- 2 slices of tofu
- 1 cup cherry tomatoes, halved
- 1 teaspoon sesame seeds

For the Dressing:
- 2 teaspoons soy sauce
- ¼ teaspoon ground black pepper
- ¼ teaspoon of sea salt
- 1 teaspoon sherry vinegar
- 1 teaspoon toasted sesame oil
- 2 tablespoons olive oil

Method:
1. Prepare the dressing and for this, place all of its ingredients in a small bowl and whisk until smooth.
2. Place cherry tomatoes in a bowl, drizzle with dressing, toss until well coated and sprinkle with sesame seeds.
3. Prepare the salad and for this, place tofu slices on a plate, top with tomato mixture and serve straight away.

Nutrition Value:
Calories: 169 Cal; Fat: 10 g; Carbs: 9 g; Protein: 11 g; Fiber: 3 g

Fennel Salad with Cucumber and Dill

Preparation time: 20 minutes; Cooking time: 0 minute; Servings: 4

Ingredients:

- 2 large fennel bulbs, cored, trimmed, cored, shaved into thin slices
- 3 small cucumbers, shaved into thin sliced
- 1/2 cup chopped dill
- 1/4 cup sliced white onion,
- 1/3 teaspoon salt
- 1/3 teaspoon ground black pepper
- 1/3 cup olive oil
- ¼ cup lemon juice

Method:
1. Take a large bowl, place all the ingredients in it, and toss until well coated.
2. Let the salad refrigerate for 15 minutes and then serve.

Nutrition Value:
Calories: 205 Cal; Fat: 19 g; Carbs: 11 g; Protein: 1.8 g; Fiber: 3.4 g

Cabbage and Mango Slaw

Preparation time: 20 minutes; Cooking time: 0 minute; Servings: 4
Ingredients:
- 1 jalapeno, chopped
- 3 cups shredded cabbage
- ¼ cup sliced red onion
- 1 large mango, destoned, cubed
- ½ cup chopped cilantro
- ½ teaspoon salt
- 1 orange, juiced, zested
- 2 teaspoons olive oil
- 1 lime, juiced, zested

Method:
1. Take a large bowl, place all the ingredients in it, and toss until well coated.
2. Let the salad refrigerate for 15 minutes and then serve.

Nutrition Value:
Calories: 120 Cal; Fat: 3 g; Carbs: 25 g; Protein: 2.2 g; Fiber: 5 g

Lemon, Basil and Orzo Salad

Preparation time: 10 minutes; Cooking time: 0 minute; Servings: 4
Ingredients:
For the Salad:
- 1 cup orzo pasta, cooked
- 2 cups sliced cucumbers
- 1 cup cherry tomatoes, halved
- 1 cup baby arugula

For the Dressing:
- 2 cloves of garlic, peeled
- 1 lemon, zested
- 1 cup basil
- 1/3 cup olive oil
- ¼ teaspoon ground black pepper
- ½ teaspoon salt
- 2 tablespoons lemon juice

Method:
1. Prepare the dressing, and for this, place all of its ingredients in a food processor and pulse until smooth.
2. Take a large bowl, place orzo pasta in it, add prepared dressing in it, toss until mixed, then add remaining ingredients for the salad in it and toss until just mixed.
3. Serve straight away.

Nutrition Value:
Calories: 233 Cal; Fat: 15 g; Carbs: 24 g; Protein: 4.5 g; Fiber: 3 g

Lentil Tabouli Salad

Preparation time: 5 minutes; Cooking time: 15 minutes; Servings: 4
Ingredients:
For the Salad:
- 1 1/2 cups puy lentils, cooked
- 1/3 cup diced red onion

- 2 cups diced tomatoes
- 1/4 cup chopped mint

- 1 1/2 cups chopped parsley

For the Dressing:
- 1/3 teaspoon ground black pepper
- 1 teaspoon cinnamon
- 1 teaspoon salt

- 2 teaspoon allspice
- 3 tablespoons olive oil
- 1 lemon, juiced, zested

Method:
1. Prepare the dressing and for this, place all of its ingredients in a small bowl and whisk until smooth.
2. Take a large bowl, place all the ingredients for the salad in it, top with prepared dressing and toss until well coated.
3. Let the salad stand for 10 minutes and then serve.

Nutrition Value:
Calories: 319 Cal; Fat: 9.5 g; Carbs: 46.6 g; Protein: 16.2 g; Fiber: 9.3 g

Kale Slaw

Preparation time: 10 minutes; Cooking time: 0 minute; Servings: 4
Ingredients:
For the Salad:
- ½ small head of cabbage, shredded
- ¼ cup mixed herbs

- ¼ of a medium red onion, peeled, sliced
- 1 small bunch of kale, cut into ribbons

For the Dressing:
- 1 teaspoon minced garlic
- ¼ teaspoon ground black pepper
- ¼ teaspoon salt

- ¼ teaspoon red chili flakes
- ¼ cup olive oil
- 1 lemon, juiced

For the Topping:
- 1 teaspoon hemp seeds
- 1 teaspoon sunflower

- 1 teaspoon pumpkin seeds

Method:
1. Prepare the dressing and for this, place all of its ingredients in a small bowl and whisk until smooth.
2. Take a large bowl, place all the ingredients for the salad in it, top with prepared dressing and toss until well coated.
3. Garnish the salad with all the seeds and then serve.

Nutrition Value:
Calories: 76 Cal; Fat: 7.1 g; Carbs: 4 g; Protein: 0.7 g; Fiber: 1 g

Moroccan Salad with Blood Oranges

Preparation time: 15 minutes; Cooking time: 0 minute; Servings: 4
Ingredients:
- 1 cup quinoa, cooked
- 3 blood oranges, divided
- 2 green onions, sliced
- ¼ cup sliced kalamata olives
- ¼ teaspoon salt
- ¼ teaspoon ground black pepper

- 1 tablespoon apple cider vinegar
- ¼ cup olive oil
- 1 teaspoon honey
- ¼ cup slivered almonds, toasted
- 12 mint leaves, torn

Method:
1. Take a large bowl, place all the ingredients in it, except the last two ones, and toss until well coated.

2. Top the salad with almonds and mint and then serve straight away.
Nutrition Value:
Calories: 344 Cal; Fat: 14 g; Carbs: 49 g; Protein: 9 g; Fiber: 9.8 g

Carrot Salad with Cashews

Preparation time: 20 minutes; Cooking time: 0 minute; Servings: 4
Ingredients:

- 4 cups grated carrots
- 3 scallions, chopped
- ½ cup cilantro, chopped
- ½ teaspoon minced garlic
- 1 teaspoon minced ginger
- ½ teaspoon salt
- ¼ teaspoon cayenne pepper
- ¼ teaspoon ground black pepper
- 1 teaspoon curry powder
- 2 tablespoons honey
- ½ teaspoon ground turmeric
- 1/3 cup raisins
- ½ cup toasted cashews
- 1 tablespoon orange zest
- 3 tablespoon lime juice
- 1/4 cup olive oil

Method:
1. Take a large bowl, place all the ingredients in it, and toss until well coated.
2. Let the salad refrigerate for 15 minutes and then serve.
Nutrition Value:
Calories: 251 Cal; Fat: 16 g; Carbs: 29 g; Protein: 3 g; Fiber: 4 g

Cucumber Salad with Chili and Lime

Preparation time: 5 minutes; Cooking time: 0 minute; Servings: 4
Ingredients:

- 1 jalapeno, deseeded, diced
- 2 large cucumbers, sliced
- ¼ of a medium red onion, sliced
- ½ bunch of cilantros
- ½ teaspoon red chili flakes
- 1/2 teaspoon salt
- ½ teaspoon coriander
- 3 tablespoons lime juice
- 2 tablespoons olive oil

Method:
1. Take a large bowl, place all the ingredients in it, and toss until well coated.
2. Serve straight away
Nutrition Value:
Calories: 91 Cal; Fat: 7.2 g; Carbs: 7.6 g; Protein: 1.2 g; Fiber: 1.1 g

Chapter 5: Beans and Grains

Falafel

Preparation time: 10 minutes; Cooking time: 30 minutes; Servings: 4

Ingredients:
- ¼ cup and 1 tablespoon olive oil
- 1 cup chickpeas, cooked
- ½ cup chopped parsley
- ½ cup chopped red onion
- ½ cup chopped cilantro
- 2 teaspoons minced garlic
- ½ teaspoon ground black pepper
- ¼ teaspoon ground cinnamon
- 1 teaspoon of sea salt
- ½ teaspoon ground cumin

Method:
1. Place all the ingredients in a food processor, reserving ¼ cup oil, and pulse until smooth.
2. Shape the mixture into small patties, place them on a rimmed baking sheet, greased with remaining oil and bake for 30 minutes until cooked and roasted on both sides, turning halfway through.
3. Serve straight away.

Nutrition Value:
Calories: 354 Cal; Fat: 20.7 g; Carbs: 34.6 g; Protein: 11 g; Fiber: 7 g

Lentil and Chickpea Salad

Preparation time: 10 minutes; Cooking time: 0 minute; Servings: 4

Ingredients:

For the Lemon Dressing:
- ¼ cup lemon juice
- 2 tablespoons olive oil
- 1 teaspoon Dijon mustard
- 1 teaspoon honey or maple syrup
- ½ teaspoon minced garlic
- ¼ teaspoon of sea salt
- ¼ teaspoon ground black pepper

For the Salad:
- 2 cups French green lentils, cooked
- 1 ½ cups cooked chickpeas
- 1 medium avocado, pitted, sliced
- 1 big bunch of radishes, chopped
- ¼ cup chopped mint and dill
- Crumbled vegan feta cheese as needed

Method:
1. Prepare the dressing and for this, place all of its ingredients in a bowl and whisk until combined.
2. Take a large bowl, place all the ingredients for the salad in it, drizzle with the dressing and toss until combined.
3. Serve straight away.

Nutrition Value:
Calories: 377 Cal; Fat: 11.1 g; Carbs: 53.4 g; Protein: 19.2 g; Fiber: 10.1 g

Lebanese Bean Salad

Preparation time: 10 minutes; Cooking time: 0 minute; Servings: 4

Ingredients:

For the Salad:
- 1 ½ cups cooked chickpeas
- 3 cups cooked kidney beans
- 1 small red onion, peeled, diced
- 1 medium cucumber, peeled, deseeded, diced
- 2 stalks celery, chopped
- ¾ cup chopped parsley

- 2 tablespoons chopped dill

For the Dressing:
- 1 ½ teaspoon minced garlic
- ¾ teaspoon salt
- ¼ cup olive oil
- 1/8 teaspoon red pepper flakes
- ¼ cup lemon juice

Method:
1. Prepare the dressing and for this, place all of its ingredients in a bowl and whisk until combined.
2. Take a large bowl, place all the ingredients for the salad in it, drizzle with the dressing and toss until combined.
3. Serve straight away.

Nutrition Value:
Calories: 249 Cal; Fat: 11.2 g; Carbs: 29.5 g; Protein: 10 g; Fiber: 8.2 g

Roasted Carrots with Farro, and Chickpeas

Preparation time: 10 minutes; Cooking time: 35 minutes; Servings: 4
Ingredients:
For the Chickpeas and Farro:
- 1 cup farro, cooked
- 1 ½ cups cooked chickpeas
- ½ teaspoon minced garlic
- 1 teaspoon lemon juice
- ½ teaspoon salt
- 1 teaspoon olive oil

For the Roasted Carrots:
- 1 pound heirloom carrots, scrubbed
- ½ teaspoon ground black pepper
- ¼ teaspoon ground cumin
- 1 teaspoon salt
- 1 tablespoon olive oil

For the Spiced Pepitas:
- 3 tablespoons green pumpkin seeds
- 1/8 teaspoon salt
- 1/8 teaspoon red chili powder
- 1/8 teaspoon cumin
- ½ teaspoon olive oil

For the Crème Fraiche:
- 1 tablespoon chopped parsley
- 1/3 cup vegan crème fraîche
- ¼ teaspoon ground black pepper
- 1/3 teaspoon salt
- 2 teaspoons water

For the Garnish:
- 1 more tablespoon chopped parsley

Method:
1. Prepare chickpeas and farro and for this, place all of its ingredients in a bowl and toss until combined.
2. Prepare the carrots and for this, arrange them on a baking sheet lined with parchment paper, drizzle with oil, sprinkle with the seasoning, toss until coated, and bake for 35 minutes until roasted and fork-tender, turning halfway.
3. Meanwhile, prepare pepitas and for this, take a skillet pan, place it over medium heat, add oil and when hot, add remaining ingredients in it and cook for 3 minutes until seeds are golden on the edges, set aside, and let it cool.
4. Prepare the crème Fraiche and for this, place all its ingredients in a bowl and whisk until combined.
5. Top chickpeas and farro with carrots, drizzle with crème Fraiche, sprinkle with pepitas and parsley and then serve.

Nutrition Value:
Calories: 249 Cal; Fat: 8.4 g; Carbs: 36 g; Protein: 7 g; Fiber: 8.4 g

Lentil Soup

Preparation time: 10 minutes; Cooking time: 50 minutes; Servings: 4

Ingredients:

- 1 cup green lentils
- 1 medium white onion, peeled, chopped
- 1 cup chopped kale leaves
- 28 ounces diced tomatoes
- 2 carrots, peeled, chopped
- 2 teaspoons minced garlic
- 1 teaspoon curry powder
- ¼ teaspoon ground black pepper
- 1 teaspoon salt
- 2 teaspoons ground cumin
- 1/8 teaspoon red pepper flakes
- ½ teaspoon dried thyme
- ¼ cup olive oil
- 4 cups vegetable broth
- 1 tablespoon lemon juice
- 2 cups of water

Method:

1. Take a large pot, place it over medium heat, add 1 tablespoon oil and when hot, add onion and carrot and cook for 5 minutes until softened.
2. Then stir in garlic, curry powder, cumin and thyme, cook for 1 minute, then stir in tomatoes and cook for 3 minutes.
3. Add lentils, pour in water and broth, season with black pepper, salt, and red pepper and bring the mixture to a boil.
4. Switch heat to medium-low, simmer lentils for 30 minutes, then puree half of the soup, return it into the pan, stir in kale and cook for 5 minutes until softened.
5. Drizzle with lemon juice and serve straight away.

Nutrition Value:

Calories: 366 Cal; Fat: 15.5 g; Carbs: 47.8 g; Protein: 14.5 g; Fiber: 10.8 g

Spaghetti Squash Burrito Bowls

Preparation time: 10 minutes; Cooking time: 60 minutes; Servings: 4

Ingredients:

For the Spaghetti Squash:

- 2 medium spaghetti squash , halved, deseeded
- 2 tablespoons olive oil

- 1 teaspoon salt
- ½ teaspoon ground black pepper

For the Slaw:

- 1/3 cup chopped green onions
- 2 cups chopped purple cabbage
- 1/3 cup chopped cilantro
- 15 ounces cooked black beans

- 1 medium red bell pepper, cored, chopped
- ¼ teaspoon salt
- 1 teaspoon olive oil
- 2 tablespoons lime juice

For the Salsa Verde:

- 1 avocado, pitted, diced
- ½ teaspoon minced garlic
- ¾ cup salsa verde

- 1/3 cup cilantro
- 1 tablespoon lime juice

Method:

1. Prepare the squash and for this, place squash halves on a baking sheet lined with parchment paper, rub them with oil, season with salt and black pepper and bake for 60 minutes until roasted and fork-tender.
2. Meanwhile, place the slaw and for this, place all of its ingredients in a bowl and toss until combined.
3. Prepare the salsa, and for this, place all of its ingredients in a food processor and pulse until smooth.

4. When squash has baked, fluff its flesh with a fork, then top with slaw and salsa and serve.
Nutrition Value:
   Calories: 301 Cal; Fat: 17.3 g; Carbs: 34.3 g; Protein: 7.7 g; Fiber: 13 g

Quinoa and Black Beans

Preparation time: 10 minutes; Cooking time: 35 minutes; Servings: 4
Ingredients:
- 3/4 cup quinoa
- 30 ounces cooked black beans
- 1 medium white onion, peeled, chopped
- 1 ½ teaspoon minced garlic
- 1 cup frozen corn kernels
- ¼ teaspoon ground black pepper
- 1/3 teaspoon salt
- 1 teaspoon ground cumin
- 1/4 teaspoon cayenne
- 1 teaspoon olive oil
- 1 1/2 cups vegetable broth
- 1/2 cup chopped cilantro

Method:
1. Take a saucepan, place it over medium heat, add oil and when hot, add onion and garlic, and cook for 10 minutes until softened.
2. Add quinoa, pour in the broth, stir in all the seasoning, then bring the mixture to a boil, switch heat to medium-low level and simmer for 20 minutes until the quinoa has absorbed all the liquid.
3. Add corn, stir until mixed, cook for 5 minutes until heated, and then stir in beans until mixed.
4. Garnish with cilantro and serve.

Nutrition Value:
   Calories: 153 Cal; Fat: 1.7 g; Carbs: 27.8 g; Protein: 7.7 g; Fiber: 7.8 g

Spanish Rice

Preparation time: 5 minutes; Cooking time: 40 minutes; Servings: 4
Ingredients:
- 1/2 of medium green bell pepper, chopped
- 1 medium white onion, peeled, chopped
- 10 ounces diced tomatoes with green chilies
- 1 teaspoon salt
- 2 teaspoons red chili powder
- 1 cup white rice
- 2 tablespoons olive oil
- 2 cups of water

Method:
1. Take a large skillet pan, place it over medium heat, add oil and when hot, add onion, pepper, and rice, and cook for 10 minutes.
2. Then add remaining ingredients, stir until mixed, bring the mixture to a boil, then simmer over medium-low heat for 30 minutes until cooked and most of the liquid has absorbed.
3. Serve straight away.

Nutrition Value:
   Calories: 270 Cal; Fat: 7.6 g; Carbs: 45.7 g; Protein: 4.8 g; Fiber: 2.5 g

Stuffed Peppers

Preparation time: 10 minutes; Cooking time: 20 minutes; Servings: 4
Ingredients:
- 2 green onions, sliced
- 2 green bell peppers, halved, cored
- 1 large tomato, diced
- 1/2 cup Arborio rice, cooked

- ¼ teaspoon ground black pepper
- 1 teaspoon Italian seasoning
- 1 teaspoon salt
- 1 teaspoon dried basil
- 1 tablespoon olive oil
- 1 cup of water
- 1/2 cup crumbled vegan feta cheese

Method:
1. Prepare the peppers and for this, cut them in half, then remove the seeds and roast them on a greased baking sheet for 20 minutes at 400 degrees F until tender.
2. Meanwhile, heat oil in a skillet pan over medium-high heat and when hot, add onion, season with seasonings and herbs, and cook for 3 minutes.
3. Add tomatoes, stir well, cook for 5 minutes, then stir in rice and cook for 3 minutes until heated.
4. When done, remove the pan from heat, stir in cheese, and stuff the mixture into roasted peppers.
5. Serve straight away.

Nutrition Value:
Calories: 385 Cal; Fat: 15.2 g; Carbs: 52.6 g; Protein: 10.8 g; Fiber: 4.5 g

Black Beans and Rice

Preparation time: 10 minutes; Cooking time: 30 minutes; Servings: 4

Ingredients:
- 3/4 cup white rice
- 1 medium white onion, peeled, chopped
- 3 1/2 cups cooked black beans
- 1 teaspoon minced garlic
- 1/4 teaspoon cayenne pepper
- 1 teaspoon ground cumin
- 1 teaspoon olive oil
- 1 1/2 cups vegetable broth

Method:
1. Take a large pot over medium-high heat, add oil and when hot, add onion and garlic and cook for 4 minutes until sauté.
2. Then stir in rice, cook for 2 minutes, pour in the broth, bring it to a boil, switch heat to the low level and cook for 20 minutes until tender.
3. Stir in remaining ingredients, cook for 2 minutes, and then serve straight away.

Nutrition Value:
Calories: 140 Cal; Fat: 0.9 g; Carbs: 27.1 g; Protein: 6.3 g; Fiber: 6.2 g

Vegetable Barley Soup

Preparation time: 5 minutes; Cooking time: 15 minutes; Servings: 8

Ingredients:
- 1 cup barley
- 14.5 ounces diced tomatoes with juice
- 2 large carrots, chopped
- 15 ounces cooked chickpeas
- 2 stalks celery, chopped
- 1 zucchini, chopped
- 1 medium white onion, peeled, chopped
- 1/2 teaspoon ground black pepper
- 1 teaspoon garlic powder
- 1 teaspoon curry powder
- 1 teaspoon salt
- 1 teaspoon paprika
- 1 teaspoon white sugar
- 1 teaspoon dried parsley
- 1 teaspoon Worcestershire sauce
- 3 bay leaves
- 2 quarts vegetable broth

Method:
1. Place all the ingredients in a pot, stir until mixed, place it over medium-high heat and bring the mixture to a boil.

2. Switch heat to medium level, simmer the soup for 90 minutes until cooked, and when done, remove bay leaf from it.
3. Serve straight away.

Nutrition Value:
    Calories: 188 Cal; Fat: 1.6 g; Carbs: 37 g; Protein: 7 g; Fiber: 8.4 g

Lentils and Rice with Fried Onions

Preparation time: 5 minutes; Cooking time: 7 minutes; Servings: 4
Ingredients:
- 3/4 cup long-grain white rice, cooked
- 1 large white onion, peeled, sliced
- 1 1/3 cups green lentils, cooked
- ½ teaspoon salt
- 1/4 cup vegan sour cream
- ¼ teaspoon ground black pepper
- 6 tablespoons olive oil

Method:
1. Take a large skillet pan, place it over medium heat, add oil and when hot, add onions, and cook for 10 minutes until browned, set aside until required.
2. Take a saucepan, place it over medium heat, grease it with oil, add lentils and beans and cook for 3 minutes until warmed.
3. Season with salt and black pepper, cook for 2 minutes, then stir in half of the browned onions, and top with cream and remaining onions.
4. Serve straight away.

Nutrition Value:
    Calories: 535 Cal; Fat: 22.1 g; Carbs: 69 g; Protein: 17.3 g; Fiber: 10.6 g

Asparagus Rice Pilaf

Preparation time: 10 minutes; Cooking time: 35 minutes; Servings: 4
Ingredients:
- 1 1/4 cups rice
- 1/2 pound asparagus, diced, boiled
- 2 ounces spaghetti, whole-grain, broken
- 1/4 cup minced white onion
- 1/2 teaspoon minced garlic
- 1/2 cup cashew halves
- ¼ teaspoon ground black pepper
- ½ teaspoon salt
- 1/4 cup vegan butter
- 2 1/4 cups vegetable broth

Method:
1. Take a saucepan, place it over medium-low heat, add butter and when it melts, stir in spaghetti and cook for 3 minutes until golden brown.
2. Add onion and garlic, cook for 2 minutes until tender, then stir in rice, cook for 5 minutes, pour in the broth, season with salt and black pepper and bring it to a boil.
3. Switch heat to medium level, cook for 20 minutes, then add cashews and asparagus and stir until combined.
4. Serve straight away.

Nutrition Value:
    Calories: 249 Cal; Fat: 10 g; Carbs: 35.1 g; Protein: 5.3 g; Fiber: 1.8 g

Mexican Stuffed Peppers

Preparation time: 10 minutes; Cooking time: 40 minutes; Servings: 4
Ingredients:
- 2 cups cooked rice
- 1/2 cup chopped onion
- 15 ounces cooked black beans
- 4 large green bell peppers, destemmed, cored
- 1 tablespoon olive oil

- 1 tablespoon salt
- 14.5-ounce diced tomatoes
- 1/2 teaspoon ground cumin
- 1 teaspoon garlic salt
- 1 teaspoon red chili powder
- 1/2 teaspoon salt
- 2 cups shredded vegan Mexican cheese blend

Method:
1. Boil the bell peppers in salty water for 5 minutes until softened and then set aside until required.
2. Heat oil over medium heat in a skillet pan, then add onion and cook for 10 minutes until softened.
3. Transfer the onion mixture in a bowl, add remaining ingredients, reserving ½ cup cheese blended, stir until mixed, and then fill this mixture into the boiled peppers.
4. Arrange the peppers in the square baking dish, sprinkle them with remaining cheese and bake for 30 minutes at 350 degrees F.
5. Serve straight away.

Nutrition Value:
Calories: 509 Cal; Fat: 22.8 g; Carbs: 55.5 g; Protein: 24 g; Fiber: 12 g

Quinoa and Black Bean Chili

Preparation time: 10 minutes; Cooking time: 32 minutes; Servings: 10
Ingredients:
- 1 cup quinoa, cooked
- 38 ounces cooked black beans
- 1 medium white onion, peeled, chopped
- 1 cup of frozen corn
- 1 green bell pepper, deseeded, chopped
- 1 zucchini, chopped
- 1 tablespoon minced chipotle peppers in adobo sauce
- 1 red bell pepper, deseeded, chopped
- 1 jalapeno pepper, deseeded, minced
- 28 ounces crushed tomatoes
- 2 teaspoons minced garlic
- 1/3 teaspoon ground black pepper
- ¾ teaspoon salt
- 1 teaspoon dried oregano
- 1 tablespoon red chili powder
- 1 tablespoon ground cumin
- 1 tablespoon olive oil
- 1/4 cup chopped cilantro

Method:
1. Take a large pot, place it over medium heat, add oil and when hot, add onion and cook for 5 minutes.
2. Then stir in garlic, cumin, and chili powder, cook for 1 minute, add remaining ingredients except for corn and quinoa, stir well and simmer for 20 minutes at medium-low heat until cooked.
3. Then stir in corn and quinoa, cook for 5 minutes until hot and then top with cilantro.
4. Serve straight away.

Nutrition Value:
Calories: 233 Cal; Fat: 3.5 g; Carbs: 42 g; Protein: 11.5 g; Fiber: 11.8 g

Mushroom Risotto

Preparation time: 10 minutes; Cooking time: 35 minutes; Servings: 4
Ingredients:
- 1 cup of rice
- 3 small white onions, peeled, chopped
- 1 teaspoon minced celery
- 1 ½ cups sliced mushrooms
- ½ teaspoon minced garlic
- 1 teaspoon minced parsley
- ½ teaspoon salt
- ¼ teaspoon ground black pepper
- 1 tablespoon olive oil
- 1 teaspoon vegan butter

- ¼ cup vegan cashew cream
- 1 cup grated vegan Parmesan cheese
- 1 cup of coconut milk
- 5 cups vegetable stock

Method:

1. Take a large skillet pan, place it over medium-high heat, add oil and when hot, add onion and garlic, and cook for 5 minutes.
2. Transfer to a plate, add celery and parsley into the pan, stir in salt and black pepper, and cook for 3 minutes.
3. Then switch heat to medium-low level, stir in mushrooms, cook for 5 minutes, then pour in cream and milk, stir in rice until combined, and bring the mixture to simmer.
4. Pour in vegetable stock, one cup at a time until it has absorbed and, when done, stir in cheese and butter.
5. Serve straight away.

Nutrition Value:

Calories: 439 Cal; Fat: 19.5 g; Carbs: 48.7 g; Protein: 17 g; Fiber: 2 g

Quinoa with Chickpeas and Tomatoes

Preparation time: 10 minutes; Cooking time: 0 minute; Servings: 6
Ingredients:

- 1 tomato, chopped
- 1 cup quinoa, cooked
- ½ teaspoon minced garlic
- ¼ teaspoon ground black pepper
- ½ teaspoon salt
- 1/2 teaspoon ground cumin
- 4 teaspoons olive oil
- 3 tablespoons lime juice
- 1/2 teaspoon chopped parsley

Method:

1. Take a large bowl, place all the ingredients in it, except for the parsley, and stir until mixed.
2. Garnish with parsley and serve straight away.

Nutrition Value:

Calories: 185 Cal; Fat: 5.4 g; Carbs: 28.8 g; Protein: 6 g; Fiber: 4.5 g

Barley Bake

Preparation time: 10 minutes; Cooking time: 98 minutes; Servings: 6
Ingredients:

- 1 cup pearl barley
- 1 medium white onion, peeled, diced
- 2 green onions, sliced
- 1/2 cup sliced mushrooms
- 1/8 teaspoon ground black pepper
- 1/4 teaspoon salt
- 1/2 cup chopped parsley
- 1/2 cup pine nuts
- 1/4 cup vegan butter
- 29 ounces vegetable broth

Method:

1. Place a skillet pan over medium-high heat, add butter and when it melts, stir in onion and barley, add nuts and cook for 5 minutes until light brown.
2. Add mushrooms, green onions and parsley, sprinkle with salt and black pepper, cook for 1 minute and then transfer the mixture into a casserole dish.
3. Pour in broth, stir until mixed and bake for 90 minutes until barley is tender and has absorbed all the liquid.
4. Serve straight away.

Nutrition Value:

Calories: 280 Cal; Fat: 14.2 g; Carbs: 33.2 g; Protein: 7.4 g; Fiber: 7 g

Zucchini Risotto

Preparation time: 10 minutes; Cooking time: 30 minutes; Servings: 6
Ingredients:

- 2 cups Arborio rice
- 10 sun-dried tomatoes, chopped
- 1 medium white onion, peeled, chopped
- 1 tablespoon chopped basil leaves
- 1/2 medium zucchini, sliced
- 1 teaspoon dried thyme
- 1/3 teaspoon ground black pepper
- 1 tablespoon vegan butter
- 6 tablespoons grated vegan Parmesan cheese
- 7 cups vegetable broth, hot

Method:
1. Take a large pot, place it over medium heat, add butter and when it melts, add onion and cook for 2 minutes.
2. Stir in rice, cook for another 2 minutes until toasted, and then stir in broth, 1 cup at a time until absorbed completely and creamy mixture comes together.
3. Then stir in remaining ingredients until combined, taste to adjust seasoning and serve.

Nutrition Value:
Calories: 363 Cal; Fat: 4.1 g; Carbs: 71.2 g; Protein: 9.1 g; Fiber: 3.1 g

Mushroom, Lentil, and Barley Stew

Preparation time: 10 minutes; Cooking time: 6 hours; Servings: 8
Ingredients:

- 3/4 cup pearl barley
- 2 cups sliced button mushrooms
- 3/4 cup dry lentils
- 1-ounce dried shiitake mushrooms
- 2 teaspoons minced garlic
- 1/4 cup dried onion flakes
- 2 teaspoons ground black pepper
- 1 teaspoon dried basil
- 2 ½ teaspoons salt
- 2 teaspoons dried savory
- 3 bay leaves
- 2 quarts vegetable broth

Method:
1. Switch on the slow cooker, place all the ingredients in it, and stir until combined.
2. Shut with lid and cook the stew for 6 hours at a high heat setting until cooked.
3. Serve straight away.

Nutrition Value:
Calories: 213 Cal; Fat: 1.2 g; Carbs: 44 g; Protein: 8.4 g; Fiber: 9 g

Tomato Barley Soup

Preparation time: 10 minutes; Cooking time: 40 minutes; Servings: 6
Ingredients:

- 1/4 cup barley
- 1 cup chopped celery
- 14.5 ounces peeled and diced tomatoes
- 1 cup chopped white onions
- 2 tomatoes, diced
- 1 cup chopped carrots
- 2 teaspoons minced garlic
- 1/8 teaspoon ground black pepper
- 1 teaspoon salt
- 2 tablespoons olive oil
- 2 1/2 cups water
- 10.75 ounces chicken broth

Method:
1. Take a large saucepan, place it over medium heat, add onion, carrot, and celery, stir in garlic and cook for 10 minutes until tender.
2. Then add remaining ingredients, stir until combined, and bring the mixture to a boil.
3. Switch heat to the level, simmer the soup for 40 minutes and then serve straight away.

Nutrition Value:

Calories: 129 Cal; Fat: 5.5 g; Carbs: 15.3 g; Protein: 4.6 g; Fiber: 3.7 g

Black Beans, Corn, and Yellow Rice

Preparation time: 10 minutes; Cooking time: 25 minutes; Servings: 8
Ingredients:

- 8 ounces yellow rice mix
- 15.25 ounces cooked kernel corn
- 1 1/4 cups water
- 15 ounces cooked black beans
- 1 teaspoon ground cumin
- 2 teaspoons lime juice
- 2 tablespoons olive oil

Method:
1. Place a saucepan over high heat, add oil, water, and rice, bring the mixture to a bowl, and then switch heat to medium-low level.
2. Simmer for 25 minutes until rice is tender and all the liquid has been absorbed and then transfer the rice to a large bowl.
3. Add remaining ingredients into the rice, stir until mixed and serve straight away.

Nutrition Value:
Calories: 100 Cal; Fat: 4.4 g; Carbs: 15.1 g; Protein: 2 g; Fiber: 1.4 g

Lemony Quinoa

Preparation time: 10 minutes; Cooking time: 0 minute; Servings: 6
Ingredients:

- 1 cup quinoa, cooked
- 1/4 of medium red onion, peeled, chopped
- 1 bunch of parsley, chopped
- 2 stalks of celery, chopped
- ¼ teaspoon of sea salt
- 1/4 teaspoon cayenne pepper
- 1/2 teaspoon ground cumin
- 1/4 cup lemon juice
- 1/4 cup pine nuts, toasted

Method:
1. Take a large bowl, place all the ingredients in it, and stir until combined.
2. Serve straight away.

Nutrition Value:
Calories: 147 Cal; Fat: 4.8 g; Carbs: 21.4 g; Protein: 6 g; Fiber: 3 g

Cuban Beans and Rice

Preparation time: 10 minutes; Cooking time: 55 minutes; Servings: 6
Ingredients:

- 1 cup uncooked white rice
- 1 green bell pepper, cored, chopped
- 15.25 ounces cooked kidney beans
- 1 cup chopped white onion
- 4 tablespoons tomato paste
- 1 teaspoon minced garlic
- 1 teaspoon salt
- 1 tablespoon olive oil
- 2 ½ cups vegetable broth

Method:
1. Take a saucepan, place it over medium heat, add oil and when hot, add onion, garlic and bell pepper and cook for 5 minutes until tender.
2. Then stir in salt and tomatoes, switch heat to the low level and cook for 2 minutes.
3. Then stir in rice and beans, pour in the broth, stir until mixed and cook for 45 minutes until rice has absorbed all the liquid.
4. Serve straight away.

Nutrition Value:
Calories: 258 Cal; Fat: 3.2 g; Carbs: 49.3 g; Protein: 7.3 g; Fiber: 5 g

Brown Rice, Broccoli, and Walnut

Preparation time: 5 minutes; Cooking time: 18 minutes; Servings: 4
Ingredients:

- 1 cup of brown rice
- 1 medium white onion, peeled, chopped
- 1 pound broccoli florets
- ½ cup chopped walnuts, toasted
- ½ teaspoon minced garlic
- ⅛ teaspoon ground black pepper
- ½ teaspoon salt
- 1 tablespoon vegan butter
- 1 cup vegetable broth
- 1 cup shredded vegan cheddar cheese

Method:

1. Take a saucepan, place it over medium heat, add butter and when it melts, add onion and garlic and cook for 3 minutes.
2. Stir in rice, pour in the broth, bring the mixture to boil, then switch heat to medium-low level and simmer until rice has absorbed all the liquid.
3. Meanwhile, take a casserole dish, place broccoli florets in it, sprinkle with salt and black pepper, cover with a plastic wrap and microwave for 5 minutes until tender.
4. Place cooked rice in a dish, top with broccoli, sprinkle with nuts and cheese, and then serve.

Nutrition Value:
Calories: 368 Cal; Fat: 23 g; Carbs: 30.4 g; Protein: 15.1 g; Fiber: 5.7 g

Pecan Rice

Preparation time: 5 minutes; Cooking time: 10 minutes; Servings: 4
Ingredients:

- 1/4 cup chopped white onion
- 1/4 teaspoon ground ginger
- 1/2 cup chopped pecans
- 1/4 teaspoon salt
- 2 tablespoons minced parsley
- 1/4 teaspoon ground black pepper
- 1/4 teaspoon dried basil
- 2 tablespoons vegan margarine
- 1 cup brown rice, cooked

Method:

1. Take a skillet pan, place it over medium heat, add margarine and when it melts, add all the ingredients except for rice and stir until mixed.
2. Cook for 5 minutes, then stir in rice until combined and continue cooking for 2 minutes.
3. Serve straight away.

Nutrition Value:
Calories: 280 Cal; Fat: 16.1 g; Carbs: 31 g; Protein: 4.3 g; Fiber: 3.8 g

Broccoli and Rice Stir Fry

Preparation time: 5 minutes; Cooking time: 10 minutes; Servings: 8
Ingredients:

- 16 ounces frozen broccoli florets, thawed
- 3 green onions, diced
- ½ teaspoon salt
- ¼ teaspoon ground black pepper
- 2 tablespoons soy sauce
- 1 tablespoon olive oil
- 1 ½ cups white rice, cooked

Method:

1. Take a skillet pan, place it over medium heat, add broccoli, and cook for 5 minutes until tender-crisp.
2. Then add scallion and other ingredients, toss until well mixed and cook for 2 minutes until hot.
3. Serve straight away.

Nutrition Value:
  Calories: 187 Cal; Fat: 3.4 g; Carbs: 33 g; Protein: 6.3 g; Fiber: 2.3 g

Lentil, Rice and Vegetable Bake

Preparation time: 10 minutes; Cooking time: 40 minutes; Servings: 6
Ingredients:
- 1/2 cup white rice, cooked
- 1 cup red lentils, cooked
- 1/3 cup chopped carrots
- 1 medium tomato, chopped
- 1 small onion, peeled, chopped
- 1/3 cup chopped zucchini
- 1/3 cup chopped celery
- 1 ½ teaspoon minced garlic
- ½ teaspoon ground black pepper
- 1 teaspoon dried basil
- 1 teaspoon ground cumin
- 1 teaspoon dried oregano
- ½ teaspoon salt
- 1 teaspoon olive oil
- 8 ounces tomato sauce

Method:
1. Take a skillet pan, place it over medium heat, add oil and when hot, add onion and garlic, and cook for 5 minutes.
2. Then add remaining vegetables, season with salt, black pepper, and half of each cumin, oregano and basil and cook for 5 minutes until vegetables are tender.
3. Take a casserole dish, place lentils and rice in it, top with vegetables, spread with tomato sauce and sprinkle with remaining cumin, oregano, and basil, and bake for 30 minutes until bubbly.
4. Serve straight away.

Nutrition Value:
  Calories: 187 Cal; Fat: 1.5 g; Carbs: 35.1 g; Protein: 9.7 g; Fiber: 8.1 g

Coconut Rice

Preparation time: 10 minutes; Cooking time: 25 minutes; Servings: 7
Ingredients:
- 2 1/2 cups white rice
- 1/8 teaspoon salt
- 40 ounces coconut milk, unsweetened

Method:
1. Take a large saucepan, place it over medium heat, add all the ingredients in it and stir until mixed.
2. Bring the mixture to a boil, then switch heat to medium-low level and simmer rice for 25 minutes until tender and all the liquid is absorbed.
3. Serve straight away.

Nutrition Value:
  Calories: 535 Cal; Fat: 33.2 g; Carbs: 57 g; Protein: 8.1 g; Fiber: 2.1 g

Quinoa and Chickpeas Salad

Preparation time: 10 minutes; Cooking time: 0 minute; Servings: 4
Ingredients:
- 3/4 cup chopped broccoli
- 1/2 cup quinoa, cooked
- 15 ounces cooked chickpeas
- ½ teaspoon minced garlic
- 1/3 teaspoon ground black pepper
- 2/3 teaspoon salt
- 1 teaspoon dried tarragon
- 2 teaspoons mustard
- 1 tablespoon lemon juice
- 3 tablespoons olive oil

Method:
1. Take a large bowl, place all the ingredients in it, and stir until well combined.

2. Serve straight away.

Nutrition Value:
    Calories: 264 Cal; Fat: 12.3 g; Carbs: 32 g; Protein: 7.1 g; Fiber: 5.1 g

Brown Rice Pilaf

Preparation time: 5 minutes; Cooking time: 25 minutes; Servings: 4
Ingredients:
- 1 cup cooked chickpeas
- 3/4 cup brown rice, cooked
- 1/4 cup chopped cashews
- 2 cups sliced mushrooms
- 2 carrots, sliced
- ½ teaspoon minced garlic
- 1 1/2 cups chopped white onion
- 3 tablespoons vegan butter
- ½ teaspoon salt
- ¼ teaspoon ground black pepper
- 1/4 cup chopped parsley

Method:
1. Take a large skillet pan, place it over medium heat, add butter and when it melts, add onions and cook them for 5 minutes until softened.
2. Then add carrots and garlic, cook for 5 minutes, add mushrooms, cook for 10 minutes until browned, add chickpeas and cook for another minute.
3. When done, remove the pan from heat, add nuts, parsley, salt and black pepper, toss until mixed, and garnish with parsley.
4. Serve straight away.

Nutrition Value:
    Calories: 409 Cal; Fat: 17.1 g; Carbs: 54 g; Protein: 12.5 g; Fiber: 6.7 g

Barley and Mushrooms with Beans

Preparation time: 5 minutes; Cooking time: 15 minutes; Servings: 6
Ingredients:
- 1/2 cup uncooked barley
- 15.5 ounces white beans
- 1/2 cup chopped celery
- 3 cups sliced mushrooms
- 1 cup chopped white onion
- 1 teaspoon minced garlic
- 1 teaspoon olive oil
- 3 cups vegetable broth

Method:
1. Take a saucepan, place it over medium heat, add oil and when hot, add vegetables and cook for 5 minutes until tender.
2. Pour in broth, stir in barley, bring the mixture to boil, and then simmer for 50 minutes until tender.
3. When done, add beans into the barley mixture, stir until mixed and continue cooking for 5 minutes until hot.
4. Serve straight away.

Nutrition Value:
    Calories: 202 Cal; Fat: 2.1 g; Carbs: 39 g; Protein: 9.1 g; Fiber: 8.8 g

Vegan Curried Rice

Preparation time: 5 minutes; Cooking time: 25 minutes; Servings: 4
Ingredients:
- 1 cup white rice
- 1 tablespoon minced garlic
- 1 tablespoon ground curry powder
- 1/3 teaspoon ground black pepper
- 1 tablespoon red chili powder
- 1 tablespoon ground cumin
- 2 tablespoons olive oil
- 1 tablespoon soy sauce
- 1 cup vegetable broth

Method:

1. Take a saucepan, place it over low heat, add oil and when hot, add garlic and cook for 3 minutes.
2. Then stir in all spices, cook for 1 minute until fragrant, pour in the broth, and switch heat to a high level.
3. Stir in soy sauce, bring the mixture to boil, add rice, stir until mixed, then switch heat to the low level and simmer for 20 minutes until rice is tender and all the liquid has absorbed.
4. Serve straight away.

Nutrition Value:

Calories: 262 Cal; Fat: 8 g; Carbs: 43 g; Protein: 5 g; Fiber: 2 g

Garlic and White Bean Soup

Cooking time: 10 minutes; Servings: 4

Ingredients:

- 45 ounces cooked cannellini beans
- 1/4 teaspoon dried thyme
- 2 teaspoons minced garlic
- 1/8 teaspoon crushed red pepper
- 1/2 teaspoon dried rosemary
- 1/8 teaspoon ground black pepper
- 2 tablespoons olive oil
- 4 cups vegetable broth

Method:

1. Place one-third of white beans in a food processor, then pour in 2 cups broth and pulse for 2 minutes until smooth.
2. Place a pot over medium heat, add oil and when hot, add garlic and cook for 1 minute until fragrant.
3. Add pureed beans into the pan along with remaining beans, sprinkle with spices and herbs, pour in the broth, stir until combined, and bring the mixture to boil over medium-high heat.
4. Switch heat to medium-low level, simmer the beans for 15 minutes, and then mash them with a fork.
5. Taste the soup to adjust seasoning and then serve.

Nutrition Value:

Calories: 222 Cal; Fat: 7 g; Carbs: 13 g; Protein: 11.2 g; Fiber: 9.1 g

Coconut Curry Lentils

Preparation time: 10 minutes; Cooking time: 40 minutes; Servings: 4

Ingredients:

- 1 cup brown lentils
- 1 small white onion, peeled, chopped
- 1 teaspoon minced garlic
- 1 teaspoon grated ginger
- 3 cups baby spinach
- 1 tablespoon curry powder
- 2 tablespoons olive oil
- 13 ounces coconut milk, unsweetened
- 2 cups vegetable broth

For Serving:

- 4 cups cooked rice
- 1/4 cup chopped cilantro

Method:

1. Place a large pot over medium heat, add oil and when hot, add ginger and garlic and cook for 1 minute until fragrant.
2. Add onion, cook for 5 minutes, stir in curry powder, cook for 1 minute until toasted, add lentils and pour in broth.
3. Switch heat to medium-high level, bring the mixture to a boil, then switch heat to the low level and simmer for 20 minutes until tender and all the liquid is absorbed.

4. Pour in milk, stir until combined, turn heat to medium level, and simmer for 10 minutes until thickened.
5. Then remove the pot from heat, stir in spinach, let it stand for 5 minutes until its leaves wilts and then top with cilantro.
6. Serve lentils with rice.

Nutrition Value:
Calories: 184 Cal; Fat: 3.7 g; Carbs: 30 g; Protein: 11.3 g; Fiber: 10.7 g

Tomato, Kale, and White Bean Skillet

Preparation time: 10 minutes; Cooking time: 10 minutes; Servings: 4
Ingredients:

- 30 ounces cooked cannellini beans
- 3.5 ounces sun-dried tomatoes, packed in oil, chopped
- 6 ounces kale, chopped
- 1 teaspoon minced garlic
- 1/4 teaspoon ground black pepper
- 1/4 teaspoon salt
- 1/2 tablespoon dried basil
- 1/8 teaspoon red pepper flakes
- 1 tablespoon apple cider vinegar
- 1 tablespoon olive oil
- 2 tablespoons oil from sun-dried tomatoes

Method:
1. Prepare the dressing and for this, place basil, black pepper, salt, vinegar, and red pepper flakes in a small bowl, add oil from sun-dried tomatoes and whisk until combined.
2. Take a skillet pan, place it over medium heat, add olive oil and when hot, add garlic and cook for 1 minute until fragrant.
3. Add kale, splash with some water and cook for 3 minutes until kale leaves have wilted.
4. Add tomatoes and beans, stir well and cook for 3 minutes until heated.
5. Remove pan from heat, drizzle with the prepared dressing, toss until mixed and serve.

Nutrition Value:
Calories: 264 Cal; Fat: 12 g; Carbs: 38 g; Protein: 9 g; Fiber: 13 g

Chard Wraps with Millet

Preparation time: 25 minutes; Cooking time: 0 minute; Servings: 4
Ingredients:

- 1 carrot, cut into ribbons
- 1/2 cup millet, cooked
- 1/2 of a large cucumber, cut into ribbons
- 1/2 cup chickpeas, cooked
- 1 cup sliced cabbage
- 1/3 cup hummus
- Mint leaves as needed for topping
- Hemp seeds as needed for topping
- 1 bunch of Swiss rainbow chard

Method:
1. Spread hummus on one side of chard, place some of millet, vegetables, and chickpeas on it, sprinkle with some mint leaves and hemp seeds and wrap it like a burrito.
2. Serve straight away.

Nutrition Value:
Calories: 152 Cal; Fat: 4.5 g; Carbs: 25 g; Protein: 3.5 g; Fiber: 2.4 g

Quinoa Meatballs

Preparation time: 10 minutes; Cooking time: 35 minutes; Servings: 4
Ingredients:

- 1 cup quinoa, cooked
- 1 tablespoon flax meal
- 1 cup diced white onion
- 1 ½ teaspoon minced garlic
- 1/2 teaspoon salt
- 1 teaspoon dried oregano

- 1 teaspoon lemon zest
- 1 teaspoon paprika
- 1 teaspoon dried basil
- 3 tablespoons water
- 2 tablespoons olive oil
- 1 cup grated vegan mozzarella cheese
- Marinara sauce as needed for serving

Method:
1. Place flax meal in a bowl, stir in water and set aside until required.
2. Take a large skillet pan, place it over medium heat, add 1 tablespoon oil and when hot, add onion and cook for 2 minutes.
3. Stir in all the spices and herbs, then stir in quinoa until combined and cook for 2 minutes.
4. Transfer quinoa mixture in a bowl, add flax meal mixture, lemon zest, and cheese, stir until well mixed and then shape the mixture into twelve 1 ½ inch balls.
5. Arrange balls on a baking sheet lined with parchment paper, refrigerate the balls for 30 minutes and then bake for 20 minutes at 400 degrees F.
6. Serve balls with marinara sauce.

Nutrition Value:
Calories: 100 Cal; Fat: 100 g; Carbs: 100 g; Protein: 100 g; Fiber: 100 g

Rice Stuffed Jalapeños

Preparation time: 5 minutes; Cooking time: 15 minutes; Servings: 6

Ingredients:
- 3 medium-sized potatoes, peeled, cubed, boiled
- 2 large carrots, peeled, chopped, boiled
- 3 tablespoons water
- 1/4 teaspoon onion powder
- 1 teaspoons salt
- 1/2 cup nutritional yeast
- 1/4 teaspoon garlic powder
- 1 lime, juiced
- 3 tablespoons water
- Cooked rice as needed
- 3 jalapeños pepper, halved
- 1 red bell pepper, sliced, for garnish
- ½ cup vegetable broth

Method:
1. Place boiled vegetables in a food processor, pour in broth and pulse until smooth.
2. Add garlic powder, onion powder, salt, water, and lime juice, pulse until combined, then add yeast and blend until smooth.
3. Tip the mixture in a bowl, add rice, and stir until incorporated.
4. Cut each jalapeno into half lengthwise, brush them with oil, season them with some salt, stuff them with rice mixture and bake them for 20 minutes at 400 degrees F until done.
5. Serve straight away.

Nutrition Value:
Calories: 148 Cal; Fat: 3.7 g; Carbs: 12.2 g; Protein: 2 g; Fiber: 2 g

Pineapple Fried Rice

Preparation time: 5 minutes; Cooking time: 12 minutes; Servings: 2

Ingredients:
- 2 cups brown rice, cooked
- 1/2 cup sunflower seeds, toasted
- 2/3 cup green peas
- 1 teaspoon minced garlic
- 1 large red bell pepper, cored, diced
- 1 tablespoon grated ginger
- 2/3 cup pineapple chunks with juice
- 2 tablespoons coconut oil
- 1 bunch of green onions, sliced

For the Sauce:
- 4 tablespoons soy sauce
- 1/2 cup pineapple juice
- 1/2 teaspoon sesame oil
- 1/2 a lime, juiced

Method:

1. Take a skillet pan, place it over medium-high heat, add oil and when hot, add red bell pepper, pineapple pieces, and two-third of onion, cook for 5 minutes, then stir in ginger and garlic and cook for 1 minute.
2. Switch heat to the high level, add rice to the pan, stir until combined and cook for 5 minutes.
3. When done, fold in sunflower seeds and peas and set aside until required.
4. Prepare the sauce and for this, place sesame oil in a small bowl, add soy sauce and pineapple juice and whisk until combined.
5. Drizzle sauce over rice, drizzle with lime juice, and serve straight away.

Nutrition Value:

Calories: 179 Cal; Fat: 5.5 g; Carbs: 30 g; Protein: 3.3 g; Fiber: 2 g

Lentil and Wild Rice Soup

Preparation time: 10 minutes; Cooking time: 40 minutes; Servings: 4

Ingredients:

- 1/2 cup cooked mixed beans
- 12 ounces cooked lentils
- 2 stalks of celery, sliced
- 1 1/2 cup mixed wild rice, cooked
- 1 large sweet potato, peeled, chopped
- 1/2 medium butternut, peeled, chopped
- 4 medium carrots, peeled, sliced
- 1 medium onion, peeled, diced
- 10 cherry tomatoes
- 1/2 red chili, deseeded, diced
- 1 ½ teaspoon minced garlic
- 1/2 teaspoon salt
- 2 teaspoons mixed dried herbs
- 1 teaspoon coconut oil
- 2 cups vegetable broth

Method:

1. Take a large pot, place it over medium-high heat, add oil and when it melts, add onion and cook for 5 minutes.
2. Stir in garlic and chili, cook for 3 minutes, then add remaining vegetables, pour in the broth, stir and bring the mixture to a boil.
3. Switch heat to medium-low heat, cook the soup for 20 minutes, then stir in remaining ingredients and continue cooking for 10 minutes until soup has reached to desired thickness.
4. Serve straight away.

Nutrition Value:

Calories: 331 Cal; Fat: 2 g; Carbs: 54 g; Protein: 13 g; Fiber: 12 g

Black Bean Meatball Salad

Preparation time: 10 minutes; Cooking time: 25 minutes; Servings: 4

Ingredients:

For the Meatballs:

- 1/2 cup quinoa, cooked
- 1 cup cooked black beans
- 3 cloves of garlic, peeled
- 1 small red onion, peeled
- 1 teaspoon ground dried coriander
- 1 teaspoon ground dried cumin
- 1 teaspoon smoked paprika

For the Salad:

- 1 large sweet potato, peeled, diced
- 1 lemon, juiced
- 1 teaspoon minced garlic
- 1 cup coriander leaves
- 1/3 cup almonds
- 1/3 teaspoon ground black pepper
- ½ teaspoon salt
- 1 1/2 tablespoons olive oil

Method:

1. Prepare the meatballs and for this, place beans and puree in a blender, pulse until pureed, and this place this mixture in a medium bowl.
2. Add onion and garlic, process until chopped, add to the bean mixture, add all the spices, stir until combined, and shape the mixture into uniform balls.
3. Bake the balls on a greased baking sheet for 25 minutes at 350 degrees F until browned.
4. Meanwhile, spread sweet potatoes on a baking sheet lined with baking paper, drizzle with ½ tablespoon oil, toss until coated and bake for 20 minutes with the meatballs.
5. Prepare the dressing, and for this, place remaining ingredients for the salad in a food processor and pulse until smooth.
6. Place roasted sweet potatoes in a bowl, drizzle with the dressing, toss until coated, and then top with meatballs.
7. Serve straight away.

Nutrition Value:
Calories: 140 Cal; Fat: 8 g; Carbs: 8 g; Protein: 10 g; Fiber: 4 g

Black Beans and Cauliflower Rice

Preparation time: 10 minutes; Cooking time: 20 minutes; Servings: 4
Ingredients:
- 3 cups cauliflower rice
- 15.5 ounces cooked black beans
- 1/2 cup diced red bell pepper
- 1/2 cup chopped onion
- 3 tablespoons chopped pickled jalapeno
- 1 ½ teaspoon minced garlic
- ¼ teaspoon ground black pepper
- 1/3 teaspoon sea salt
- 1/4 teaspoon ground cayenne pepper
- 2 tablespoons olive oil
- 1/2 cup diced parsley

Method:
1. Take a large skillet pan, place it over medium heat, add oil and garlic and cook for 2 minutes.
2. Then add onion and bell pepper, season with black pepper, salt, and cayenne pepper, cook for 5 minutes, then stir in jalapeno pepper and top with cauliflower rice.
3. Season with salt and black pepper, cook for 7 minutes, turning halfway, then add beans and cook for 2 minutes until hot.
4. Garnish with parsley and serve.

Nutrition Value:
Calories: 270.3 Cal; Fat: 1.6 g; Carbs: 52.7 g; Protein: 13.5 g; Fiber: 13.1 g

Black Bean Stuffed Sweet Potatoes

Preparation time: 15 minutes; Cooking time: 65 minutes; Servings: 4
Ingredients:
- 4 large sweet potatoes
- 15 ounces cooked black beans
- 1/2 teaspoon ground black pepper
- 1/2 of a medium red onion, peeled, diced
- 1/2 teaspoon sea salt
- 1/4 teaspoon onion powder
- 1/4 teaspoon garlic powder
- 1/4 teaspoon red chili powder
- 1/4 teaspoon cumin
- 1 teaspoon lime juice
- 1 1/2 tablespoons olive oil
- 1/2 cup cashew cream sauce

Method:
1. Spread sweet potatoes on a baking tray greased with oil and bake for 65 minutes at 350 degrees F until tender.
2. Meanwhile, prepare the sauce, and for this, whisk together the cream sauce, black pepper and lime juice until combined, set aside until required.

3. When 10 minutes of the baking time of potatoes are left, heat a skillet pan with oil, then add onion and cook for 5 minutes until golden.
4. Then stir in spice, cook for another 3 minutes, stir in bean until combined and cook for 5 minutes until hot.
5. Let roasted sweet potatoes cool for 10 minutes, then cut them open, mash the flesh and top with bean mixture, cilantro and avocado, and then drizzle with cream sauce.
6. Serve straight away.

Nutrition Value:
Calories: 387 Cal; Fat: 16.1 g; Carbs: 53 g; Protein: 10.4 g; Fiber: 17.6 g

Black Bean and Quinoa Salad

Preparation time: 10 minutes; Cooking time: 0 minute; Servings: 10
Ingredients:
- 15 ounces cooked black beans
- 1 medium red bell pepper, cored, chopped
- 1 cup quinoa, cooked
- 1 medium green bell pepper, cored, chopped
- 1/2 cup vegan feta cheese, crumbled

Method:
1. Place all the ingredients in a large bowl, except for cheese, and stir until incorporated.
2. Top the salad with cheese and serve straight away.

Nutrition Value:
Calories: 64 Cal; Fat: 1 g; Carbs: 8 g; Protein: 3 g; Fiber: 3 g

Chickpea Fajitas

Preparation time: 10 minutes; Cooking time: 30 minutes; Servings: 4
Ingredients:
For the Chickpea Fajitas:
- 1 1/2 cups cooked chickpeas
- 1 medium white onion, peeled, sliced
- 2 medium green bell peppers, cored, sliced
- 1 tablespoon fajita seasoning
- 2 tablespoons olive oil

For the Cream:
- 1/2 cup cashews, soaked
- 1 clove of garlic, peeled
- ½ teaspoon salt
- 1/2 teaspoon ground cumin
- 1/4 cup lime juice
- 1/4 cup water
- 1 tablespoon olive oil

To serve:
- Sliced avocado for topping
- Chopped lettuce for topping
- 4 flour tortillas
- Chopped tomatoes for topping
- Salsa for topping
- Chopped cilantro for topping

Method:
1. Prepare chickpeas and for this, whisk together seasoning and oil until combined, add onion, pepper, and chickpeas, toss until well coated, then spread them in a baking sheet and roast for 30 minutes at 400 degrees F until crispy and browned, stirring halfway.
2. Meanwhile, prepare the cream and for this, place all of its ingredients in a food processor and pulse until smooth, set aside until required.
3. When chickpeas and vegetables have roasted, top them evenly on tortillas, then top them evenly with avocado, lettuce, tomatoes, salsa, and cilantro and serve.

Nutrition Value:
Calories: 391 Cal; Fat: 16 g; Carbs: 43 g; Protein: 8 g; Fiber: 9 g

Coconut Chickpea Curry

Preparation time: 10 minutes; Cooking time: 30 minutes; Servings: 4
Ingredients:

- 2 teaspoons coconut flour
- 16 ounces cooked chickpeas
- 14 ounces tomatoes, diced
- 1 large red onion, sliced
- 1 ½ teaspoon minced garlic
- ½ teaspoon of sea salt
- 1 teaspoon curry powder
- 1/3 teaspoon ground black pepper
- 1 ½ tablespoons garam masala
- 1/4 teaspoon cumin
- 1 small lime, juiced
- 13.5 ounces coconut milk, unsweetened
- 2 tablespoons coconut oil

Method:

1. Take a large pot, place it over medium-high heat, add oil and when it melts, add onions and tomatoes, season with salt and black pepper and cook for 5 minutes.
2. Switch heat to medium-low level, cook for 10 minutes until tomatoes have released their liquid, then add chickpeas and stir in garlic, curry powder, garam masala, and cumin until combined.
3. Stir in milk and flour, bring the mixture to boil, then switch heat to medium heat and simmer the curry for 12 minutes until cooked.
4. Taste to adjust seasoning, drizzle with lime juice, and serve.

Nutrition Value:

Calories: 225 Cal; Fat: 9.4 g; Carbs: 28.5 g; Protein: 7.3 g; Fiber: 9 g

Mediterranean Chickpea Casserole

Preparation time: 10 minutes; Cooking time: 60 minutes; Servings: 4
Ingredients:

- 3 cups baby spinach
- 2 medium red onions, peeled, diced
- 2 1/2 cups tomatoes
- 3 cups cooked chickpeas
- 1 ½ teaspoon minced garlic
- 1/3 teaspoon ground black pepper
- 1 ¼ teaspoon salt
- 1/4 teaspoon allspice
- 1 tablespoon coconut sugar
- 1 teaspoon dried oregano
- 1/4 teaspoon cayenne
- 1/4 teaspoon cloves
- 2 bay leaves
- 1 tablespoon coconut oil
- 2 tablespoons olive oil
- 1 cup vegetable stock
- 1 lemon, juiced
- 2 ounces vegan feta cheese

Method:

1. Take a large skillet pan, place it over medium-high heat, add coconut oil and when it melts, add onion and cook for 5 minutes until softened.
2. Switch heat to medium-low level, stir in garlic, cook for 2 minutes, then stir in tomatoes, add all the spices and bay leaves, pour in the stock, stir until mixed and cook for 20 minutes.
3. Then stir in chickpeas, simmer cooking for 15 minutes until the cooking liquid has reduced by one-third, stir in spinach and cook for 3 minutes until it begins to wilt.
4. Then stir in olive oil, sugar and lemon juice, taste to adjust seasoning, and remove and discard bay leaves.
5. When done, top chickpeas with cheese, broil for 5 minutes until cheese has melted and golden brown, then garnish with parsley and serve.

Nutrition Value:

Calories: 257.8 Cal; Fat: 3.8 g; Carbs: 47.1 g; Protein: 10.3 g; Fiber: 9.4 g

Zoodles with White Beans

Preparation time: 10 minutes; Cooking time: 20 minutes; Servings: 4

Ingredients:

- 15 ounces cooked cannellini beans
- 2 medium zucchinis, spiralized into noodles
- 3 teaspoons minced garlic
- 1 cup chopped Roma tomatoes
- 2/3 teaspoon salt
- 1/8 teaspoon red pepper flakes
- 1/4 cup olive oil
- 1/4 cup chopped parsley
- 4 ounces whole-grain spaghetti, cooked

Method:

1. Cook the pasta, drain it, transfer it into a bowl, add zucchini noodles and toss until mixed.
2. Take a pot, place it over low heat, add oil, garlic, and red pepper flakes, stir until cook for 5 minutes until garlic is golden brown.
3. Then add all the ingredients, except for parsley and salt, toss until mixed and cook for 5 minutes until thoroughly heated.
4. When done, season with salt, top with parsley and serve.

Nutrition Value:

Calories: 301 Cal; Fat: 15 g; Carbs: 34 g; Protein: 11 g; Fiber: 7 g

Sweet Potato and White Bean Skillet

Preparation time: 10 minutes; Cooking time: 45 minutes; Servings: 4

Ingredients:

- 1 large bunch of kale, chopped
- 2 large sweet potatoes, peeled, ¼-inch cubes
- 12 ounces cannellini beans
- 1 small onion, peeled, diced
- 1/8 teaspoon red pepper flakes
- 1 teaspoon salt
- 1 teaspoon cumin
- ½ teaspoon ground black pepper
- 1 teaspoon curry powder
- 1 1/2 tablespoons coconut oil
- 6 ounces coconut milk, unsweetened

Method:

1. Take a large skillet pan, place it over medium heat, add ½ tablespoon oil and when it melts, add onion and cook for 5 minutes.
2. Then stir in sweet potatoes, stir well, cook for 5 minutes, then season with all the spices, cook for 1 minute and remove the pan from heat.
3. Take another pan, add remaining oil in it, place it over medium heat and when oil melts, add kale, season with some salt and black pepper, stir well, pour in the milk and cook for 15 minutes until tender.
4. Then add beans, beans, and red pepper, stir until mixed and cook for 5 minutes until hot.
5. Serve straight away.

Nutrition Value:

Calories: 263 Cal; Fat: 4 g; Carbs: 44 g; Protein: 13 g; Fiber: 12 g

Chapter 6: Vegetables

Beans Curry

Preparation time: 10 minutes; Cooking time: 8 hours and 10 minutes; Servings: 5

Ingredients:

- 2 cups kidney beans, dried, soaked
- 1-inch of ginger, grated
- 1 ½ cup diced tomatoes
- 1 medium red onion, peeled, sliced
- 1 tablespoon tomato paste
- 1 teaspoon minced garlic
- 1 small bunch cilantro, chopped
- ½ teaspoon cumin powder
- 1 teaspoon salt
- 1 ½ teaspoon curry powder
- 2 tablespoons olive oil
- 2 tablespoons lemon juice

Method:

1. Place onion in a food processor, add ginger and garlic, and pulse for 1 minute until blended.
2. Take a skillet pan, place it over medium heat, add oil and when hot, add the onion-garlic mixture, and cook for 5 minutes until softened and light brown.
3. Then add tomatoes and tomato paste, stir in ½ teaspoon salt, cumin and curry powder and cook for 5 minutes until cooked.
4. Drain the soaked beans, add them to the slow cooker, add cooked tomato mixture, and remaining ingredients except for cilantro and lemon juice and stir until mixed.
5. Switch on the slow cooker, then shut with lid and cook for 8 hours at high heat setting until tender.
6. When done, transfer 1 cup of beans to the blender, process until creamy, then return it into the slow cooker and stir until mixed.
7. Drizzle with lemon juice, top with cilantro, and serve.

Nutrition Value:

Calories: 252 Cal; Fat: 6.5 g; Carbs: 38 g; Protein: 13 g; Fiber: 9.3 g

Pasta with Kidney Bean Sauce

Preparation time: 5 minutes; Cooking time: 15 minutes; Servings: 4

Ingredients:

- 12 ounces cooked kidney beans
- 7 ounces whole-wheat pasta, cooked
- 1 medium white onion, peeled, diced
- 1 cup arugula
- 2 tablespoons tomato paste
- 1 teaspoon minced garlic
- ½ teaspoon smoked paprika
- 1 teaspoon dried oregano
- ½ teaspoon cayenne pepper
- 1/3 teaspoon ground black pepper
- 2/3 teaspoon salt
- 2 tablespoons balsamic vinegar

Method:

1. Take a large skillet pan, place it over medium-high heat, add onion and garlic, splash with some water and cook for 5 minutes.
2. Then add remaining ingredients, except for pasta and arugula, stir until mixed and cook for 10 minutes until thickened.
3. When done, mash with the fork, top with arugula and serve with pasta.
4. Serve straight away

Nutrition Value:

Calories: 236 Cal; Fat: 1.6 g; Carbs: 46 g; Protein: 12 g; Fiber: 12.3 g

Stuffed Peppers with Kidney Beans

Preparation time: 5 minutes; Cooking time: 35 minutes; Servings: 4
Ingredients:

- 3.5 ounces cooked kidney beans
- 1 big tomato, diced
- 3.5 ounces sweet corn, canned
- 2 medium bell peppers, deseeded, halved
- ½ of medium red onion, peeled, diced
- 1 teaspoon garlic powder
- 1/3 teaspoon ground black pepper
- 2/3 teaspoon salt
- ½ teaspoon dried basil
- 3 teaspoons parsley
- ½ teaspoon dried thyme
- 3 tablespoons cashew
- 1 teaspoon olive oil

Method:
1. Switch on the oven, then set it to 400 degrees F and let it preheat.
2. Take a large skillet pan, place it over medium heat, add oil and when hot, add onion and cook for 2 minutes until translucent.
3. Add beans, tomatoes, and corn, stir in garlic and cashews and cook for 5 minutes.
4. Stir in salt, black pepper, parsley, basil, and thyme, remove the pan from heat and evenly divide the mixture between bell peppers.
5. Bake the peppers for 25 minutes until tender, then top with parsley and serve.

Nutrition Value:
Calories: 139 Cal; Fat: 1.6 g; Carbs: 18 g; Protein: 5.1 g; Fiber: 3.3 g

Chickpea Shakshuka

Preparation time: 5 minutes; Cooking time: 30 minutes; Servings: 6
Ingredients:

- 22 ounces cooked chickpeas
- 1/2 cup diced white onion
- 5 green olives
- 1/2 medium red bell pepper, chopped
- 1 1/2 Tbsp minced garlic
- 1 Tbsp coconut sugar
- 2 teaspoons red chili powder
- 2 teaspoons smoked paprika
- 1/8 teaspoon cayenne pepper
- 1 teaspoon salt
- 3 Tbsp tomato paste
- 1 tsp ground cumin
- 1/4 teaspoon ground cinnamon
- 1/8 teaspoon cardamom
- 1/8 teaspoon coriander
- 28-ounces tomato puree
- 1 Tbsp avocado oil

Method:
1. Take a large skillet pan, place it over medium heat, add oil and when hot, add garlic, onion and bell pepper and cook for 5 minutes until fragrant.
2. Then stir in the tomato puree and tomato paste, stir in all the spices until combined, bring the mixture to simmer, and cook for 3 minutes.
3. Add olives and chickpeas, stir to combine, switch heat to medium-low level and simmer for 20 minutes until cooked.
4. Serve straight away.

Nutrition Value:
Calories: 211 Cal; Fat: 5.1 g; Carbs: 36.3 g; Protein: 8.8 g; Fiber: 8.8 g

Thai Tofu

Preparation time: 5 minutes; Cooking time: 7 minutes; Servings: 4
Ingredients:

- 14 ounces tofu, firm, drained, 3/4 inch cubed
- 1/3 cup chopped green onion
- 2 teaspoons grated ginger
- 3 tablespoons coconut flakes
- 1 teaspoon soy sauce

- 1 ½ teaspoon olive oil
- ¼ cup peanut butter
- ½ teaspoon sesame oil
- 1 teaspoon sesame seeds

Method:
1. Take a skillet pan, place it over medium-high heat. Reduce heat to medium, add both oils and when hot, add green onions and cook for 1 minute.
2. Then add tofu cubes, cook for 4 minutes and stir in soy sauce halfway.
3. Stir in ginger and peanut butter, stir gently until well incorporated, and then remove the pan from heat.
4. Sprinkle with sesame seeds and serve.

Nutrition Value:
Calories: 285 Cal; Fat: 20.5 g; Carbs: 10.6 g; Protein: 20.1 g; Fiber: 4.3 g

Avocado Burrito Bowl

Preparation time: 5 minutes; Cooking time: 10 minutes; Servings: 4
Ingredients:
- 1 cup brown rice, cooked

For Marinated Kale:
- 1 bunch of kale, chopped
- ¼ cup lime juice
- 2 tablespoons olive oil
- ½ jalapeño, deseeded, chopped
- ½ teaspoon cumin
- ¼ teaspoon salt

For Avocado Salsa:
- 1 avocado, pitted, sliced
- ½ cup cilantro leaves
- ½ cup salsa verde
- 2 tablespoons lime juice

For Seasoned Black Beans:
- 1/3 cup chopped red onion
- 4 cups cooked black beans
- 1 ½ teaspoon minced garlic
- ¼ teaspoon cayenne pepper
- ¼ teaspoon red chili powder
- 1 tablespoon olive oil

For Garnish:
- 6 Cherry tomatoes, sliced into thin rounds
- 4 teaspoons hot sauce

Method:
1. Prepare kale and for this, place all its ingredients in a large bowl and toss until combined, set aside until required.
2. Prepare the salsa, and for this, place all its ingredients in a blender, process until smooth, and set aside until required.
3. Prepare beans and for this, take a saucepan, place it over medium-low heat, add oil and when hot, add onion and garlic and cook for 2 minutes.
4. Then add remaining ingredients, stir until mixed and cook for 7 minutes until beans are heated and tender.
5. Top rice with beans, kale, and salsa, drizzle with hot sauce and serve with tomatoes.

Nutrition Value:
Calories: 494 Cal; Fat: 14.7 g; Carbs: 80.8 g; Protein: 17.7 g; Fiber: 21.1 g

Butternut Squash Linguine

Preparation time: 10 minutes; Cooking time: 35 minutes; Servings: 4
Ingredients:
- 1 medium white onion, peeled, chopped
- 3 cups diced butternut squash, peeled, deseeded
- 1 teaspoon minced garlic
- ½ teaspoon salt
- ⅛ teaspoon red pepper flakes
- ¼ teaspoon ground black pepper

- 1 tablespoon chopped sage
- 2 tablespoons olive oil
- 2 cups vegetable broth
- 12 ounces linguine, whole-grain, cooked

Method:

1. Take a large skillet pan, place it over medium heat, add oil and when hot, add sage and cook for 3 minutes until crispy.
2. Transfer sage to a bowl, sprinkle with some salt and set aside until required.
3. Add onion, squash pieces, and garlic into the pan, season with salt, red pepper and black pepper, stir until mixed and cook for 10 minutes.
4. Pour in broth, stir, bring the mixture to boil, then switch heat to medium-low level and simmer for 20 minutes.
5. When done, remove the pan from heat, puree by using an immersion blender until smooth, taste to adjust seasoning and return it into the pan.
6. Heat the pan over medium heat, add cooked pasta, toss until well coated and cook for 2 minutes until hot.
7. Serve straight away.

Nutrition Value:

Calories: 380 Cal; Fat: 9 g; Carbs: 68.4 g; Protein: 10.7 g; Fiber: 10.8 g

Sweet Potato and Bean Burgers

Preparation time: 10 minutes; Cooking time: 50 minutes; Servings: 8

Ingredients:

- 1 cup oats, old-fashioned, ground
- 1 ½ pounds sweet potatoes
- 1 cup cooked millet
- 15 ounces cooked black beans
- ½ cup cilantro, chopped
- ½ small red onion, peeled, diced
- ½ teaspoon salt
- 1 teaspoon chipotle powder
- 2 teaspoons cumin powder
- ½ teaspoon cayenne powder
- 1 teaspoon red chili powder
- 2 tablespoons olive oil
- 8 hamburger buns, whole-wheat, toasted

Method:

1. Prepare sweet potatoes, and for this, slice them lengthwise and roast for 40 minutes at 400 degrees F, cut-side up.
2. Prepare the burgers and for this, place all the ingredients in the bowl, except for oil and buns, stir until combined, and then shape the mixture into eight patties.
3. Take a skillet pan, place it over medium heat, add oil and when hot, add patties and cook for 4 minutes per side until browned.
4. Sandwich patties between buns, and serve.

Nutrition Value:

Calories: 255 Cal; Fat: 12.7 g; Carbs: 29 g; Protein: 10 g; Fiber: 7.3 g

Thai Peanut Sauce over Roasted Sweet Potatoes

Preparation time: 10 minutes; Cooking time: 35 minutes; Servings: 4

Ingredients:

For the Thai Peanut Sauce:

- 1 teaspoon grated ginger
- 1 teaspoon garlic
- ¼ cup of soy sauce
- 3 tablespoons apple cider vinegar
- ¼ teaspoon red pepper flakes
- 2 tablespoons honey
- ½ cup peanut butter
- 2 tablespoons water

For the Roasted vegetables:

- 1 red bell pepper, cored, deseeded, sliced into strips
- 2 sweet potatoes, peeled, 1-inch
- 1 teaspoon salt
- ¼ teaspoon cumin powder
- 2 tablespoons olive oil

For the Garnish:
- 3 green onions, sliced
- 1 ¼ cup brown rice, cooked
- ½ cup cilantro
- ¼ cup peanuts, crushed

Method:
1. Prepare the vegetables and for this, place sweet potatoes on a baking sheet, drizzle with 1 tablespoon oil, season with ½ teaspoon salt and 1/8 teaspoon cumin, toss until mixed and roast for 35 minutes at 425 degrees F, tossing halfway.
2. In the meantime, place bell pepper strips on another baking sheet, drizzle with remaining oil, season with remaining salt, and toss until mixed and roast for 20 minutes at 425 degrees F, tossing halfway.
3. While vegetables are roasting, prepare the sauce and for this, place all its ingredients in a bowl and whisk until combined.
4. Distribute rice between four bowls, top with roasted vegetables, drizzle with sauce, garnish with peanuts, cilantro, and green onions, and serve.

Nutrition Value:
Calories: 295 Cal; Fat: 11.2 g; Carbs: 38.8 g; Protein: 9.8 g; Fiber: 9.2 g

Burrito-Stuffed Sweet Potatoes

Preparation time: 10 minutes; Cooking time: 45 minutes; Servings: 4
Ingredients:
For Sweet Potatoes:
- 1 cup cooked black beans
- 4 small sweet potatoes
- ½ cup of brown rice
- ½ teaspoon minced garlic
- 1 teaspoon tomato paste
- 1 teaspoon ground cumin
- ¼ teaspoon salt
- ½ teaspoon olive oil
- 1 ¼ cup water

For the Salsa:
- 1 cup cherry tomatoes, halved
- 1 medium red bell pepper, deseeded, chopped
- ¾ cup chopped red onion
- 2 tablespoon chopped cilantro leaves
- ½ teaspoon salt
- ¼ teaspoon ground black pepper
- 1 ½ teaspoon olive oil
- 1 tablespoon lime juice

For the Guacamole:
- 1 medium avocado, pitted, peeled
- ½ teaspoon minced garlic
- 2 tablespoons chopped cilantro leaves
- ¼ teaspoon salt
- 1 tablespoon lime juice

For Serving:
- Shredded cabbage as needed

Method:
1. Prepare sweet potatoes and for this, place them in a baking dish, prick them with a fork and bake for 45 minutes at 400 degrees F until very tender.
2. Meanwhile, place a medium saucepan over medium heat, add rice and beans, stir in salt, oil, and tomatoes paste, pour in water and bring the mixture to boil.
3. Switch heat to medium-low level, simmer for 40 minutes until all the liquid has absorbed and set aside until required.
4. Prepare the salsa and for this, place all its ingredients in a bowl and stir until combined, set aside until required.

5. Prepare the guacamole and for this, place the avocado in a bowl, mash well, then add remaining ingredients, stir until combined, and set aside until required.
6. When sweet potatoes are baked, cut them along the top, pull back the skin, then split and top with rice and beans mixture.
7. Top with salsa and guacamole and cabbage and serve.

Nutrition Value:
Calories: 388 Cal; Fat: 11 g; Carbs: 67.1 g; Protein: 10.5 g; Fiber: 15.7 g

Butternut Squash Chipotle Chili

Preparation time: 10 minutes; Cooking time: 60 minutes; Servings: 4
Ingredients:

- 3 cups cooked black beans
- 2 Avocados, pitted, peeled, diced
- 1 small butternut squash, peeled, ½-inch cubed
- 1 medium red onion, peeled, chopped
- 2 teaspoons minced garlic
- 1 tablespoon chopped chipotle pepper in adobo
- 14 ounces diced tomatoes with the juices
- 2 medium red bell peppers, chopped
- ¼ teaspoon ground cinnamon
- 1 tablespoon red chili powder
- 1 ½ teaspoon salt
- 1 teaspoon ground cumin
- 1 bay leaf
- 2 tablespoons olive oil
- 2 cups vegetable broth
- 3 corn tortillas

Method:
1. Cook onion, squash, and bell pepper in oil into a large stockpot placed over medium heat for 5 minutes.
2. Switch heat to medium-low level, add peppers, garlic, cumin, cinnamon, and chili powder, stir until mixed and cook for 30 seconds.
3. Then add remaining ingredients, except for tortilla, stir until combined and cook for 1 hour until done, adjusting the taste halfway.
4. Meanwhile, prepare the tortilla chips and for this, cut tortillas into 2 by ¼ inch strips, place a skillet pan over medium heat, add oil and when hot, toss in tortilla strips, sprinkle with some salt and cook for 7 minutes until golden.
5. When done, transfer tortilla chips to a plate lined with paper towels and serve with cooked chili.

Nutrition Value:
Calories: 202 Cal; Fat: 1.4 g; Carbs: 41 g; Protein: 10.2 g; Fiber: 13.5 g

Sweet Potato, Kale and Chickpea Soup

Preparation time: 10 minutes; Cooking time: 50 minutes; Servings: 6
Ingredients:

- 3 cups cooked farro
- 3 cups chopped kale
- 1 ½ cups cooked chickpeas
- 3 cups diced sweet potatoes
- 1 red bell pepper, cored, chopped
- 1 large white onion, peeled, chopped
- ¼ teaspoon salt
- ¼ teaspoon cayenne pepper
- 2 tablespoons Thai red curry paste
- 2 tablespoons olive oil
- 2 cups of water
- 4 cups vegetable broth

Method:
1. Take a large pot, place it over medium heat, add oil and when hot, add onion, potato and bell pepper, season with salt, and cook for 5 minutes until onions have softened.
2. Stir in curry paste, cook for 1 minute, then stir in farro, pour in water and broth, and stir until combined.

3. Bring the mixture to boil, switch heat to the low level and cook for 35 minutes.
4. Stir in kale and chickpeas, cook for 5 minutes and then stir in cayenne pepper.
5. Serve straight away.

Nutrition Value:
Calories: 339 Cal; Fat: 7 g; Carbs: 58.4 g; Protein: 10.3 g; Fiber: 11.2 g

Hummus Quesadillas

Preparation time: 5 minutes; Cooking time: 8 minutes; Servings: 1
Ingredients:
- 1 tortilla, whole-grain, about 8-inches
- 1/3 cup hummus
- ¼ cup sautéed spinach
- 2 tablespoons chopped sun-dried tomatoes
- 2 tablespoons sliced Kalamata olives
- 1 teaspoon olive oil

Method:
1. Take a tortilla, spread hummus on its one side, then cover its one-half with spinach, tomatoes, and olives and fold it.
2. Take a medium skillet pan, place it over medium heat and when hot, place folded quesadilla in it, cook for 2 minutes and then flip it carefully.
3. Brush with oil, continue cooking for 2 minutes, flip again and cook for 2 minutes until golden brown.
4. When done, transfer quesadilla to a cutting board, slice it into wedges and serve.

Nutrition Value:
Calories: 187 Cal; Fat: 9 g; Carbs: 16.3 g; Protein: 10.4 g; Fiber: 0 g

Pesto with Squash Ribbons and Fettuccine

Preparation time: 10 minutes; Cooking time: 0 minute; Servings: 4
Ingredients:
For the Pesto
- 1/3 cup pumpkin seeds, toasted
- 1 cup cilantro leaves
- 2 teaspoons chopped jalapeño, deseeded
- 1 teaspoon minced garlic
- 1 lime, juiced
- ½ teaspoon of sea salt
- ⅓ cup olive oil

For Pasta and Squash Ribbons
- 8 ounces fettuccine, whole-grain, cooked
- 2 small zucchinis
- 1 yellow squash

Method:
1. Prepare ribbons, and for this, slice zucchini and squash by using a vegetable peeler and then set aside until required.
2. Prepare pesto, and for this, place all its ingredients in a food processor and pulse for 2 minutes until blended.
3. Place vegetable ribbons in a bowl, add cooked pasta, then add prepared pesto and toss until well coated.
4. Serve straight away.

Nutrition Value:
Calories: 351 Cal; Fat: 20 g; Carbs: 38.8 g; Protein: 8 g; Fiber: 6.1 g

Kale Salad

Preparation time: 10 minutes; Cooking time: 0 minute; Servings: 4
Ingredients:
For the Salad:

- ½ of avocado, sliced
- ½ bunch of kale, chopped
- 2 carrots, sliced into long ribbons
- 1 radish, chopped

For Green Tahini:
- 1 small jalapeño, deseeded, chopped
- ½ cup cilantro
- ½ teaspoon minced garlic
- ½ teaspoon ground cumin
- ¼ teaspoon red pepper flakes

- ¼ cup cherry tomatoes
- 2 tablespoons green pumpkin seeds, toasted
- 1 cup cooked brown rice

- ¼ teaspoon of sea salt
- 1/3 cup olive oil
- 2 tablespoons tahini
- 1/3 cup lime juice
- 1 ½ teaspoon honey

Method:
1. Prepare the tahini, and for this, place all its ingredients in a food processor and pulse for 2 minutes until blended.
2. Then prepare the salad and for this, place all its ingredients in a bowl and toss until mixed.
3. Add prepared tahini dressing, toss until coated, and serve.

Nutrition Value:
Calories: 484 Cal; Fat: 20.4 g; Carbs: 66.2 g; Protein: 14.6 g; Fiber: 13 g

Thai Red Curry with Vegetables

Preparation time: 10 minutes; Cooking time: 25 minutes; Servings: 4
Ingredients:
- 1 ¼ cups brown rice, cooked
- 1 cup sliced carrots
- 1 medium red bell pepper, cored, sliced into strips
- 1 green bell pepper, cored, sliced into strips
- 1 ½ cups sliced kale
- 1 teaspoon minced garlic
- 1 cup chopped white onion
- 1 tablespoon grated ginger

- 1/8 teaspoon salt
- 2 tablespoons Thai red curry paste
- 1 ½ teaspoon coconut sugar
- 1 tablespoon olive oil
- 1 tablespoon soy sauce
- 2 teaspoons lime juice
- 14 ounces of coconut milk
- ½ cup of water
- ¼ cup chopped cilantro

Method:
1. Prepare the curry and for this, take a large skillet pan, place it over medium heat, add oil and when hot, add onion, season with salt, and cook for 5 minutes.
2. Stir in ginger and garlic, cook for 1 minute until fragrant, then add carrot and bell pepper and cook for 5 minutes.
3. Stir in curry paste, cook for 2 minutes, then add kale, stir in sugar, pour in coconut milk, stir until combined and bring the mixture to simmer.
4. Switch heat to the low level, simmer for 10 minutes until vegetables are tender, and then stir in soy sauce and lime juice.
5. Garnish with cilantro and serve with brown rice.

Nutrition Value:
Calories: 340 Cal; Fat: 11.3 g; Carbs: 56.3 g; Protein: 8.3 g; Fiber: 5.6 g

Peanut Slaw with Soba Noodles

Preparation time: 40 minutes; Cooking time: 0 minute; Servings: 4
Ingredients:
For the Slaw:
- ½ pound Brussels sprouts

- 1 bunch of green onions, sliced into thin rounds
- 6 cups shredded green cabbage

For the Peanut Dressing:
- 1 teaspoon minced garlic
- 1 tablespoon grated ginger
- 2 tablespoons honey
- 3 tablespoons rice vinegar

For the Garnish:
- ¼ cup chopped cilantro
- 2 tablespoons chopped peanuts

- 4 medium carrots, grated
- 4 ounces soba noodles, cooked

- 3 tablespoons soy sauce
- ½ cup peanut butter
- 3 tablespoons toasted sesame oil

- 1 lime, sliced into wedges

Method:
1. Prepare the dressing and for this, place all its ingredients in a large bowl and whisk until smooth.
2. Place noodles in a large bowl, add all the vegetables, pour in the prepared dressing and toss until well coated.
3. Let the slaw marinate for 30 minutes, top with peanuts and cilantro and serve with lime wedges.

Nutrition Value:
Calories: 265 Cal; Fat: 14 g; Carbs: 31.2 g; Protein: 9 g; Fiber: 4.6 g

Thai Green Curry with Spring Vegetables

Preparation time: 10 minutes; Cooking time: 35 minutes; Servings: 4
Ingredients:
- 2 cups sliced asparagus
- 1 small white onion, peeled, diced
- 2 cups baby spinach, chopped
- 1 cup sliced carrots
- 1 teaspoon minced garlic
- 1 tablespoon chopped ginger
- 1 cup brown rice, cooked
- 2 tablespoons Thai green curry paste

- 1 ½ teaspoon coconut sugar
- 1/8 teaspoon salt
- 1 ½ teaspoon lime juice
- 2 teaspoons olive oil
- 1 ½ teaspoons soy sauce
- 14 ounces coconut milk, unsweetened
- ½ cup of water

Method:
1. Take a large skillet pan, place it over medium heat, add oil and when hot, add ginger, onion, and garlic and cook for 5 minutes.
2. Then add carrots and asparagus, cook for 3 minutes, stir in curry paste and continue cooking for 2 minutes.
3. Pour in milk and water, stir in sugar and bring the curry to simmer.
4. Switch heat to the low level, simmer for 10 minutes until cooked, then stir in spinach and cook for 30 seconds until spinach leaves wilt.
5. When done, remove the pan from heat, stir in lime juice and soy sauce, taste to adjust seasoning and garnish with cilantro.
6. Serve curry with boiled rice.

Nutrition Value:
Calories: 400 Cal; Fat: 22.1 g; Carbs: 49 g; Protein: 8.6 g; Fiber: 6.1 g

Mango Cabbage Wraps

Preparation time: 15 minutes; Cooking time: 35 minutes; Servings: 4
Ingredients:

- 2 tablespoons chopped peanuts, toasted
- 1 small head of green cabbage

For the Baked Tofu:
- 15 ounces tofu, extra-firm, drained, cut into ½-inch cubed
- 2 teaspoons cornstarch

For the Peanut Sauce:
- 1 teaspoon minced garlic
- 2 tablespoons soy sauce
- 2 tablespoons apple cider vinegar
- 4 tablespoons lime juice

For the Mango Pico:
- 4 green onions, chopped
- 2 mangos, peeled, stoned, diced
- 1 medium red bell pepper, cored, chopped

- 2 tablespoons coconut flakes, unsweetened, toasted

- 1 tablespoon soy sauce
- 1 tablespoon olive oil

- 2 tablespoons honey
- 1/3 cup peanut butter
- 2 teaspoons toasted sesame oil

- 1 jalapeño, minced
- 1/3 cup cilantro leaves, chopped
- ¼ teaspoon salt
- 2 tablespoons lime juice

Method:
1. Prepare tofu and for this, place tofu pieces on a baking sheet, drizzle with 1 tablespoon oil and soy sauce, and toss until coated.
2. Sprinkle with 1 teaspoon cornstarch, toss until incorporated, sprinkle with remaining corn starch, toss until well coated, arrange tofu pieces in a single layer and bake for 35 minutes at 400 degrees F until crispy and golden brown.
3. Meanwhile, prepare the peanut sauce and for this, place all its ingredients in a food processor and pulse for 2 minutes until blended, set aside until required.
4. Prepare the salsa and for this, place all its ingredients in a bowl and toss until mixed.
5. When tofu has baked, take a pan, place it over medium heat, add toast peanuts and coconut flakes in it, and then add tofu pieces.
6. Pour in two-third of the peanut sauce, toss until well coated, cook for 5 minutes until its edges begin to bowl, then transfer tofu to a plate and let cool for 10 minutes.
7. Prepare the wrap and for this, pull out one leaf at a time from the cabbage, add some salsa, top with tofu, drizzle with remaining peanut sauce and serve.

Nutrition Value:
Calories: 448 Cal; Fat: 26 g; Carbs: 40 g; Protein: 20 g; Fiber: 6.6 g

Zucchanoush

Preparation time: 10 minutes; Cooking time: 10 minutes; Servings: 7
Ingredients:
- 1 pound small zucchini, quartered lengthwise
- 3 tablespoons mint leaves, divided
- ½ teaspoon minced garlic
- 1/3 teaspoon ground black pepper

- 2/3 teaspoon salt
- 2 tablespoons lemon juice
- 3 tablespoons olive oil, divided
- 1/4 cup tahini
- 1 tablespoon pine nuts, toasted

Method:
1. Place zucchini pieces in a bowl, add 1 tablespoon oil, season with ½ teaspoon salt, toss until well coated, and then grill for 10 minutes over medium heat until evenly charred.
2. Then transfer grilled zucchini to a food processor, add remaining ingredients, except for mint and nuts, and process for 2 minutes until blended.
3. Tip the mixture in a bowl, garnish with mint and nuts and then serve.

Nutrition Value:

Calories: 125 Cal; Fat: 11.5 g; Carbs: 4.5 g; Protein: 3 g; Fiber: 1 g

Grilled Asparagus and Shiitake Tacos

Preparation time: 5 minutes; Cooking time: 15 minutes; Servings: 4

Ingredients:

- 8 ounces shiitake mushrooms, destemmed
- 1 bunch of green onions
- 2 teaspoons minced garlic
- 1 teaspoon ground chipotle chili
- 1/2 teaspoon salt
- 3 tablespoons olive oil
- 8 corn tortillas, warmed
- 4 lime wedges
- 1 cup guacamole
- ¼ cup cilantro sprigs
- 4 tablespoons hot sauce

Method:

1. Take a large baking dish, add garlic, salt, and chipotle and stir in oil until combined.
2. Add all the vegetables, toss until well coated, and then grill over medium heat until lightly charred, 6 minutes grilling time for asparagus, 5 minutes for onions and mushrooms.
3. When done, cut vegetables for 2-inch pieces, distribute them evenly between tortillas, top with cilantro, guacamole, and hot sauce and serve with lime wedges.

Nutrition Value:

Calories: 350 Cal; Fat: 21 g; Carbs: 36 g; Protein: 7 g; Fiber: 11 g

Mushroom and Quinoa Burger

Preparation time: 15 minutes; Cooking time: 40 minutes; Servings: 5

Ingredients:

For the Burgers:

- 1 cup cooked quinoa
- 4 medium caps of Portobello mushroom, gills removed, chopped
- 1/4 cup chopped red onion
- ½ teaspoon minced garlic
- 3 green onions, chopped
- 1/2 cup cornstarch
- 1/2 cup walnuts
- 2 teaspoons rice wine vinegar
- 2 tablespoons olive oil
- 5 whole-grain burger buns

For Toppings:

- Sprouts as needed
- Lettuce as needed
- Sliced tomatoes as needed
- Vegan mayonnaise as needed

Method:

1. Prepare the burgers and for this, place mushrooms in a baking dish, add garlic and nuts, drizzle with 1 tablespoon oil, season with ¾ teaspoon salt and ¼ teaspoon black pepper, and then bake for 20 minutes until tender.
2. Then transfer the mushroom mixture in a food processor, add remaining ingredients for a burger, except for buns, stir until well mixed and then shape the mixture into five patties.
3. Fry the patties in batches for 5 minutes until browned and then bake for 10 minutes at 375 degrees F until thoroughly cooked.
4. Sandwich patties in burger buns, top with mayonnaise, sprouts, lettuce and tomatoes, and then serve.

Nutrition Value:

Calories: 495 Cal; Fat: 31 g; Carbs: 49 g; Protein: 9 g; Fiber: 7 g

BBQ Chickpea and Cauliflower Flatbreads

Preparation time: 5 minutes; Cooking time: 15 minutes; Servings: 4

Ingredients:

- 2 avocados, peeled, pitted, sliced
- 1 cup BBQ chickpeas

- 12 ounces chopped cauliflower florets
- 1 teaspoon salt
- 2 tablespoons roasted pumpkin seeds, salted
- 1 tablespoon olive oil
- 2 tablespoons lemon juice
- 4 flatbreads, toasted
- Hot sauce as needed for serving

Method:
1. Place a large baking sheer]t, place cauliflower in it, add oil, season with ¼ teaspoon salt, toss until well coated, and then bake for 25 minutes at 425 degrees F until don't.
2. Meanwhile, place the avocado in a bowl, add remaining salt and lemon juice, mash well with a fork and then spread on one side of flatbreads.
3. Distribute roasted cauliflower between flatbreads, top with chickpeas and pumpkin seeds, drizzle with hot sauce and then serve.

Nutrition Value:
Calories: 500 Cal; Fat: 25 g; Carbs: 65 g; Protein: 11 g; Fiber: 13 g

Summer Minestrone

Preparation time: 5 minutes; Cooking time: 15 minutes; Servings: 4
Ingredients:
- 1 medium yellow squash, cut into 1/2-inch pieces
- 1/2 cup frozen peas
- 1 small carrot, peeled, sliced
- 1 small zucchini, cut into 1/2-inch pieces
- 8 ounces red potatoes, peeled, cut into 1/2-inch pieces
- 1 large onion, peeled, chopped
- 1 tablespoon olive oil
- 1 teaspoon minced garlic
- 1/3 teaspoon ground black pepper
- 2/3 teaspoon salt
- 1 cup chopped basil
- 4 cups vegetable broth
- 1/4 cup grated vegan parmesan cheese

Method:
1. Take a large saucepan, place it over medium heat, add oil and when hot, add onion, stir in black pepper and salt and cook for 8 minutes.
2. Then stir in garlic, cook for 1 minute, stir in potatoes, pour in broth and simmer for 5 minutes.
3. Add carrot, squash, and zucchini, continue simmer for 3 minutes, and then add peas, simmer for another 3 minutes.
4. Stir in basil and cheese and then serve with bread.

Nutrition Value:
Calories: 185 Cal; Fat: 6 g; Carbs: 29 g; Protein: 7 g; Fiber: 5 g

Potatoes with Nacho Sauce

Preparation time: 10 minutes; Cooking time: 30 minutes; Servings: 4
Ingredients:
- 2 pounds mixed baby potatoes, halved
- 1/2 jalapeno chili, deseeded, chopped
- 1 cup cashews, soaked, drained
- 1/2 teaspoon garlic powder
- 1/2 teaspoon red chili powder
- 1 teaspoon of sea salt
- 1/2 teaspoon sweet paprika
- 1/2 teaspoon ground cumin
- 1/4 cup nutritional yeast
- 3 tablespoons lemon juice
- 3 tablespoons olive oil
- 1 cup of water
- Tortilla chips for serving

Method:
1. Place potatoes in a baking sheet, drizzle with oil, season with ½ teaspoon salt and ¼ teaspoon black pepper, and roast for 30 minutes at 450 degrees F until crispy and golden.

2. Meanwhile, place the remaining ingredients in a blender and pulse for 2 minutes until smooth.
3. Tip the sauce in a saucepan and cook for 5 minutes at the medium-low level until warm and then serve with roasted potatoes and tortilla chips.

Nutrition Value:

Calories: 380 Cal; Fat: 18 g; Carbs: 47 g; Protein: 10 g; Fiber: 6 g

Veggie Kabobs

Preparation time: 10 minutes; Cooking time: 10 minutes; Servings: 10

Ingredients:

- 8 ounces button mushrooms, halved
- 2 pounds summer squash, peeled, 1-inch cubed
- 12 ounces small broccoli florets
- 2 cups grape tomatoes
- 1 teaspoon salt
- 1/2 teaspoon smoked paprika
- 1 teaspoon ground cumin
- 6 tablespoons olive oil
- 1/2 teaspoon ground coriander
- 1 lime, juiced

Method:

1. Toss broccoli florets with 1 tablespoon oil, toss tomatoes and squash pieces with 2 tablespoons oil, then toss mushrooms with 1 tablespoon oil and thread these vegetables onto skewers.
2. Grill mushrooms and broccoli for 7 to 10 minutes, squash and tomatoes and 8 minutes, and when done, transfer the skewers to a plate and drizzle with lime juice and remaining oil.
3. Prepared the spice mix and for this, stir together salt, paprika, cumin, and coriander, sprinkle half of the mixture over grilled veggies, cover them with foil for 5 minutes, and then sprinkle with the remaining spice mix.
4. Serve straight away.

Nutrition Value:

Calories: 110 Cal; Fat: 9 g; Carbs: 8 g; Protein: 3 g; Fiber: 3 g

Summer Pesto Pasta

Preparation time: 10 minutes; Cooking time: 10 minutes; Servings: 4

Ingredients:

- 1 pound whole-grain spaghetti, cooked
- 2 cups grape tomatoes, halved
- 2 ears corn, shucked
- 1 medium yellow squash, ½ inch sliced
- 1 small bell pepper, deseeded, cut into sixths
- 1 medium zucchini, ½ inch sliced
- 1/4 cup chopped parsley
- 4 green onions
- 1 teaspoon salt
- 1 teaspoon ground black pepper
- 1 lemon, juiced, zested
- 2 tablespoons olive oil
- 1/2 cup vegan pesto

Method:

1. Place corn, onions, bell pepper, zucchini and squash in a bowl, season with ½ teaspoon each of salt and black pepper, and toss until coated.
2. Grill the corn for 10 minutes, and grill remaining vegetables for 6 minutes until lightly charred and when done, chop vegetables and place them in a bowl.
3. Place pesto in another bowl, add lemon juice and zest, season with remaining salt and black pepper, and whisk until combined.
4. Pour pesto over vegetables, toss until mixed, then cut kernels from grilled cobs, add them to the vegetables, then add pasta, parsley, and tomatoes and toss until combined.

5. Serve straight away.
Nutrition Value:
   Calories: 370 Cal; Fat: 12 g; Carbs: 54 g; Protein: 12 g; Fiber: 5 g

Linguine with Wild Mushrooms

Preparation time: 5 minutes; Cooking time: 3 minutes; Servings: 4
Ingredients:
- 12 ounces mixed mushrooms, sliced
- 2 green onions, sliced
- 1 ½ teaspoon minced garlic
- 1 pound whole-grain linguine pasta, cooked
- 1/4 cup nutritional yeast
- ½ teaspoon salt
- ¾ teaspoon ground black pepper
- 6 tablespoons olive oil
- ¾ cup vegetable stock, hot

Method:
1. Take a skillet pan, place it over medium-high heat, add garlic and mushroom and cook for 5 minutes until tender.
2. Transfer the vegetables to a pot, add pasta and remaining ingredients, except for green onions, toss until combined and cook for 3 minutes until hot.
3. Garnish with green onions and serve.
Nutrition Value:
   Calories: 430 Cal; Fat: 15 g; Carbs: 62 g; Protein: 15 g; Fiber: 5 g

Edamame and Noodle Salad

Preparation time: 5 minutes; Cooking time: 5 minutes; Servings: 4
Ingredients:
- 24 ounces shirataki noodles
- 1 medium apple, sliced
- 2 cups grape tomatoes, halved
- 3 cups frozen edamame, shelled
- 3 cups shredded carrots
- 2 cups frozen corn
- 1/2 teaspoon salt
- 1/2 cup rice vinegar
- 1 tablespoon Sriracha hot sauce and more for serving
- 1/2 cup peanut butter
- 2 tablespoons water
- 1/2 cup chopped cilantro

Method:
1. Take a large pot, place it over high heat, pour in water, bring it to boil, then add noodles, corn and edamame, boil for 2 minutes and drain when done.
2. Place remaining ingredients in a large bowl, whisk until combined, then add boiled vegetables and toss until well coated.
3. Drizzle with more Sriracha sauce and toss until combined.
Nutrition Value:
   Calories: 455 Cal; Fat: 22 g; Carbs: 50 g; Protein: 22 g; Fiber: 13 g

Pilaf with Garbanzos and Dried Apricots

Preparation time: 10 minutes; Cooking time: 15 minutes; Servings: 4
Ingredients:
- 1 cup bulgur
- 6 ounces cooked chickpeas
- 1/2 cup Dried apricot
- 1 small white onion, peeled, diced
- ½ teaspoon minced garlic
- 2 teaspoons curry powder
- 1/2 teaspoon salt
- 1 tablespoon olive oil
- 1/4 cup fresh parsley leaves
- 2 cups vegetable broth
- 3/4 cup water

Method:

1. Take a saucepan, place it over high heat, pour in water and 1 ½ cup broth, and bring it to a boil.
2. Then stir in bulgur, switch heat to medium-low level and simmer for 15 minutes until most of the liquid has absorbed.
3. Meanwhile, take a skillet pan, place it over medium heat, add oil and when hot, add onion, cook for 10 minutes, then stir in garlic and curry powder and cook for another minute.
4. Then add apricots, beans, and salt, pour in remaining broth and bring the mixture to boiling.
5. Remove pan from heat, fluff the bulgur with a fork, add to the onion-apricot mixture and stir until mixed.
6. Garnish with parsley and serve.

Nutrition Value:
Calories: 222 Cal; Fat: 4.5 g; Carbs: 35 g; Protein: 9.5 g; Fiber: 7 g

Avocado and Lime Bean Bowl

Preparation time: 10 minutes; Cooking time: 0 minute; Servings: 1
Ingredients:

- 1/2 cup mint berries
- 1/4 of medium avocado, pitted, sliced
- 1/2 cup breakfast beans
- 12 ounces roasted vegetable mix
- 1/8 teaspoon salt
- 1/8 teaspoon cumin
- 1 teaspoon sunflower seeds
- 1 teaspoon lime juice
- Lime wedges for serving

Method:
1. Place avocado in a bowl, mash with a fork and then stir in lime juice, salt, and cumin until combined.
2. Place roasted vegetable mix in a dish, top with mashed avocado mixture, beans, and sunflower seeds.
3. Serve with lime wedges and berries.

Nutrition Value:
Calories: 292 Cal; Fat: 10.4 g; Carbs: 45.6 g; Protein: 9.7 g; Fiber: 12.1 g

Kung Pao Brussels Sprouts

Preparation time: 10 minutes; Cooking time: 25 minutes; Servings: 1
Ingredients:

- 2 pounds Brussels sprouts, halved
- 1 teaspoon minced garlic
- ¾ teaspoon ground black pepper
- 1 tablespoon cornstarch
- 1 ½ teaspoon salt
- 1 tablespoon brown sugar
- 1/8 teaspoon red pepper flakes
- 1 tablespoon sesame oil
- 2 tablespoons olive oil
- 2 teaspoons apple cider vinegar
- 1/2 cup soy sauce
- 1 tablespoon hoisin sauce
- 2 teaspoons garlic chili sauce
- 1/2 cup water
- Sesame seeds as needed for garnish
- Green onions as needed for garnish
- Chopped roasted peanuts as needed for garnish

Method:
1. Place sprouts on a baking sheet, drizzle with oil, season with salt and black pepper, and then bake for 20 minutes at 425 degrees F until crispy and tender.
2. Meanwhile, take a skillet pan, place it over medium heat, add oil and when hot, add garlic and cook for 1 minute until fragrant.

3. Then stir in cornstarch and remaining ingredients, except for garnishing ingredients and simmer for 3 minutes, set aside until required.
4. When Brussel sprouts have roasted, add them to the sauce, toss until mixed and broil for 5 minutes until glazed.
5. When done, garnish with nuts, sesame seeds, and green onions and then serve.

Nutrition Value:
Calories: 272 Cal; Fat: 17 g; Carbs: 26 g; Protein: 10 g; Fiber: 7 g

Balsamic-Glazed Roasted Cauliflower

Preparation time: 10 minutes; Cooking time: 1 hour and 5 minutes; Servings: 4
Ingredients:
- 1 large head cauliflower, cut into florets
- 1/2-pound green beans, trimmed
- 1 medium red onion, peeled, cut into wedges
- 2 cups cherry tomatoes
- ½ teaspoon salt
- 1/4 cup brown sugar
- 3 tablespoons olive oil
- 1 cup balsamic vinegar
- 2 tablespoons chopped parsley, for garnish

Method:
1. Place cauliflower florets in a baking dish, add tomatoes, green beans and onion wedges around it, season with salt, and drizzle with oil.
2. Pour vinegar in a saucepan, stir in sugar, bring the mixture to a boil and simmer for 15 minutes until reduced by half.
3. Brush the sauce generously over cauliflower florets and then roast for 1 hour at 400 degrees F until cooked, brushing sauce frequently.
4. When done, garnish vegetables with parsley and then serve.

Nutrition Value:
Calories: 86 Cal; Fat: 5.7 g; Carbs: 7.7 g; Protein: 3.1 g; Fiber: 3.3 g

Stuffed Sweet Potato

Preparation time: 10 minutes; Cooking time: 45 minutes; Servings: 4
Ingredients:
- 4.5 pounds sweet potatoes
- 1/3 cup corn kernels
- 1 cup chopped kale
- 1/4 cup diced green onion
- 3/4 cup diced tomato
- ½ teaspoon minced garlic
- 1/2 teaspoon sea salt
- 1/2 teaspoon chipotle flakes
- 1/2 teaspoon Dijon mustard
- 1/2 teaspoon smoked paprika
- 1/2 teaspoon liquid smoke
- 1/4 teaspoon ground turmeric
- 1/2 tablespoon lemon juice
- 3 tablespoons nutritional yeast
- 1/3 cup cashews, soaked, drained
- 1 1/2 cup pasta, cooked
- 1 cup baked pumpkin puree
- 1/2 cup vegetable broth

Method:
1. Wrap each potato in a foil and then bake for 45 minutes at 375 degrees F until tender.
2. Meanwhile, prepare the cheese sauce and for this, place pumpkin and cashews in a food processor, add garlic, yeast, salt, paprika, chipotle flakes, liquid smoke, turmeric, mustard, and lemon juice, pour in broth and puree until smooth.
3. Take a pot, place it over medium-low heat, add prepared sauce, then add remaining ingredients, toss until coated, and cook for 5 minutes until kale has wilted.
4. Season the mixture with salt and black pepper, then switch heat to the low level and cook until sweet potatoes have roasted.

5. When sweet potatoes are roasted, let them stand for 10 minutes, then unwrap them, split them by slicing down the center and spoon prepared sauce generously in the center.
6. Serve straight away.

Nutrition Value:
   Calories: 330 Cal; Fat: 3.5 g; Carbs: 58 g; Protein: 13 g; Fiber: 15.2 g

Split Pea Pesto Stuffed Shells

Preparation time: 15 minutes; Cooking time: 60 minutes; Servings: 6
Ingredients:
- 12 ounces jumbo pasta shells, whole-grain, cooked
- Marinara sauce as needed for serving

For the Split Pea Pesto:
- 1 cup green split peas
- 1/4 cup basil leaves
- 1 teaspoon minced garlic
- 1 teaspoon of sea salt
- 2 tablespoons lemon juice
- 2 1/4 cups water, divided

Method:
1. Take a small saucepan, place it over high heat, add peas, pour in 2 cups water, and bring the beans to boil.
2. Switch heat to the low level, simmer beans for 30 minutes, and when done, drain the beans then transfer them to a food processor.
3. Pour in remaining ingredients for the pesto and pulse until blended.
4. Take a baking dish, spread the marinara sauce in the bottom, then stuffed shell with prepared pesto, arrange them into the prepared baking dish, spread with some marinara sauce over the top and bake for 30 minutes until heated.
5. Garnish with basil and serve.

Nutrition Value:
   Calories: 82 Cal; Fat: 0 g; Carbs: 15 g; Protein: 6 g; Fiber: 6 g

Tofu Tikka Masala

Preparation time: 10 minutes; Cooking time: 4 hours and 10 minutes; Servings: 4
Ingredients:
- 16 ounces tofu, extra-firm, drained, ½ inch cubed
- 1 ½ teaspoon minced garlic
- 2 medium carrots, peeled sliced
- 1 medium white onion, peeled, diced
- 1 1/2 cups diced potatoes
- 1 medium red bell pepper, cored, cut into chunks
- ¾ cup frozen peas
- 2 cups cauliflower florets
- ½ tablespoon grated ginger
- ¼ teaspoon ground black pepper
- ½ teaspoon salt
- ½ teaspoon ground turmeric
- 1 ½ teaspoons cumin
- ¼ teaspoon cayenne pepper
- 1 tablespoon garam masala
- 1 teaspoon coriander
- ¼ teaspoon paprika
- ½ tablespoon maple syrup
- 15 ounces tomato sauce
- 15 ounces of coconut milk
- 2 tablespoons chopped cilantro

Method:
1. Take a slow cooker, place all the ingredients in it, except for cilantro and peas, and stir until combined.
2. Switch on the slow cooker, shut with lid, and cook for 4 hours at a high heat setting.
3. When done, stir in peas, cook for 10 minutes, uncovering the cooker, and, when done, serve with cooked brown rice.

Nutrition Value:

Calories: 303 Cal; Fat: 11.5 g; Carbs: 36 g; Protein: 15 g; Fiber: 8.7 g

Thai Peanut and Sweet Potato Buddha Bowl

Preparation time: 10 minutes; Cooking time: 20 minutes; Servings: 2
Ingredients:

- 1 cup quinoa, cooked
- 4 cups sweet potato, peeled, small dice
- ½ cup carrots shredded
- ¼ cup cilantro
- 2 teaspoons minced garlic
- 2 teaspoons chopped the rosemary

For the Thai Peanut Sauce

- ¼ cup Thai red curry paste
- ¼ cup brown sugar
- 2 tablespoons soy sauce
- 1 tablespoon lime juice

- 1 teaspoon salt
- 1 teaspoon ground cinnamon
- 1 teaspoon ground black pepper
- ¼ cup peanuts, chopped
- ¼ cup olive oil
- ½ cup Thai Peanut Sauce

- 1 ½ cups coconut milk
- 2 tablespoons apple cider vinegar
- 1 cup peanut butter

Method:

1. Place sweet potatoes in a baking dish, add garlic, drizzle with oil, sprinkle with salt, rosemary, black pepper, and cinnamon and bake for 20 minutes at 425 degrees F until roasted.
2. Meanwhile, prepare the peanut sauce, and for this, place all its ingredients in a food processor and pulse until smooth.
3. When sweet potatoes have cooked, distribute them between two bowls along with peanuts, quinoa, cilantro, and carrots and then drizzle with sauce generously.
4. Serve straight away.

Nutrition Value:
Calories: 202 Cal; Fat: 1.3 g; Carbs: 47 g; Protein: 4 g; Fiber: 7.4 g

Buffalo Cauliflower Tacos

Preparation time: 10 minutes; Cooking time: 20 minutes; Servings: 4
Ingredients:
For the Cauliflower:

- 1/2 head cauliflower, cut into florets
- 1 teaspoon garlic powder
- ¼ teaspoon ground black pepper

For the Tacos:

- 1 medium head of romaine lettuce, chopped
- 8 flour tortillas

- 1 teaspoon red chili powder
- 4 teaspoons olive oil
- 3/4 cup buffalo sauce

- 1 medium avocado, pitted, diced
- Vegan ranch as needed
- Chopped cilantro as needed

Method:

1. Place cauliflower florets in a bowl, add garlic powder, black pepper, red chili powder, olive oil, and ¼ cup buffalo sauce and toss until combined.
2. Spread cauliflower florets on a baking sheet in a single layer and cook for 20 minutes until roasted, flipping halfway.
3. When done, transfer cauliflower in a large bowl, then heat remaining buffalo sauce, add to cauliflower florets and toss until combined.
4. Assemble tacos and for this, top tortilla with cauliflower, lettuce, and avocado, drizzle with ranch dressing and then top with green onions.
5. Serve straight away.

Nutrition Value:

Calories: 250 Cal; Fat: 9 g; Carbs: 37 g; Protein: 9 g; Fiber: 5.4 g

Meatball Sub

Preparation time: 10 minutes; Cooking time: 22 minutes; Servings: 3
Ingredients:
For the Meatballs:
- 1/3 cup sunflower seeds, ground
- 1 1/2 cups cooked kidney beans
- 1/2 cup mushrooms, chopped
- 1/2 cup rolled oats
- ½ teaspoon minced garlic
- 1 small red onion, peeled, chopped
- 2/3 teaspoon salt
- 1 teaspoon dried oregano
- 1/3 teaspoon ground black pepper
- 1 teaspoon dried basil
- 1 teaspoon soy sauce
- 1 tablespoon olive oil
- 1 tablespoon tomato paste

For the Subs:
- 3 Italian sub rolls
- 1/4 cup chopped parsley
- 2 cups marinara sauce
- 3 tablespoons grated vegan Parmesan

Method:
1. Place beans in a bowl, mash them with a fork and set aside until required.
2. Then place a medium pan over medium heat, add oil and when hot, add onions, cook for 3 minutes, stir in garlic and mushrooms and cook for another 2 minutes.
3. Then stir in mashed beans, add oats, sunflower seeds, tomato paste, all the spices and soy sauce, stir until well combined, and shape the mixture into 14 meatballs.
4. Arrange meatballs onto a baking sheet lined with parchment paper and bake for 15 minutes at 350 degrees F until cooked.
5. Sandwich the meatballs evenly between sub rolls, top with marinara, parmesan cheese, and parsley, and then serve.

Nutrition Value:
Calories: 404 Cal; Fat: 14 g; Carbs: 60 g; Protein: 13 g; Fiber: 10 g

Pumpkin Penne

Preparation time: 10 minutes; Cooking time: 60 minutes; Servings: 4
Ingredients:
- ½ of medium white onion, sliced into wedges
- 2 cloves of garlic, unpeeled
- 1 cup cooked and mashed sugar pie pumpkin
- ½ cup unsalted cashews, soaked, drained
- ½ teaspoon of sea salt
- 1/3 teaspoon ground black pepper
- 5 fresh sage leaves
- 2 tablespoons olive oil and more as needed for drizzling
- 1 cup vegetable broth
- 16 ounces penne pasta, cooked

Method:
1. Take a baking sheet, place onion, pumpkin and garlic in it, drizzle with salt, season with salt and black pepper, pierce pumpkin with a fork, cover the baking sheet and bake for 45 minutes until vegetables are very tender.
2. Then add sage in the last five minutes and after 45 minutes of baking, uncover the baking sheet and continue baking for 15 minutes.
3. When done, peel the pumpkin add to the food processor along with remaining vegetables and ingredients, except for pasta and puree until blended.
4. Place pasta in a pot, add half of the blended pumpkin mixture, stir until coated, then stir in remaining pumpkin mixture and serve.

Nutrition Value:

Calories: 301 Cal; Fat: 6.1 g; Carbs: 46.2 g; Protein: 16.3 g; Fiber: 6.3 g

White Bean and Mushroom Meatballs Subs

Preparation time: 15 minutes; Cooking time: 30 minutes; Servings: 20

Ingredients:

For The Meatballs:

- 1 1/4 cups bread crumbs
- 15 ounces cooked white beans
- 1 small white onion, peeled, diced
- 8 ounces button mushrooms, chopped
- 1 teaspoon minced garlic
- 1/2 teaspoon ground black pepper
- 1 teaspoon salt
- 1/2 teaspoon red chili flake
- 1 teaspoon oregano
- 1 lemon, juiced
- 1 tablespoon olive oil
- 2 tablespoons parsley, chopped

For the Subs:

- 15 ounces marinara sauce
- 20 sub rolls

Method:

1. Take a large skillet pan, place it over medium heat, add oil and when hot, add onion and cook for 5 minutes.
2. Then add garlic and mushrooms, cook for 2 minutes, add beans, season with salt, red chili flakes, oregano, and black pepper, stir in lemon juice and cook for 1 minute.
3. Transfer the mixture into the food processor, puree until smooth, add 1 cup crumbs and parsley and pulse until well combined.
4. Let the mixture stand for five minutes, shape the mixture into twenty meatballs, cover with remaining breadcrumbs until coated, and cook for 20 minutes until nicely browned on all sides.
5. Sandwich the meatballs in sub rolls, top with marinara sauce and serve.

Nutrition Value:

Calories: 404 Cal; Fat: 14 g; Carbs: 60 g; Protein: 13 g; Fiber: 10 g

Sweet Potato Fries

Preparation time: 10 minutes; Cooking time: 30 minutes; Servings: 4

Ingredients:

- 3 large sweet potatoes
- 1/2 teaspoon sea salt
- ¼ teaspoon cayenne pepper
- 1 teaspoon cumin
- 1/4 teaspoon paprika
- 1 tablespoon olive oil

Method:

1. Peel the potatoes, cut into wedges lengthwise, place them in a bowl, drizzle with oil and toss until combined.
2. Stir together remaining ingredients, sprinkle over sweet potatoes, spread the potatoes evenly on a baking sheet greased with oil in a single layer, and bake for 30 minutes at 400 degrees F until done, tossing twice.
3. Serve straight away.

Nutrition Value:

Calories: 78 Cal; Fat: 4 g; Carbs: 11 g; Protein: 1 g; Fiber: 2 g

Vegetarian Biryani

Preparation time: 10 minutes; Cooking time: 33 minutes; Servings: 6

Ingredients:

- 12 ounces chickpeas
- 2 cups rice, rinsed
- 1 large onion, peeled, sliced
- 2 cups sliced mixed veggies
- 1 ½ teaspoon minced garlic
- 1 tablespoon grated ginger

- 1 tablespoon cumin
- 1/2 teaspoon turmeric
- 1 tablespoon coriander
- 3/4 teaspoon salt
- 1 teaspoon cinnamon
- 1 teaspoon red chili powder

- 1/2 teaspoon cardamom
- 1 bay leaf
- 1/2 cup raisins
- 2 tablespoons olive oil
- 4 cups vegetable stock

Garnishing
- 1/4 cup cashews

- 1/4 cup chopped parsley

Method:
1. Take a large skillet pan, place it over medium-high heat, add oil and when hot, add onion and cook for 5 minutes.
2. Then add vegetables, ginger, and garlic, continue cooking for 5 minutes, reserve 1 cup of the mixture and set it aside.
3. Add bay leaf into the pan, stir in all the spices, cook for 1 minute, stir in rice and cook for 1 minute.
4. Season with salt, pour in the stock, then top with reserved vegetables, chickpeas and raisins, switch heat to a high level, and bring the mixture to simmer.
5. Then switch heat to the low level, cover the pan with a towel, place lid on top of it to seal the pan completely, and simmer for 20 minutes until all the liquid has soaked by the rice.
6. When done, fluff the rice with a fork, top with cilantro and cashews, and then serve.

Nutrition Value:
Calories: 385 Cal; Fat: 6.8 g; Carbs: 73.6 g; Protein: 8.6 g; Fiber: 5.5 g

Roasted Cauliflower

Preparation time: 10 minutes; Cooking time: 1 hour and 20 minutes; Servings: 4
Ingredients:
- 1 medium head of cauliflower
- ½ teaspoon salt
- 1 teaspoon dried parsley
- 1 teaspoon dried dill

- 1 teaspoon dried mint
- 1 tablespoon zaatar spice
- 2 tablespoons olive oil, divided
- 1 cup of water

Method:
1. Trim the cauliflower, then slice from the bottom, drizzle it with 1 tablespoon oil, season with salt and zaatar spice, cover cauliflower with a foil and bake for 55 minutes.
2. When done, uncover the cauliflower, drizzle with remaining oil and bake for 30 minutes until roasted, turning halfway.
3. When done, sprinkle with parsley, dill, and milk and serve cauliflower with lemon wedges and tahini sauce.

Nutrition Value:
Calories: 127 Cal; Fat: 8 g; Carbs: 13 g; Protein: 5 g; Fiber: 5.1 g

Chinese Eggplant with Szechuan Sauce

Preparation time: 10 minutes; Cooking time: 25 minutes; Servings: 4
Ingredients:
- 1 1/2 pound Eggplant
- 2 teaspoons minced garlic
- 2 teaspoons grated ginger
- 2 tablespoons cornstarch

- 2 teaspoons salt
- 4 tablespoons peanut oil
- 10 dried red chilies

For the Szechuan Sauce:
- 1 teaspoon Szechuan peppercorns, toasted, crushed

- 1/2 teaspoon five-spice
- 1 tablespoon mirin

- 3 tablespoons brown sugar
- 1 teaspoon red chili flakes
- 1/4 cup soy sauce
- 1 tablespoon rice vinegar
- 1 tablespoon sesame oil

Method:
1. Cut eggplant into bite-size pieces, place them in a large bowl, cover them with water, stir in salt and let them stand for 15 minutes.
2. Prepare the Szechuan sauce and for this, place all its ingredients in a small bowl except for Szechuan peppercorns and whisk until combined and set aside until required.
3. Pat dry eggplant with paper towels, sprinkle with corn starch and then fry them in a single layer over medium heat for 10 minutes until golden brown.
4. When eggplants are done, transfer them to a plate, add some more oil into the pan, add garlic and ginger and cook for 2 minutes.
5. Add Szechuan peppercorns and prepared sauce, stir until combined and simmer for 20 seconds.
6. Return eggplant pieces into the pan, toss until mixed, cook for 1 minute and then garnish with green onions.
7. Serve straight away.

Nutrition Value:
Calories: 323 Cal; Fat: 22 g; Carbs: 30 g; Protein: 6 g; Fiber: 7.4 g

Quinoa Cakes

Preparation time: 20 minutes; Cooking time: 25 minutes; Servings: 4
Ingredients:
For the Quinoa Cakes:
- 1 cup quinoa, rinsed
- 1 teaspoon garlic powder
- 1/2 teaspoon salt
- 1 teaspoon cumin
- 1/2 teaspoon Italian dried herbs
- 1 lemon, zested
- 2 teaspoons olive oil
- 2 cups of water
- 1/4 cup chopped parsley

For the Tomato Chickpea Relish
- 1 ½ cup cooked chickpeas
- 1/4 cup chopped scallions
- 2 cups grape tomatoes, halved
- 1/4 cup chopped fresh basil
- 1 cup cucumber, diced
- ¼ teaspoon minced garlic
- 1/4 teaspoon salt
- 3 tablespoons balsamic vinegar
- 3 tablespoons olive oil

Method:
1. Take a pot over high heat, add all the ingredients for quinoa in it except for lime zest and parsley, stir, bring the mixture to boil, then switch heat to the low level and simmer for 20 minutes.
2. Meanwhile, prepare tomato relish and for this, place all its ingredients in a bowl and stir until combined.
3. When quinoa has cooked, let it stand for 5 minutes, then fluff it with a fork, cool it for 15 minutes, stir in parsley and lemon zest and shape the mixture into four balls.
4. Fry the balls over medium heat on a greased pan for 5 minutes until browned, then transfer them on a plate, top with chickpea relish and serve.

Nutrition Value:
Calories: 388 Cal; Fat: 17.6 g; Carbs: 48.3 g; Protein: 12.3 g; Fiber: 9 g

Ramen with Miso Shiitake

Preparation time: 10 minutes; Cooking time: 35 minutes; Servings: 4

Ingredients:

For Ramen Broth:

- 1 large white onion, peeled, diced
- 1/3 teaspoon ground black pepper
- 1/2 cup dried Shiitake Mushrooms, chopped
- 2 tablespoons white miso paste
- 1 teaspoon minced garlic
- 2 tablespoons olive oil
- 1/8 cup mirin
- 4 cups vegetable stock
- 4 cups of water

For the Ramen:

- 8 ounces cubed tofu, crispy as needed
- 8 ounces cooked ramen noodles as needed
- Sautéed bok choy as needed
- Fresh spinach as needed
- Shredded carrots as needed
- Roasted winter squash as needed
- Roasted cauliflower as needed
- Roasted carrots as needed
- Roasted sweet potato as needed
- Sautéed mushrooms as needed
- Smoked mushrooms as needed
- Pickled radish as needed
- Mix herbs as needed

For Garnish:

- Scallions as needed
- Sesame seeds as needed
- Sriracha as needed
- Sesame oil as needed

Method:

1. Prepare the broth and for this, place a pot over medium-high heat, add 1 tablespoon oil and when hot, add onion and cook for 3 minutes.
2. Switch heat to medium level, stir in garlic, cook for 1 minute, then add remaining ingredients for the broth and simmer for 30 minutes until done.
3. Distribute all the ingredients for ramen evenly between four bowls, then pour in broth and top evenly with garnishing ingredients.
4. Serve straight away.

Nutrition Value:

Calories: 408 Cal; Fat: 14 g; Carbs: 60 g; Protein: 14 g; Fiber: 4.3 g

Ratatouille

Preparation time: 5 minutes; Cooking time: 15 minutes; Servings: 4

Ingredients:

- 2 medium zucchinis, sliced into ½-inch sliced moons
- 1 large eggplant, cut into ½-inch pieces
- 2 medium tomatoes, cut into ¾-inch wedges
- 1 red bell pepper, sliced into ½-inch strips
- 1 medium white onion, sliced
- 12 cloves of garlic, peeled
- 1 teaspoon salt
- 1 teaspoon balsamic vinegar
- 1/3 teaspoon ground black pepper
- 3 tablespoons rosemary and thyme
- Olive oil as needed

Method:

1. Prepare all the vegetables, then spread them in a single layer on a greased sheet pan, add garlic and herbs, drizzle with oil, toss until coated and season with salt with black pepper.
2. Toss the vegetables, roast them for 40 minutes at 400 degrees F, tossing halfway, and then continue roasting for 20 minutes at 300 degrees F until tender.
3. When done, taste to adjust salt, drizzle with vinegar and serve.

Nutrition Value:

Calories: 147 Cal; Fat: 9.7 g; Carbs: 15.1 g; Protein: 2.5 g; Fiber: 4.2 g

Tofu with Bok Choy

Preparation time: 10 minutes; Cooking time: 15 minutes; Servings: 2

Ingredients:

- 6 ounces baby bok choy, quartered lengthwise
- 12 ounces tofu, firm, drained, cut it into 1-inch cubes
- 1 shallot, peeled, sliced

For the Black Pepper Sauce:

- ½ teaspoon ground black pepper
- 2 tablespoons soy sauce
- 1 teaspoon brown sugar

- 2 teaspoons minced garlic
- 1 teaspoon ground black pepper
- ¼ teaspoon salt
- 2 tablespoons peanut oil
- Corn starch as needed for dredging

- 2 tablespoons of rice wine
- 1 teaspoon red chili paste
- 2 tablespoons water

Method:

1. Prepare the sauce and for this, take a skillet pan, add all the ingredients in it and whisk until combined.
2. Take another skillet pan, place it over medium-high heat, add 1 tablespoon peanut oil and when hot, add salt and black pepper and cook for 1 minute.
3. Dredge tofu pieces in cornstarch, add them into the skillet pan, and cook for 6 minutes until seared and crispy on all sides.
4. When done, transfer tofu pieces to a plate lined with paper towels and set aside until required.
5. Add remaining oil into the pan and when hot, add bok choy, shallots and garlic, stir and cook for 4 minutes.
6. Pour in the prepared sauce, toss until mixed and simmer for 3 minutes until bok choy is tender.
7. Then add crispy tofu pieces, toss until coated, cook for 3 minutes until heated, and then serve.

Nutrition Value:

Calories: 463 Cal; Fat: 24.4 g; Carbs: 37.5 g; Protein: 25 g; Fiber: 6.5 g

Blackened Tempeh

Preparation time: 10 minutes; Cooking time: 10 minutes; Servings: 2

Ingredients:

For the Ranch Dressing:

- 1 teaspoon Cajun spice blend

For the Blackened Tempeh:

- 4 radishes, sliced
- 3 cups shredded kale
- 1 medium avocado, pitted, sliced
- 1 block of tempeh
- 3 tablespoons Cajun Spice
- ½ a lemon, zested

- 1/3 cup vegan ranch dressing

- ¼ cup pickled onions
- ¼ teaspoon salt
- 1 teaspoon peanut oil
- 2 tablespoons olive oil
- 1 scallion, sliced

Method:

1. Prepare the ranch dressing and for this, place all its ingredients in a bowl and stir until combined, set aside until required.
2. Take a sauté pan, place it over medium heat, add tempeh, pour in salted water to cover it, and simmer for 8 minutes until its bitterness has reduced.
3. When done, transfer tempeh to a cutting board, then cut it ½-inch slices and season with Cajun spices until coated on both sides.
4. Place shredded kale in a bowl, drizzle with peanut oil, season with salt and lemon zest, massage with fingers, then add remaining ingredients along with ranch dressing and toss until coated.

5. Distribute the kale salad between the bowl, top with tempeh and scallions and then serve.

Nutrition Value:

Calories: 281 Cal; Fat: 18.1 g; Carbs: 17.1 g; Protein: 17 g; Fiber: 11.4 g

Veggie Lo Mein

Preparation time: 5 minutes; Cooking time: 15 minutes; Servings: 2

Ingredients:

- 5 ounces lo mein noodles or whole-wheat linguine, cooked

For the Lo Mein Sauce:

- 1/8 teaspoon ground white pepper
- 1 teaspoon sriracha
- 1 teaspoon maple syrup
- 1/4 teaspoon liquid smoke
- 1 tablespoon oyster sauce
- 3 tablespoons soy sauce
- 2 tablespoons Chinese cooking wine
- 2 teaspoons sesame oil

For the Lo Mein Stir Fry:

- 1/2 a white onion, peeled, sliced
- 1 teaspoon grated ginger
- 2 cups sliced mushrooms
- 1 ½ teaspoon minced garlic
- 1 cup shredded cabbage
- 1/2 of medium red bell pepper, sliced
- 1 cup carrot, cut into matchstick
- 1 cup snow peas
- ¼ cup baby spinach
- ¼ cup bok choy
- ¼ cup shredded Brussel sprouts
- ¼ cup bean sprouts
- 2 tablespoons peanut oil

For the Garnish:

- Scallions, sliced, as needed

Method:

1. Prepare the sauce and for this, place all its ingredients in a small bowl and whisk until combined.
2. Take a large skillet pan, place it over medium-high heat, add oil and when hot, add onion and mushrooms and cook for 4 minutes, stirring constantly.
3. Switch heat to medium level, add garlic and ginger, cook for 2 minutes, then add remaining vegetables and continue cooking for 4 minutes until crispy.
4. Add noodles, toss until mixed, stir in the sauce until coated, cook for 2 minutes until hot and then divide evenly between bowls.
5. Top with scallions and serve.

Nutrition Value:

Calories: 464 Cal; Fat: 16.6 g; Carbs: 67.8 g; Protein: 13.8 g; Fiber: 7.2 g

Szechuan Tofu and Veggies

Preparation time: 10 minutes; Cooking time: 20 minutes; Servings: 2

Ingredients:

- 8 ounces tofu, drained, cubed
- 1 cup shredded carrots
- 4 ounces sliced mushrooms
- ½ cup sliced white onion
- 2 cups shredded cabbage
- 1 cup asparagus
- ½ of medium red bell pepper, cored, sliced
- 8 dried red Chinese chilies, small
- 1/3 teaspoon ground black pepper
- 2/3 teaspoon salt
- 2 tablespoons olive oil

For Garnish:

- Chopped scallions as needed
- Sesame seeds as needed
- Red chili flakes as needed
- ¼ cup Szechuan Sauce
- Zucchini noodles as needed for serving

Method:

1. Take a large skillet pan, place it over medium heat, add oil, season with salt and black pepper, then season tofu with ½ teaspoon, add it to the pan in an even layer and cook for 5 minutes until golden on both sides.
2. Transfer tofu pieces to a plate, switch heat to medium-high level, add onion and mushrooms, cook for 3 minutes, then switch heat to medium level, add remaining vegetables along with chilies, toss until mixed and cook for 5 minutes until tender-crisp.
3. Pour in the sauce, toss until coated, cook for 2 minutes, then add tofu pieces, stir until coated, and cook for 2 minutes until warm.
4. When done, sprinkle with scallions and sesame seeds and serve over zucchini noodles.

Nutrition Value:
Calories: 307 Cal; Fat: 20.3 g; Carbs: 24 g; Protein: 14.2 g; Fiber: 7 g

Middle Eastern Salad Tacos

Preparation time: 10 minutes; Cooking time: 5 minutes; Servings: 3
Ingredients:
For the Spiced Chickpeas:
- 12 ounces cooked chickpeas
- ½ cup hummus
- ½ teaspoon salt
- 1 teaspoon cumin
- 1 teaspoon sumac

- 2 teaspoons olive oil
- 1 teaspoon sesame seeds
- 6 tortillas, warmed, about 6-inches
- Scallions for topping

For the Salad:
- 2 cucumbers, diced
- 1 tomato, diced
- ½ cup arugula
- ¼ teaspoon salt

- 1 teaspoon ground coriander
- 2 tablespoons olive oil
- 2 tablespoons lemon juice

Method:
1. Take a skillet pan, place it over medium heat, add oil and when hot, add chickpeas, stir in salt and all the spices and cook for 3 minutes until warm.
2. When done, remove the pan from heat, sprinkle with sesame seeds and set aside.
3. Take a bowl, place all the ingredients for the salad in it, and toss until mixed.
4. Spread hummus on one side of the tortilla, top with chickpeas and salad, sprinkle with scallion, and then serve.

Nutrition Value:
Calories: 405 Cal; Fat: 16 g; Carbs: 56.7 g; Protein: 13.4 g; Fiber: 12 g

Lentil Meatballs with Coconut Curry Sauce

Preparation time: 15 minutes; Cooking time: 60 minutes; Servings: 14
Ingredients:
For the Lentil Meatballs:
- 6 ounces tofu, firm, drained
- 1 cup black lentils
- ½ cup quinoa
- 1 teaspoon garlic powder

- 1 teaspoon salt
- 1/3 cup chopped cilantro
- 1 teaspoon fennel seed
- 1 Tablespoon olive oil

For the Curry:
- 1 large tomato, diced
- 2 teaspoons minced garlic
- 1 tablespoon grated ginger
- 1 teaspoon brown sugar
- ½ teaspoon ground turmeric

- ¼ teaspoon cayenne pepper
- ½ teaspoon salt
- ¼ teaspoon ground black pepper
- 1 tablespoon lime juice
- 2 tablespoons olive oil

- 1 tablespoon dried fenugreek leaves
- 13.5 ounces coconut milk, unsweetened

Method:
1. Boil lentils and fennel in 3 cups water over high heat, then simmer for 25 minutes, and when done, drain them and set aside until required.
2. Meanwhile, boil the quinoa in 1 cup water over high heat and then simmer for 15 minutes over low heat until cooked.
3. Prepare the sauce and for this, place a pot over medium heat, add oil, ginger, and garlic, cook for 2 minutes, then stir in turmeric, cook for 1 minute, add tomatoes and cook for 5 minutes.
4. Add remaining ingredients for the sauce, stir until mixed and simmer until ready to serve.
5. Transfer half of the lentils in a food processor, add quinoa and pulse until the mixture resembles sand.
6. Tip the mixture into a bowl, add remaining ingredients for the meatballs and stir until well mixed.
7. Place tofu in a food processor, add 1 tablespoon oil, process until the smooth paste comes together, add to lentil mixture, stir until well mixed and shape the mixture into small balls.
8. Place the balls on a baking sheet, spray with oil and bake for 20 minutes until golden brown.
9. Add balls into the warm sauce, toss until coated, sprinkle with cilantro, and serve.

Nutrition Value:
Calories: 150.8 Cal; Fat: 4.6 g; Carbs: 18 g; Protein: 10.2 g; Fiber: 6.8 g

Zaatar Roasted Eggplant

Preparation time: 10 minutes; Cooking time: 60 minutes; Servings: 2
Ingredients:
- 1-pound eggplant, destemmed
- ½ teaspoon minced garlic
- ¼ teaspoon salt
- 1 tablespoon zaatar spice mix
- 1 ½ tablespoon olive oil

For Serving:
- 2 cups chopped tomatoes
- 2 cups cooked brown rice
- Tahini sauce as needed
- Parsley for serving

Method:
1. Prepare the eggplant, and for this, cut it into half, then make deep diagonals in it at 1-inch interval, but not cutting through the skin and season with 1/8 teaspoon salt.
2. Place remaining ingredients in a bowl, stir until the smooth paste comes together, then brush it well on the eggplant, bake for 1 hour until tender, rotating halfway, and when done, pierce it with a fork.
3. When done, top eggplant with rice and tomatoes, drizzle with tahini sauce, top with parsley and serve.

Nutrition Value:
Calories: 268 Cal; Fat: 12 g; Carbs: 32 g; Protein: 8 g; Fiber: 12 g

Stir-Fry Tofu with Mushrooms and Broccoli

Preparation time: 5 minutes; Cooking time: 12 minutes; Servings: 2
Ingredients:
- 10 ounces tofu, pressed, drained, cubed
- 8 ounces broccoli florets, steamed
- 8 ounces shiitake mushrooms, destemmed, sliced
- 1 medium shallot, peeled, diced

- 5 dried red chilies
- 2 ½ teaspoons minced garlic
- 2/3 teaspoon salt
- 2 tablespoons black vinegar, sweetened
- 2 tablespoons chopped peanuts
- 2 tablespoons soy sauce
- 2 tablespoons peanut oil
- 2 tablespoons water

For the Garnish:
- Sliced scallions as needed
- Sesame seeds as needed

Method:
1. Take a skillet pan, place it over medium-high heat, add oil and when hot, add some and black pepper, then add tofu cubes and cook for 6 minutes until browned on all sides.
2. When done, transfer tofu cubes to a plate, add garlic and shallots, cook for 2 minutes, then add mushrooms and cook for 3 minutes until tender, add nuts and chilies, and cook for 1 minute.
3. Stir in soy sauce, vinegar and water, add steamed broccoli, toss until well coated, add tofu, toss until mixed, season with salt, and garnish with scallion and sesame seeds.
4. Serve straight away.

Nutrition Value:
Calories: 184 Cal; Fat: 6.8 g; Carbs: 22 g; Protein: 16.2 g; Fiber: 11.4 g

Vegetarian fajitas

Preparation time: 10 minutes; Cooking time: 15 minutes; Servings: 6
Ingredients:
For the Vegetables:
- 12 ounces cooked black beans
- 1 yellow bell pepper, cored, sliced
- 2 green bell peppers, cored, sliced
- 1 medium-sized white onion, peeled, sliced
- 1 red bell pepper, cored, sliced
- 3 tablespoons olive oil

For the Fajita Seasoning:
- 1/2 teaspoon onion powder
- 1/2 teaspoon garlic powder
- 1/2 teaspoon ground black pepper
- 1/2 teaspoon salt
- 2 teaspoons red chili powder
- 1/8 teaspoon cayenne pepper
- 1 teaspoon paprika

For the Toppings:
- 6 small tortillas
- Guacamole as needed
- 1 lime, cut into wedges
- 2 tablespoons chopped cilantro

Method:
1. Prepare the fajita seasoning and for this, stir all its ingredients, then sprinkle with over onion and bell peppers, drizzle with oil, toss until well coated, spread them evenly on a sheet pan and bake for 15 minutes until roasted, tossing halfway.
2. When done, heat beans over low heat until hot, then distribute it evenly on the tortilla, top with roasted vegetables, guacamole, and cilantro and serve with lime wedges.

Nutrition Value:
Calories: 288 Cal; Fat: 6.7 g; Carbs: 49 g; Protein: 10.1 g; Fiber: 11 g

Roasted Spaghetti Squash with Mushrooms

Preparation time: 10 minutes; Cooking time: 60 minutes; Servings: 4
Ingredients:
- 2 pounds spaghetti squash, halved
- 1 tablespoon unsalted butter
- 2 tablespoons olive oil
- ½ of a white onion, peeled, chopped
- 16 ounces sliced cremini mushrooms
- 2 teaspoons minced garlic
- 3 tablespoons sage
- 2/3 teaspoon salt

- 1/3 teaspoon ground black pepper
- 1/8 teaspoon nutmeg
- ¼ cup grated vegan parmesan cheese

Method:

1. Bake squash on a parchment-lined baking sheet or 50 minutes at 400 degrees F until tender.
2. Meanwhile, take a large skillet pan, place it medium-high heat, add oil and butter and when hot, add onion and cook for 3 minutes until tender.
3. Then add mushrooms, switch heat to medium level, and cook for 7 minutes.
4. Stir in sage and garlic, cook for 4 minutes until mushrooms have turned brown, and then season with black pepper, nutmeg and salt.
5. When squash has roasted, pierce it with a fork, let it cool for 10 minutes, then remove its seeds and scoop the flesh of the squash to a saucepan.
6. Add mushrooms, stir until mixed, season with some more salt, and stir in cheese until incorporated.
7. Serve straight away.

Nutrition Value:

Calories: 313 Cal; Fat: 14 g; Carbs: 47.8 g; Protein: 8.2 g; Fiber: 11.4 g

Tikka Masala with Cauliflower

Preparation time: 10 minutes; Cooking time: 22 minutes; Servings: 4

Ingredients:

- 1 medium head of cauliflower, cut into small florets
- 1 medium shallot, peeled, chopped
- 1 medium red bell pepper, cored, diced
- 2 teaspoons minced garlic
- 2 medium tomatoes, diced
- 1 tablespoon grated ginger
- 1 teaspoon salt
- ½ teaspoon red chili powder
- 1 teaspoon curry powder
- 1 teaspoon turmeric
- 1 teaspoon cumin
- 1 teaspoon coriander
- 1 teaspoon fenugreek leaves
- 1 lemon, juiced
- 2 tablespoons olive oil
- 12 ounces coconut milk, unsweetened
- 2 tablespoons chopped cilantro

Method:

1. Take a large pot, place it over medium-high heat, add oil and when hot, add shallot, ginger, and garlic and cook for 3 minutes.
2. Switch heat to medium level, add all the spices and seeds, cook for 2 minutes, then stir in tomatoes and cook for 2 minutes.
3. Pour in milk, stir until incorporated, bring the mixture to simmer, switch heat to medium-low level, add bell pepper and florets, stir until mixed and simmer for 12 minutes until tender.
4. Stir in lemon juice and serve straight away.

Nutrition Value:

Calories: 358 Cal; Fat: 13.6 g; Carbs: 48.1 g; Protein: 14.3 g; Fiber: 14.3 g

Avocado Linguine

Preparation time: 10 minutes; Cooking time: 0 minute; Servings: 4

Ingredients:

- ½ cup arugula
- 2 medium avocados
- 2 cloves of garlic, peeled
- 1/4 teaspoon ground white pepper
- 3/4 teaspoons salt
- 1 teaspoon lemon zest
- 3 tablespoons lemon juice
- 3 tablespoons olive oil

- 8 ounces linguine, whole-wheat, boiled

Method:
1. Prepare the avocado sauce, and for this, place all the ingredients in a food processor, except for pasta, arugula, pepper, and lemon zest and pulse until smooth.
2. Tip the puree in a large bowl, add remaining ingredients, toss until well mixed and taste to adjust seasoning.
3. Serve straight away.

Nutrition Value:
Calories: 387 Cal; Fat: 16.6 g; Carbs: 54.3 g; Protein: 9.4 g; Fiber: 8.6 g

Sweetcorn and Zucchini Fritters

Preparation time: 10 minutes; Cooking time: 20 minutes; Servings: 2
Ingredients:
- 1 1/2 cups corn kernels, cooked
- 4 cups shredded zucchini
- 3/4 cup chopped green onions
- 1 1/4 cup chickpea flour
- 1 ½ teaspoon minced garlic
- 1 teaspoon salt
- 1 teaspoon dried oregano
- 1 teaspoon dried thyme
- 2 teaspoons cumin
- ½ teaspoon ground black pepper
- 2 tablespoons olive oil
- Salsa for serving

Method:
1. Place all the ingredients in a large bowl, except for oil and salsa, stir until well combined, and let it stand for 5 minutes.
2. Take a large skillet pan, place it over medium heat, add oil and when hot, scoop ¼ cup of zucchini mixture per fritter in the pan and cook for 5 minutes per side until golden brown.
3. When done, serve fritters with salsa.

Nutrition Value:
Calories: 158 Cal; Fat: 3 g; Carbs: 27 g; Protein: 8 g; Fiber: 7 g

Scallion Pancakes

Preparation time: 40 minutes; Cooking time: 8 minutes; Servings: 2
Ingredients:
- 2 large bunches of green onions, sliced
- 4 cups all-purpose flour
- 1/4 teaspoon salt
- 1/4 cup and 1 tablespoon olive oil
- 1 1/2 cups chilled water

Method:
1. Place flour in a bowl, stir in water until a smooth dough comes together, knead it for 5 minutes, then cover it with plastic wrap and let it stand for 30 minutes.
2. Then roll the dough into 1/8 thick crust, brush the top with 1 tablespoon oil, season with salt, and scatter with some green onion.
3. Roll the dough into a cigar shape, roll it again into 1/8 inch thick crust and fry it into remaining hot oil for 3 minutes per side until cooked and golden.
4. When done, transfer pancake to a plate lined with paper towels, let it stand for 5 minutes, then cut it into 3 wedges and serve.

Nutrition Value:
Calories: 136 Cal; Fat: 7 g; Carbs: 17 g; Protein: 2 g; Fiber: 2 g

Spiced Carrot and Lentil Soup

Preparation time: 5 minutes; Cooking time: 20 minutes; Servings: 4
Ingredients:

- 22 ounces carrots, grated
- 5 ounces split red lentils
- ½ teaspoon salt
- 2 teaspoons cumin seeds, toasted
- 1/8 teaspoon red chili flakes
- 2 tablespoons olive oil
- 4 cups vegetable stock, hot
- ½ cup of coconut milk

Method:
1. Take a large saucepan, add 1 teaspoon cumin seeds, half of the red chili flakes along with remaining ingredients, stir until combined, and bring the mixture to a boil over medium-high heat.
2. Switch heat to medium level, simmer for 15 minutes until lentils have softened, and when done, puree the soup by using an immersion blender until smooth.
3. Serve straight away.

Nutrition Value:
Calories: 238 Cal; Fat: 7 g; Carbs: 34 g; Protein: 11 g; Fiber: 5 g

Mushroom and Broccoli Noodles

Preparation time: 10 minutes; Cooking time: 10 minutes; Servings: 4
Ingredients:
- 2 linguine pasta, whole-grain, cooked
- 8 ounces chestnut mushroom, sliced
- 4 spring onions, sliced
- 1 small head of broccoli, cut into florets, steamed
- ½ teaspoon minced garlic
- ½ teaspoon red chili flakes
- 1 tablespoon sesame oil
- 2 teaspoons hoisin sauce
- ¼ cup roasted cashew
- 3 tablespoons stock

Method:
1. Take a large frying pan, place it over medium heat, add oil and when hot, add mushrooms and cook for 2 minutes until golden.
2. Stir in garlic, onion and chili flakes, cook for 1 minute, stir in broccoli and toss in pasta until hot.
3. Drizzle with hoisin sauce and 3 tablespoons of stock, toss until mixed, cook for 1 minute and remove the pan from heat.
4. Top with cashews, drizzle with some more sesame oil and serve.

Nutrition Value:
Calories: 624 Cal; Fat: 14 g; Carbs: 105 g; Protein: 25 g; Fiber: 8 g

Tomato and Basil Sauce

Preparation time: 5 minutes; Cooking time: 10 minutes; Servings: 4
Ingredients:
- 14 ounces chopped tomatoes
- ½ teaspoon minced garlic
- 1 teaspoon vegetable stock powder
- 1 teaspoon sugar
- 1 tablespoon tomato purée
- 5 basil leaves
- 1 tablespoon olive oil
- ¼ cup vegetable stock

Method:
1. Take a skillet pan, place it over medium heat, add oil and when hot, add garlic and cook for 1 minute until fragrant.
2. Then stir in tomatoes and remaining ingredients until combined, except for basil, and bring the mixture to boil.
3. Switch heat to the low level, simmer the mixture for 5 minutes, and when done, top with basil.
4. Serve straight away.

Nutrition Value:

Calories: 52 Cal; Fat: 3 g; Carbs: 5 g; Protein: 2 g; Fiber: 1 g

Pasta with Creamy Greens and Lemon

Preparation time: 5 minutes; Cooking time: 10 minutes; Servings: 4

Ingredients:

- 5 ounces broccoli, cut into florets
- 3.5 ounces frozen soya beans
- ¼ cup basil leaves
- 3.5 ounces frozen peas
- 3.5 ounces mange tout
- 2/3 teaspoon salt
- 1/3 teaspoon ground black pepper
- 1 lemon, juiced, zested
- 5.3 ounces vegan mascarpone
- 3 ounces grated vegan parmesan cheese
- 12 ounces whole-grain pasta, cooked

Method:

1. Cook the pasta in a saucepan, add all the vegetables in the last 3 minutes, and, when done, drain the pasta and vegetables.
2. Return the pasta and vegetables into the pan, add remaining ingredients and stir until well combined.
3. Serve straight away.

Nutrition Value:

Calories: 635 Cal; Fat: 28 g; Carbs: 75 g; Protein: 26 g; Fiber: 7 g

Chapter 7: Snack and Sides

Black Bean Lime Dip

Preparation time: 5 minutes; Cooking time: 6 minutes; Servings: 4
Ingredients:

- 15.5 ounces cooked black beans
- 1 teaspoon minced garlic
- ½ of a lime, juiced
- 1 inch of ginger, grated
- 1/3 teaspoon salt
- 1/3 teaspoon ground black pepper
- 1 tablespoon olive oil

Method:

1. Take a frying pan, add oil and when hot, add garlic and ginger and cook for 1 minute until fragrant.
2. Then add beans, splash with some water and fry for 3 minutes until hot.
3. Season beans with salt and black pepper, drizzle with lime juice, then remove the pan from heat and mash the beans until smooth pasta comes together.
4. Serve the dip with whole-grain breadsticks or vegetables.

Nutrition Value:
Calories: 374 Cal; Fat: 14 g; Carbs: 46 g; Protein: 15 g; Fiber: 17 g

Beetroot Hummus

Preparation time: 10 minutes; Cooking time: 60 minutes; Servings: 4
Ingredients:

- 15 ounces cooked chickpeas
- 3 small beets
- 1 teaspoon minced garlic
- 1/2 teaspoon smoked paprika
- 1 teaspoon of sea salt
- 1/4 teaspoon red chili flakes
- 2 tablespoons olive oil
- 1 lemon, juiced
- 2 tablespoon tahini
- 1 tablespoon chopped almonds
- 1 tablespoon chopped cilantro

Method:

1. Drizzle oil over beets, season with salt, then wrap beets in a foil and bake for 60 minutes at 425 degrees F until tender.
2. When done, let beet cool for 10 minutes, then peel and dice them and place them in a food processor.
3. Add remaining ingredients and pulse for 2 minutes until smooth, tip the hummus in a bowl, drizzle with some more oil, and then serve straight away.

Nutrition Value:
Calories: 50.1 Cal; Fat: 2.5 g; Carbs: 5 g; Protein: 2 g; Fiber: 1 g

Zucchini Hummus

Preparation time: 5 minutes; Cooking time: 0 minute; Servings: 8
Ingredients:

- 1 cup diced zucchini
- 1/2 teaspoon sea salt
- 1 teaspoon minced garlic
- 2 teaspoons ground cumin
- 3 tablespoons lemon juice
- 1/3 cup tahini

Method:

1. Place all the ingredients in a food processor and pulse for 2 minutes until smooth.
2. Tip the hummus in a bowl, drizzle with oil and serve.

Nutrition Value:

Calories: 65 Cal; Fat: 5 g; Carbs: 3 g; Protein: 2 g; Fiber: 1 g

Chipotle and Lime Tortilla Chips

Preparation time: 10 minutes; Cooking time: 15 minutes; Servings: 4
Ingredients:

- 12 ounces whole-wheat tortillas
- 4 tablespoons chipotle seasoning
- 1 tablespoon olive oil
- 4 limes, juiced

Method:
1. Whisk together oil and lime juice, brush it well on tortillas, then sprinkle with chipotle seasoning and bake for 15 minutes at 350 degrees F until crispy, turning halfway.
2. When done, let the tortilla cool for 10 minutes, then break it into chips and serve.

Nutrition Value:
Calories: 150 Cal; Fat: 7 g; Carbs: 18 g; Protein: 2 g; Fiber: 2 g

Carrot and Sweet Potato Fritters

Preparation time: 10 minutes; Cooking time: 8 minutes; Servings: 10
Ingredients:

- 1/3 cup quinoa flour
- 1½ cups shredded sweet potato
- 1 cup grated carrot
- 1/3 teaspoon ground black pepper
- 2/3 teaspoon salt
- 2 teaspoons curry powder
- 2 flax eggs
- 2 tablespoons coconut oil

Method:
1. Place all the ingredients in a bowl, except for oil, stir well until combined and then shape the mixture into ten small patties
2. Take a large pan, place it over medium-high heat, add oil and when it melts, add patties in it and cook for 3 minutes per side until browned.
3. Serve straight away

Nutrition Value:
Calories: 70 Cal; Fat: 3 g; Carbs: 8 g; Protein: 1 g; Fiber: 1 g

Buffalo Quinoa Bites

Preparation time: 15 minutes; Cooking time: 30 minutes; Servings: 20
Ingredients:
For the Bites:

- 1 cup cooked quinoa
- 15 ounces cooked white beans
- 3 tablespoons chickpea flour
- 1 medium shallot, peeled, chopped
- 3 cloves of garlic, peeled
- ½ teaspoon ground black pepper
- 1/2 teaspoon salt
- 1 teaspoon smoked paprika
- 1/4 cup vegan buffalo sauce

For the Dressing:

- 1/4 cup chives
- 2 tablespoons hemp hearts
- 1 tablespoon nutritional yeast
- 1 teaspoon garlic powder
- 1 teaspoon onion powder
- 1/2 teaspoon salt
- ½ teaspoon ground black pepper
- 2 teaspoons dried dill
- 1 lemon, juiced
- 1/4 cup tahini
- 3/4 cup water

Method:
1. Prepare the bites, and for this, place half of the beans in a food processor, add garlic and shallots, and pulse for 2 minutes until mixture comes together.

2. Then add all the spices of the bites and buffalo sauce and pulse for 2 minutes until smooth. Add remaining beans along with chickpea flour and quinoa and pulse until just combined.
3. Tip the mixture in a dish, shape it in the dough, shape it into twenty balls, about the golf-ball size, and bake for 30 minutes at 350 degrees F until crispy and browned, turning halfway.
4. Meanwhile, prepare the dressing and for this, place all of its ingredients in a food processor and pulse for 2 minutes until smooth.
5. Serve bites with prepared dressing.

Nutrition Value:
Calories: 78 Cal; Fat: 3 g; Carbs: 9 g; Protein: 4 g; Fiber: 2 g

Tomato and Pesto Toast

Preparation time: 5 minutes; Cooking time: 0 minute; Servings: 4
Ingredients:
- 1 small tomato, sliced
- ¼ teaspoon ground black pepper
- 1 tablespoon vegan pesto
- 2 tablespoons hummus
- 1 slice of whole-grain bread, toasted
- Hemp seeds as needed for garnishing

Method:
1. Spread hummus on one side of the toast, top with tomato slices and then drizzle with pesto.
2. Sprinkle black pepper on the toast along with hemp seeds and then serve straight away.

Nutrition Value:
Calories: 214 Cal; Fat: 7.2 g; Carbs: 32 g; Protein: 6.5 g; Fiber: 3 g

Avocado and Sprout Toast

Preparation time: 5 minutes; Cooking time: 0 minute; Servings: 4
Ingredients:
- 1/2 of a medium avocado, sliced
- 1 slice of whole-grain bread, toasted
- 2 tablespoons sprouts
- 2 tablespoons hummus
- ¼ teaspoon lemon zest
- ½ teaspoon hemp seeds
- ¼ teaspoon red pepper flakes

Method:
1. Spread hummus on one side of the toast and then top with avocado slices and sprouts.
2. Sprinkle with lemon zest, hemp seeds, and red pepper flakes and then serve straight away.

Nutrition Value:
Calories: 200 Cal; Fat: 10.5 g; Carbs: 22 g; Protein: 7 g; Fiber: 7 g

Apple and Honey Toast

Preparation time: 5 minutes; Cooking time: 0 minute; Servings: 4
Ingredients:
- ½ of a small apple, cored, sliced
- 1 slice of whole-grain bread, toasted
- 1 tablespoon honey
- 2 tablespoons hummus
- 1/8 teaspoon cinnamon

Method:
1. Spread hummus on one side of the toast, top with apple slices and then drizzle with honey.
2. Sprinkle cinnamon on it and then serve straight away.

Nutrition Value:
Calories: 212 Cal; Fat: 7 g; Carbs: 35 g; Protein: 4 g; Fiber: 5.5 g

Thai Snack Mix

Preparation time: 15 minutes; Cooking time: 90 minutes; Servings: 4
Ingredients:

- 5 cups mixed nuts
- 1 cup chopped dried pineapple
- 1 cup pumpkin seed
- 1 teaspoon onion powder
- 1 teaspoon garlic powder
- 2 teaspoons paprika
- 1/2 teaspoon ground black pepper
- 1 teaspoon of sea salt
- 1/4 cup coconut sugar
- 1/2 teaspoon red chili powder
- 1 tablespoon red pepper flakes
- 1/2 tablespoon red curry powder
- 2 tablespoons soy sauce
- 2 tablespoons coconut oil

Method:
1. Switch on the slow cooker, add all the ingredients in it except for dried pineapple and red pepper flakes, stir until combined and cook for 90 minutes at high heat setting, stirring every 30 minutes.
2. When done, spread the nut mixture on a baking sheet lined with parchment paper and let it cool.
3. Then spread dried pineapple on top, sprinkle with red pepper flakes and serve.

Nutrition Value:
Calories: 230 Cal; Fat: 17.5 g; Carbs: 11.5 g; Protein: 6.5 g; Fiber: 2 g

Zucchini Fritters

Preparation time: 10 minutes; Cooking time: 6 minutes; Servings: 12
Ingredients:

- 1/2 cup quinoa flour
- 3 1/2 cups shredded zucchini
- 1/2 cup chopped scallions
- 1/3 teaspoon ground black pepper
- 1 teaspoon salt
- 2 tablespoons coconut oil
- 2 flax eggs

Method:
1. Squeeze moisture from the zucchini by wrapping it in a cheesecloth and then transfer it to a bowl.
2. Add remaining ingredients, except for oil, stir until combined and then shape the mixture into twelve patties.
3. Take a skillet pan, place it over medium-high heat, add oil and when hot, add patties and cook for 3 minutes per side until brown.
4. Serve the patties with favorite vegan sauce.

Nutrition Value:
Calories: 37 Cal; Fat: 1 g; Carbs: 4 g; Protein: 2 g; Fiber: 1 g

Zucchini Chips

Preparation time: 10 minutes; Cooking time: 120 minutes; Servings: 4
Ingredients:

- 1 large zucchini, thinly sliced
- 1 teaspoon salt
- 2 tablespoons olive oil

Method:
1. Pat dry zucchini slices and then spread them in an even layer on a baking sheet lined with parchment sheet.
2. Whisk together salt and oil, brush this mixture over zucchini slices on both sides and then bake for 2 hours or more until brown and crispy.
3. When done, let the chips cool for 10 minutes and then serve straight away.

Nutrition Value:

Calories: 54 Cal; Fat: 5 g; Carbs: 1 g; Protein: 0 g; Fiber: 0.3 g

Rosemary Beet Chips

Preparation time: 10 minutes; Cooking time: 20 minutes; Servings: 3
Ingredients:
- 3 large beets, scrubbed, thinly sliced
- 1/8 teaspoon ground black pepper
- ¼ teaspoon of sea salt
- 3 sprigs of rosemary, leaves chopped
- 4 tablespoons olive oil

Method:
1. Spread beet slices in a single layer between two large baking sheets, brush the slices with oil, then season with spices and rosemary, toss until well coated, and bake for 20 minutes at 375 degrees F until crispy, turning halfway.
2. When done, let the chips cool for 10 minutes and then serve.

Nutrition Value:
Calories: 79 Cal; Fat: 4.7 g; Carbs: 8.6 g; Protein: 1.5 g; Fiber: 2.5 g

Quinoa Broccoli Tots

Preparation time: 10 minutes; Cooking time: 20 minutes; Servings: 16
Ingredients:
- 2 tablespoons quinoa flour
- 2 cups steamed and chopped broccoli florets
- 1/2 cup nutritional yeast
- 1 teaspoon garlic powder
- 1 teaspoon miso paste
- 2 flax eggs
- 2 tablespoons hummus

Method:
1. Place all the ingredients in a bowl, stir until well combined, and then shape the mixture into sixteen small balls.
2. Arrange the balls on a baking sheet lined with parchment paper, spray with oil and bake at 400 degrees F for 20 minutes until brown, turning halfway.
3. When done, let the tots cool for 10 minutes and then serve straight away.

Nutrition Value:
Calories: 19 Cal; Fat: 0 g; Carbs: 2 g; Protein: 1 g; Fiber: 0.5 g

Spicy Roasted Chickpeas

Preparation time: 10 minutes; Cooking time: 20 minutes; Servings: 6
Ingredients:
- 30 ounces cooked chickpeas
- ½ teaspoon salt
- 2 teaspoons mustard powder
- ½ teaspoon cayenne pepper
- 2 tablespoons olive oil

Method:
1. Place all the ingredients in a bowl and stir until well coated and then spread the chickpeas in an even layer on a baking sheet greased with oil.
2. Bake the chickpeas for 20 minutes at 400 degrees F until golden brown and crispy and then serve straight away.

Nutrition Value:
Calories: 187.1 Cal; Fat: 7.4 g; Carbs: 24.2 g; Protein: 7.3 g; Fiber: 6.3 g

Nacho Kale Chips

Preparation time: 10 minutes; Cooking time: 14 hours; Servings: 10
Ingredients:
- 2 bunches of curly kale
- 2 cups cashews, soaked, drained

- 1/2 cup chopped red bell pepper
- 1 teaspoon garlic powder
- 1 teaspoon salt
- 2 tablespoons red chili powder
- 1/2 teaspoon smoked paprika
- 1/2 cup nutritional yeast
- 1 teaspoon cayenne
- 3 tablespoons lemon juice
- 3/4 cup water

Method:
1. Place all the ingredients except for kale in a food processor and pulse for 2 minutes until smooth.
2. Place kale in a large bowl, pour in the blended mixture, mix until coated, and dehydrate for 14 hours at 120 degrees F until crispy.
3. If dehydrator is not available, spread kale between two baking sheets and bake for 90 minutes at 225 degrees F until crispy, flipping halfway.
4. When done, let chips cool for 15 minutes and then serve.

Nutrition Value:
Calories: 191 Cal; Fat: 12 g; Carbs: 16 g; Protein: 9 g; Fiber: 2 g

Red Salsa

Preparation time: 10 minutes; Cooking time: 0 minute; Servings: 8
Ingredients:
- 30 ounces diced fire-roasted tomatoes
- 4 tablespoons diced green chilies
- 1 medium jalapeño pepper, deseeded
- 1/2 cup chopped green onion
- 1 cup chopped cilantro
- 1 teaspoon minced garlic
- ½ teaspoon of sea salt
- 1 teaspoon ground cumin
- ¼ teaspoon stevia
- 3 tablespoons lime juice

Method:
1. Place all the ingredients in a food processor and process for 2 minutes until smooth.
2. Tip the salsa in a bowl, taste to adjust seasoning and then serve.

Nutrition Value:
Calories: 71 Cal; Fat: 0.2 g; Carbs: 19 g; Protein: 2 g; Fiber: 4.1 g

Tomato Hummus

Preparation time: 5 minutes; Cooking time: 0 minute; Servings: 4
Ingredients:
- 1/4 cup sun-dried tomatoes, without oil
- 1 ½ cups cooked chickpeas
- 1 teaspoon minced garlic
- 1/2 teaspoon salt
- 2 tablespoons sesame oil
- 1 tablespoon lemon juice
- 1 tablespoon olive oil
- 1/4 cup of water

Method:
1. Place all the ingredients in a food processor and process for 2 minutes until smooth.
2. Tip the hummus in a bowl, drizzle with more oil, and then serve straight away.

Nutrition Value:
Calories: 122.7 Cal; Fat: 4.1 g; Carbs: 17.8 g; Protein: 5.1 g; Fiber: 3.5 g

Marinated Mushrooms

Preparation time: 10 minutes; Cooking time: 7 minutes; Servings: 6
Ingredients:
- 12 ounces small button mushrooms
- 1 teaspoon minced garlic
- 1/4 teaspoon dried thyme
- 1/2 teaspoon sea salt
- 1/2 teaspoon dried basil
- 1/2 teaspoon red pepper flakes

- 1/4 teaspoon dried oregano
- 1/2 teaspoon maple syrup
- 1/4 cup apple cider vinegar
- 1/4 cup and 1 teaspoon olive oil
- 2 tablespoons chopped parsley

Method:
1. Take a skillet pan, place it over medium-high heat, add 1 teaspoon oil and when hot, add mushrooms and cook for 5 minutes until golden brown.
2. Meanwhile, prepare the marinade and for this, place remaining ingredients in a bowl and whisk until combined.
3. When mushrooms have cooked, transfer them into the bowl of marinade and toss until well coated.
4. Serve straight away

Nutrition Value:
Calories: 103 Cal; Fat: 9 g; Carbs: 2 g; Protein: 1 g; Fiber: 1 g

Hummus Quesadillas

Preparation time: 5 minutes; Cooking time: 15 minutes; Servings: 1
Ingredients:
- 1 tortilla, whole wheat
- 1/4 cup diced roasted red peppers
- 1 cup baby spinach
- 1/3 teaspoon minced garlic
- ¼ teaspoon salt
- ¼ teaspoon ground black pepper
- 1/4 teaspoon olive oil
- 1/4 cup hummus
- Oil as needed

Method:
1. Place a large pan over medium heat, add oil and when hot, add red peppers and garlic, season with salt and black pepper and cook for 3 minutes until sauté.
2. Then stir in spinach, cook for 1 minute, remove the pan from heat and transfer the mixture in a bowl.
3. Prepare quesadilla and for this, spread hummus on one-half of the tortilla, then spread spinach mixture on it, cover the filling with the other half of the tortilla and cook in a pan for 3 minutes per side until browned.
4. When done, cut the quesadilla into wedges and serve.

Nutrition Value:
Calories: 187 Cal; Fat: 9 g; Carbs: 16.3 g; Protein: 10.4 g; Fiber: 0 g

Nacho Cheese Sauce

Preparation time: 5 minutes; Cooking time: 10 minutes; Servings: 4
Ingredients:
- 3 tablespoons flour
- 1/4 teaspoon garlic salt
- 1/4 teaspoon salt
- 1/2 teaspoon cumin
- 1/4 teaspoon paprika
- 1 teaspoon red chili powder
- 1/8 teaspoon cayenne powder
- 1 cup vegan cashew yogurt
- 1 1/4 cups vegetable broth

Method:
1. Take a small saucepan, place it over medium heat, pour in vegetable broth, and bring it to a boil.
2. Then whisk together flour and yogurt, add to the boiling broth, stir in all the spices, switch heat to medium-low level and cook for 5 minutes until thickened.
3. Serve straight away.

Nutrition Value:
Calories: 282 Cal; Fat: 1 g; Carbs: 63 g; Protein: 3 g; Fiber: 12 g

Avocado Tomato Bruschetta

Preparation time: 10 minutes; Cooking time: 0 minute; Servings: 4
Ingredients:

- 3 slices of whole-grain bread
- 6 chopped cherry tomatoes
- ½ of sliced avocado
- ½ teaspoon minced garlic
- ½ teaspoon ground black pepper
- 2 tablespoons chopped basil
- ½ teaspoon of sea salt
- 1 teaspoon balsamic vinegar

Method:

1. Place tomatoes in a bowl, and then stir in vinegar until mixed.
2. Top bread slices with avocado slices, then top evenly with tomato mixture, garlic and basil, and season with salt and black pepper.
3. Serve straight away

Nutrition Value:

Calories: 131 Cal; Fat: 7.3 g; Carbs: 15 g; Protein: 2.8 g; Fiber: 3.2 g

Cinnamon Bananas

Preparation time: 5 minutes; Cooking time: 8 minutes; Servings: 2
Ingredients:

- 2 bananas, peeled, sliced
- 1 teaspoon cinnamon
- 2 tablespoons granulated Splenda
- 1/4 teaspoon nutmeg

Method:

1. Prepare the cinnamon mixture and for this, place all the ingredients in a bowl, except for banana, and stir until mixed.
2. Take a large skillet pan, place it over medium heat, spray with oil, add banana slices and sprinkle with half of the prepared cinnamon mixture.
3. Cook for 3 minutes, then sprinkle with remaining prepared cinnamon mixture and continue cooking for 3 minutes until tender and hot.
4. Serve straight away.

Nutrition Value:

Calories: 155 Cal; Fat: 2 g; Carbs: 39 g; Protein: 1 g; Fiber: 3 g

Salted Almonds

Preparation time: 5 minutes; Cooking time: 20 minutes; Servings: 4
Ingredients:

- 2 cups almonds
- 4 tablespoons salt
- 1 cup boiling water

Method:

1. Stir the salt into the boiling water in a pan, then add almonds in it and let them soak for 20 minutes.
2. Then drain the almonds, spread them in an even layer on a baking sheet lined with baking paper and sprinkle with salt.
3. Roast the almonds for 20 minutes at 300 degrees F, then cool them for 10 minutes and serve.

Nutrition Value:

Calories: 170 Cal; Fat: 16 g; Carbs: 5 g; Protein: 6 g; Fiber: 3 g

Pumpkin Cake Pops

Preparation time: 10 minutes; Cooking time: 10 minutes; Servings: 4
Ingredients:

- 1 cup coconut flour
- ¼ teaspoon cinnamon

- 1/4 cup coconut sugar
- 1/4 cup chocolate chips, unsweetened
- 3/4 cup pumpkin puree

Method:
1. Place all the ingredients in a bowl, except for chocolate chips, stir until incorporated, and then fold in chocolate chips until combined.
2. Shape the mixture into small balls, then place them on a cookie sheet greased with oil and bake for 10 minutes at 350 degrees F until done.
3. Let the balls cool completely and then serve.

Nutrition Value:
Calories: 82.5 Cal; Fat: 3.4 g; Carbs: 12.3 g; Protein: 0.7 g; Fiber: 0.05 g

Honey-Almond Popcorn

Preparation time: 5 minutes; Cooking time: 10 minutes; Servings: 4
Ingredients:
- 1/2 cup popcorn kernels
- 2 tablespoons honey
- 1/2 teaspoon sea salt
- 2 tablespoons coconut sugar
- 1 cup roasted almonds
- 1/4 cup walnut oil

Method:
1. Take a pot, place it over medium-low heat, add oil and when it melts, add four kernels and wait until they sizzle.
2. Then add remaining kernel, toss until coated, sprinkle with sugar, drizzle with honey, shut the pot with the lid, and shake the kernels until popped completely, adding almonds halfway.
3. Once all the kernels have popped, season them with salt and serve straight away.

Nutrition Value:
Calories: 120 Cal; Fat: 4.5 g; Carbs: 19 g; Protein: 1 g; Fiber: 1 g

Turmeric Snack Bites

Preparation time: 35 minutes; Cooking time: 0 minute; Servings: 10
Ingredients:
- 1 cup Medjool dates, pitted, chopped
- 1/2 cup walnuts
- 1 teaspoon ground turmeric
- 1 tablespoon cocoa powder, unsweetened
- 1/2 teaspoon ground cinnamon
- 1/2 cup shredded coconut, unsweetened

Method:
1. Place all the ingredients in a food processor and pulse for 2 minutes until a smooth mixture comes together.
2. Tip the mixture in a bowl and then shape it into ten small balls, 1 tablespoon of the mixture per ball and then refrigerate for 30 minutes.
3. Serve straight away.

Nutrition Value:
Calories: 109 Cal; Fat: 2 g; Carbs: 13 g; Protein: 1 g; Fiber: 0 g

Watermelon Pizza

Preparation time: 10 minutes; Cooking time: 0 minute; Servings: 10
Ingredients:
- 1/2 cup strawberries, halved
- 1/2 cup blueberries
- 1 watermelon
- 1/2 cup raspberries
- 1 cup of coconut yogurt
- 1/2 cup pomegranate seeds

- 1/2 cup cherries
- Maple syrup as needed

Method:
1. Cut watermelon into 3-inch thick slices, then spread yogurt on one side, leaving some space in the edges and then top evenly with fruits and drizzle with maple syrup.
2. Cut the watermelon into wedges and then serve.

Nutrition Value:
Calories: 150 Cal; Fat: 4 g; Carbs: 21 g; Protein: 10 g; Fiber: 2 g

Rosemary Popcorn

Preparation time: 10 minutes; Cooking time: 10 minutes; Servings: 4
Ingredients:
- 1/2 cup popcorn kernels
- 1/2 teaspoon sea salt
- 1 tablespoon and 1/2 teaspoon minced rosemary
- 3 tablespoons unsalted vegan butter
- 1/4 cup olive oil
- 1/3 teaspoon ground black pepper

Method:
1. Take a pot, place it over medium-low heat, add oil and when it melts, add four kernels and wait until they sizzle.
2. Then add remaining kernel, toss until coated, add 1 tablespoon minced rosemary, shut the pot with the lid, and shake the kernels until popped completely.
3. Once all the kernels have popped, transfer them in a bowl, cook remaining rosemary into melted butter, then drizzle this mixture over popcorn and toss until well coated.
4. Season popcorn with salt and black pepper, toss until mixed and serve.

Nutrition Value:
Calories: 160 Cal; Fat: 6 g; Carbs: 28 g; Protein: 3 g; Fiber: 4 g

Queso Dip

Preparation time: 5 minutes; Cooking time: 0 minute; Servings: 6
Ingredients:
- 1 cup cashews
- ½ teaspoon minced garlic
- 1/2 teaspoon salt
- 1/2 teaspoon ground cumin
- 1 teaspoon red chili powder
- 2 tablespoons nutritional yeast
- 1 tablespoon harissa
- 1 cup hot water

Method:
1. Place all the ingredients in a food processor and pulse for 2 minutes until smooth and well combined.
2. Tip the dip in a bowl, taste to adjust seasoning and then serve.

Nutrition Value:
Calories: 133 Cal; Fat: 9 g; Carbs: 8 g; Protein: 5 g; Fiber: 1 g

Nooch Popcorn

Preparation time: 10 minutes; Cooking time: 10 minutes; Servings: 4
Ingredients:
- 1/3 cup nutritional yeast
- 1 teaspoon of sea salt
- 3 tablespoons coconut oil
- ½ cup popcorn kernels

Method:
1. Place yeast in a large bowl, stir in salt, and set aside until required.
2. Take a medium saucepan, place it over medium-high heat, add oil and when it melts, add four kernels and wait until they sizzle.

3. Then add remaining kernel, toss until coated, shut the pan with the lid, and shake the kernels until popped completely.
4. When done, transfer popcorns tot eh yeast mixture, shut with lid and shape well until coated.
5. Serve straight away

Nutrition Value:
Calories: 160 Cal; Fat: 6 g; Carbs: 28 g; Protein: 3 g; Fiber: 4 g

Masala Popcorn

Preparation time: 5 minutes; Cooking time: 15 minutes; Servings: 4

Ingredients:

- 3 cups popped popcorn
- 2 hot chili peppers, sliced
- 1 teaspoon ground cumin
- 6 curry leaves
- 1 teaspoon ground coriander
- 1/3 teaspoon salt
- 1/8 teaspoon chaat masala
- 1/4 teaspoon turmeric powder
- ¼ teaspoon red pepper flakes
- 1/4 teaspoon garam masala
- 1/3 cup olive oil

Method:
1. Take a large pot, place it over medium heat, add half of the oil and when hot, add chili peppers and curry leaves and cook for 3 minutes until golden.
2. When done, transfer curry leaves and pepper to a plate lined with paper towels and set aside until required.
3. Add remaining oil into the pot, add remaining ingredients except for popcorns, stir until mixed and cook for 1 minute until fragrant.
4. Then tip in popcorns, remove the pan from heat, stir well until coated, and then sprinkle with bay leaves and red chili.
5. Toss until mixed and serve straight away.

Nutrition Value:
Calories: 150 Cal; Fat: 9 g; Carbs: 15 g; Protein: 2 g ;Fiber: 4 g

Applesauce

Preparation time: 10 minutes; Cooking time: 15 minutes; Servings: 6

Ingredients:

- 4 pounds mixed apples, cored, ½-inch chopped
- 1 strip of orange peel, about 3-inch
- 1/2 cup coconut sugar
- 1/2 teaspoon salt
- 1 cinnamon stick, about 3-inch
- 2 tablespoons apple cider vinegar
- Apple cider as needed for consistency of the sauce

Method:
1. Take a large pot, place apples in it, then add remaining ingredients except for cider, stir until mixed and cook for 15 minutes over medium heat until apples have wilted, stirring every 10 minutes.
2. When done, remove the cinnamon stick and orange peel and puree the mixture by using an immersion blender until smooth and stir in apple cider until sauce reaches to desired consistency.
3. Serve straight away.

Nutrition Value:
Calories: 75 Cal; Fat: 0.2 g; Carbs: 19 g; Protein: 0.2 g; Fiber: 1.3 g

Avocado Toast with Herbs and Peas

Preparation time: 10 minutes; Cooking time: 0 minute; Servings: 4
Ingredients:
- ½ of a medium avocado, peeled, pitted, mashed
- 6 slices of radish
- 2 tablespoons baby peas
- ¼ teaspoon ground black pepper
- 1 teaspoon chopped basil
- ¼ teaspoon salt
- 1/2 lemon, juiced
- 1 slice of bread, whole-grain, toasted

Method:
1. Spread mashed avocado on the one side of the toast and then top with peas, pressing them into the avocado.
2. Layer the toast with radish slices, season with salt and black pepper, sprinkle with basil, and drizzle with lemon juice.
3. Serve straight away.

Nutrition Value:
Calories: 250 Cal; Fat: 12 g; Carbs: 22 g; Protein: 7 g; Fiber: 9 g

Oven-Dried Grapes

Preparation time: 5 minutes; Cooking time: 4 hours; Servings: 4
Ingredients:
- 3 large bunches of grapes, seedless
- Olive oil as needed for greasing

Method:
1. Spread grapes into two greased baking sheets and bake for 4 hours at 225 degrees F until semi-dried.
2. When done, let the grape cool completely and then serve.

Nutrition Value:
Calories: 299 Cal; Fat: 1 g; Carbs: 79 g; Protein: 3.1 g; Fiber: 3.7 g

Black Bean and Corn Quesadillas

Preparation time: 15 minutes; Cooking time: 30 minutes; Servings: 4
Ingredients:
For the Black Beans and Corn:
- 1/2 of a medium white onion, peeled, chopped
- 1/2 cup cooked black beans
- 1/2 cup cooked corn kernels
- 1 teaspoon minced garlic
- ½ of jalapeno, deseeded, diced
- 1/2 teaspoon salt
- 1 teaspoon red chili powder
- 1 teaspoon cumin
- 1 tablespoon olive oil

For the Quesadillas:
- 4 large corn tortillas
- 4 green onions, chopped
- ½ cup vegan nacho cheese sauce
- ½ cup chopped cilantro
- 1 large tomato, diced
- Salsa as needed for dipping

Method:
1. Prepare beans and for this, take a frying pan, place it over medium-high heat, add oil and when hot, add onion, jalapeno, and garlic and cook for 3 minutes.
2. Then add remaining ingredients, stir until mixed and cook for 2 minutes until hot.
3. Take a large skillet pan, place over medium heat, place the tortilla in it and cook for 1 minute until toasted and then flip it.
4. Spread some of the cheese sauce on one half of the top, spread with beans mixture, top with cilantro, onion, and tomato and then fold the filling with the other side of the tortilla.

5. Pat down the tortilla, cook it for 2 minutes, then carefully flip it, continue cooking for 2 minutes until hot, and then slide to a plate.
6. Cook remaining quesadilla in the same manner, then cut them into wedges and serve.

Nutrition Value:
Calories: 251 Cal; Fat: 9.5 g; Carbs: 30.6 g; Protein: 15.6 g; Fiber: 12.1 g

Zaatar Popcorn

Preparation time: 10 minutes; Cooking time: 0 minute; Servings: 8
Ingredients:
- 8 cups popped popcorns
- 1/4 cup za'atar spice blend
- ¾ teaspoon salt
- 4 tablespoons olive oil

Method:
1. Place all the ingredients except for popcorns in a large bowl and whisk until combined.
2. Then add popcorns, toss until well coated, and serve straight away.

Nutrition Value:
Calories: 150 Cal; Fat: 9 g; Carbs: 15 g; Protein: 2 g; Fiber: 4 g

Potato Chips

Preparation time: 10 minutes; Cooking time: 20 minutes; Servings: 2
Ingredients:
- 3 medium potatoes, scrubbed, thinly sliced, soaked in warm water for 10 min
- ½ teaspoon garlic powder
- ½ teaspoon onion powder
- ½ teaspoon red chili powder
- ½ teaspoon curry powder
- 1 teaspoon of sea salt
- 1 tablespoon apple cider vinegar
- 2 tablespoons olive oil

Method:
1. Drain the potato slices, pat dry, then place them in a large bowl, add remaining ingredients and toss until well coated.
2. Spread the potatoes in a single layer on a baking sheet and bake for 20 minutes until crispy, turning halfway.
3. Serve straight away.

Nutrition Value:
Calories: 600 Cal; Fat: 30 g; Carbs: 78 g; Protein: 9 g; Fiber: 23 g

Spinach and Artichoke Dip

Preparation time: 10 minutes; Cooking time: 25 minutes; Servings: 10
Ingredients:
- 28 ounces artichokes
- 1 small white onion, peeled, diced
- 1 1/2 cups cashews, soaked, drained
- 4 cups spinach
- 4 cloves of garlic, peeled
- 1 1 1/2 teaspoons salt
- 1/4 cup nutritional yeast
- 1 tablespoon olive oil
- 2 tablespoons lemon juice
- 1 1/2 cups coconut milk, unsweetened

Method:
1. Cook onion and garlic in hot oil for 3 minutes until saute and then set aside until required.
2. Place cashews in a food processor; add 1 teaspoon salt, yeast, milk, and lemon juice and pulse until smooth.
3. Add spinach, onion mixture, and artichokes and pulse until the chunky mixture comes together.

4. Tip the dip in a heatproof dish and bake for 20 minutes at 425 degrees F until the top is browned and dip bubbles.
5. Serve straight away with vegetable sticks.

Nutrition Value:
   Calories: 124 Cal; Fat: 9 g; Carbs: 8 g; Protein: 5 g; Fiber: 1 g

Chocolate-Covered Almonds

Preparation time: 1 hour and 45 minutes; Cooking time: 30 seconds; Servings: 4
Ingredients:
- 8 ounces almonds
- 1/2 teaspoon sea salt
- 6 ounces chocolate disks, semisweet, melted

Method:
1. Microwave chocolate in a heatproof bowl for 30 seconds until it melts, then dip almonds in it, four at a time, and place them on a baking sheet.
2. Let almonds stand for 1 hour until hardened, then sprinkle with salt, and cool them in the refrigerator for 30 minutes.
3. Serve straight away.

Nutrition Value:
   Calories: 286 Cal; Fat: 22 g; Carbs: 17 g; Protein: 7 g; Fiber: 5 g

Beans and Spinach Tacos

Preparation time: 10 minutes; Cooking time: 15 minutes; Servings: 4
Ingredients:
- 12 ounces spinach
- 4 tablespoons cooked kidney beans
- ½ of medium red onion, peeled, chopped
- ½ teaspoon minced garlic
- 1 medium tomato, chopped
- 3 tablespoons chopped parsley
- ½ of avocado, sliced
- ½ teaspoon ground black pepper
- 1 teaspoon salt
- 2 tablespoons olive oil
- 4 slices of vegan brie cheese
- 4 tortillas, about 6-inches

Method:
1. Take a skillet pan, place it over medium heat, add oil and when hot, add onion and cook for 10 minutes until softened.
2. Then stir in spinach, cook for 4 minutes until its leaves wilts, then drain it and distribute evenly between tortillas.
3. Top evenly with remaining ingredients, season with black pepper and salt, drizzle with lemon juice and then serve.

Nutrition Value:
   Calories: 219.8 Cal; Fat: 6 g; Carbs: 34 g; Protein: 9.9 g; Fiber: 10 g

Loaded Baked Potatoes

Preparation time: 10 minutes; Cooking time: 32 minutes; Servings: 2
Ingredients:
- 1/2 cup cooked chickpeas
- 2 medium potatoes, scrubbed
- 1 cup broccoli florets, steamed
- 1/4 cup vegan bacon bits
- 2 tablespoons all-purpose seasoning
- ¼ cup vegan cheese sauce
- 1/2 cup vegan sour cream

Method:
1. Pierce hole in the potatoes, microwave them for 12 minutes over high heat setting until soft to touch, and then bake them for 20 minutes at 450 degrees F until very tender.

2. Open the potatoes, mash the flesh with a fork, then top evenly with remaining ingredients and serve.

Nutrition Value:
Calories: 422 Cal; Fat: 16 g; Carbs: 59 g; Protein: 9 g; Fiber: 6 g

Coconut Rice

Preparation time: 5 minutes; Cooking time: 20 minutes; Servings: 4

Ingredients:
- 1 1/2 cups white rice
- 1 teaspoon coconut sugar
- 1/8 teaspoon salt
- 14 ounces coconut milk, unsweetened
- 1 1/4 cups water

Method:
1. Take a saucepan, place it over medium heat, add all the ingredients in it, stir well and bring the mixture to a boil.
2. Switch heat to medium-low level, simmer the rice for 20 minutes until tender, and then serve straight away.

Nutrition Value:
Calories: 453 Cal; Fat: 21 g; Carbs: 61.4 g; Protein: 6.8 g; Fiber: 2 g

Zucchini and Amaranth Patties

Preparation time: 10 minutes; Cooking time: 30 minutes; Servings: 14

Ingredients:
- 1 1/2 cups shredded zucchini
- ½ of a medium onion, shredded
- 1 1/2 cups cooked white beans
- 1/2 cup amaranth seeds
- 1 teaspoon red chili powder
- 1/2 teaspoon cumin
- 1/2 cup cornmeal
- 1/4 cup flax meal
- 1 tablespoon salsa
- 1 1/2 cups vegetable broth

Method:
1. Stir together stock and amaranth on a pot, bring it to a boil over medium-high heat, then switch heat to medium-low level and simmer until all the liquid is absorbed.
2. Mash the white beans in a bowl, add remaining ingredients including cooked amaranth and stir until well mixed.
3. Shape the mixture into patties, then place them on a baking sheet lined with parchment sheet and bake for 30 minutes until browned and crispy, turning halfway.
4. Serve straight away.

Nutrition Value:
Calories: 152 Cal; Fat: 3 g; Carbs: 29 g; Protein: 7 g; Fiber: 6 g

Rice Pizza

Preparation time: 10 minutes; Cooking time: 35 minutes; Servings: 6

Ingredients:
For the Crust:
- 1 1/2 cup short-grain rice, cooked
- 1/2 teaspoon garlic powder
- 1 teaspoon coconut sugar
- 1 tablespoon red chili flakes

For the Sauce:
- 1/4 teaspoon onion powder
- 1 tablespoon nutritional yeast
- 1/4 teaspoon garlic powder
- 1/4 teaspoon ginger powder
- 1 tablespoon red chili flakes
- 1 teaspoon soy sauce
- 1/2 cup tomato purée

For the Toppings:

- 2 1/2 cups oyster mushrooms
- 1 chili pepper, deseeded, sliced
- 2 scallions, sliced
- 1 teaspoon coconut sugar
- 1 teaspoon soy sauce
- Baby corn as needed

Method:
1. Prepare the crust and for this, place all of its ingredients in a bowl and stir until well combined.
2. Then take a pizza pan, line it with parchment sheet, place rice mixture in it, spread it evenly, and then bake for 20 minutes at 350 degrees F.
3. Then spread tomato sauce over the crust, top evenly with remaining ingredients for the topping and continue baking for 15 minutes.
4. When done, slice the pizza into wedges and serve.

Nutrition Value:
Calories: 140.1 Cal; Fat: 5 g; Carbs: 30 g; Protein: 3 g; Fiber: 1 g

Quinoa and Black Bean Burgers

Preparation time: 10 minutes; Cooking time: 6 minutes; Servings: 5
Ingredients:
- 1/4 cup quinoa, cooked
- 15 ounces cooked black beans
- 2 tablespoons minced white onion
- 1/4 cup minced bell pepper
- ½ teaspoon minced garlic
- 1/2 teaspoon salt
- 1 1/2 teaspoons ground cumin
- 1/2 cup bread crumbs
- 1 teaspoon hot pepper sauce
- 3 tablespoons olive oil
- 1 flax egg

Method:
1. Place all the ingredients in a bowl, except for oil, stir until well combined, and then shape the mixture into five patties.
2. Heat oil in a frying pan over medium heat, add patties and cook for 3 minutes per side until browned.
3. Serve straight away.

Nutrition Value:
Calories: 245 Cal; Fat: 10.6 g; Carbs: 29 g; Protein: 9.3 g; Fiber: 7.2 g

Jalapeno and Cilantro Hummus

Preparation time: 5 minutes; Cooking time: 0 minute; Servings: 4
Ingredients:
- ½ cup cilantro
- 1 1/2 cups chickpeas, cooked
- 1/2 of jalapeno pepper, sliced
- ½ teaspoon salt
- ½ teaspoon minced garlic
- 1 tablespoon lime juice
- 1/4 cup tahini
- ¼ water

Method:
1. Place all the ingredients in a bowl and pulse for 2 minutes until smooth.
2. Tip the hummus in a bowl, drizzle with oil sprinkle with cilantro, and then serve.

Nutrition Value:
Calories: 137 Cal; Fat: 2.3 g; Carbs: 23.3 g; Protein: 7.3 g; Fiber: 6.6 g

Carrot Cake Bites

Preparation time: 15 minutes; Cooking time: 0 minute; Servings: 15
Ingredients:
- 2 cups oats, old-fashioned
- ½ cup grated carrot
- 2 cups coconut flakes, unsweetened
- 1/2 teaspoon salt

- 1 teaspoon cinnamon
- 1/2 cup maple syrup
- 1/2 teaspoon vanilla extract, unsweetened
- 1/2 cup almond butter
- 2 tablespoons white chocolate chips

Method:
1. Place oats in a food processor, add coconut and pulse until ground.
2. Then add remaining ingredients except for chocolate chips and pulse for 3 minutes until a sticky dough comes together.
3. Add chocolate chips, pulse for 1 minute until just mixed, and then shape the mixture into fifteen small balls.
4. Refrigerate the balls for 30 minutes and then serve.

Nutrition Value:
Calories: 87 Cal; Fat: 5 g; Carbs: 9.2 g; Protein: 1.8 g; Fiber: 1.6 g

Cinnamon Bun Balls

Preparation time: 15 minutes; Cooking time: 0 minute; Servings: 10
Ingredients:
- 5 Medjool dates, pitted
- 1/2 cup whole walnuts
- 1 tablespoon chopped walnuts
- 3 tablespoons ground cinnamon
- 1 teaspoon ground cardamom

Method:
1. Place all the ingredients in a food processor, except for 1 tablespoon walnuts, and then process until smooth.
2. Shape the mixture into ten balls, then roll them into chopped walnuts and serve.

Nutrition Value:
Calories: 62 Cal; Fat: 4.5 g; Carbs: 5.8 g; Protein: 1.2 g; Fiber: 2 g

Kale Hummus

Preparation time: 5 minutes; Cooking time: 0 minute; Servings: 4
Ingredients:
- 2 cups cooked chickpeas
- 5 cloves of garlic, peeled
- 4 cups kale, torn into pieces
- 1 teaspoon of sea salt
- 1/3 cup lemon juice
- 1/4 cup olive oil
- 1/4 cup tahini

Method:
1. Place all the ingredients in a bowl and pulse for 2 minutes until smooth.
2. Tip the hummus in a bowl, drizzle with oil, and then serve.

Nutrition Value:
Calories: 173 Cal; Fat: 10 g; Carbs: 14 g; Protein: 6 g; Fiber: 5 g

Chapter 8: Desserts

Chocolate and Avocado Pudding

Preparation time: 3 hours and 10 minutes; Cooking time: 0 minute; Servings: 1
Ingredients:

- 1 small avocado, pitted, peeled
- 1 small banana, mashed
- 1/3 cup cocoa powder, unsweetened
- 1 tablespoon cacao nibs, unsweetened
- 1/4 cup maple syrup
- 1/3 cup coconut cream

Method:

1. Add avocado in a food processor along with cream and then pulse for 2 minutes until smooth.
2. Add remaining ingredients, blend until mixed, and then tip the pudding in a container.
3. Cover the container with a plastic wrap; it should touch the pudding and refrigerate for 3 hours.
4. Serve straight away.

Nutrition Value:
   Calories: 87 Cal; Fat: 7 g; Carbs: 9 g; Protein: 1.5 g; Fiber: 3.2 g

Chocolate Avocado Ice Cream

Preparation time: 1 hour and 10 minutes; Cooking time: 0 minute; Servings: 2
Ingredients:

- 4.5 ounces avocado, peeled, pitted
- 1/2 cup cocoa powder, unsweetened
- 1 tablespoon vanilla extract, unsweetened
- 1/2 cup and 2 tablespoons maple syrup
- 13.5 ounces coconut milk, unsweetened
- 1/2 cup water

Method:

1. Add avocado in a food processor along with milk and then pulse for 2 minutes until smooth.
2. Add remaining ingredients, blend until mixed, and then tip the pudding in a freezer-proof container.
3. Place the container in a freezer and chill for freeze for 4 hours until firm, whisking every 20 minutes after 1 hour.
4. Serve straight away.

Nutrition Value:
   Calories: 80.7 Cal; Fat: 7.1 g; Carbs: 6 g; Protein: 0.6 g; Fiber: 2 g

Watermelon Mint Popsicles

Preparation time: 8 hours and 5 minutes; Cooking time: 0 minute; Servings: 8
Ingredients:

- 20 mint leaves, diced
- 6 cups watermelon chunks
- 3 tablespoons lime juice

Method:

1. Add watermelon in a food processor along with lime juice and then pulse for 15 seconds until smooth.
2. Pass the watermelon mixture through a strainer placed over a bowl, remove the seeds and then stir mint into the collected watermelon mixture.

3. Take eight Popsicle molds, pour in prepared watermelon mixture, and freeze for 2 hours until slightly firm.
4. Then insert popsicle sticks and continue freezing for 6 hours until solid.
5. Serve straight away

Nutrition Value:
Calories: 90 Cal; Fat: 0 g; Carbs: 23 g; Protein: 0 g; Fiber: 0 g

Mango Coconut Chia Pudding

Preparation time: 2 hours and 5 minutes; Cooking time: 0 minute; Servings: 1
Ingredients:
- 1 medium mango, peeled, cubed
- 1/4 cup chia seeds
- 2 tablespoons coconut flakes
- 1 cup coconut milk, unsweetened
- 1 1/2 teaspoons maple syrup

Method:
1. Take a bowl, place chia seeds in it, whisk in milk until combined, and then stir in maple syrup.
2. Cover the bowl with a plastic wrap; it should touch the pudding mixture and refrigerate for 2 hours until the pudding has set.
3. Then puree mango until smooth, top it evenly over pudding, sprinkle with coconut flakes and serve.

Nutrition Value:
Calories: 159 Cal; Fat: 9 g; Carbs: 17 g; Protein: 3 g; Fiber: 6 g

Brownie Energy Bites

Preparation time: 1 hour and 10 minutes; Cooking time: 0 minute; Servings: 2
Ingredients:
- 1/2 cup walnuts
- 1 cup Medjool dates, chopped
- 1/2 cup almonds
- 1/8 teaspoon salt
- 1/2 cup shredded coconut flakes
- 1/3 cup and 2 teaspoons cocoa powder, unsweetened

Method:
1. Place almonds and walnuts in a food processor and pulse for 3 minutes until the dough starts to come together.
2. Add remaining ingredients, reserving ¼ cup of coconut and pulse for 2 minutes until incorporated.
3. Shape the mixture into balls, roll them in remaining coconut until coated, and refrigerate for 1 hour.
4. Serve straight away

Nutrition Value:
Calories: 174.6 Cal; Fat: 8.1 g; Carbs: 25.5 g; Protein: 4.1 g; Fiber: 4.4 g

Strawberry Coconut Ice Cream

Preparation time: 5 minutes; Cooking time: 0 minute; Servings: 4
Ingredients:
- 4 cups frouncesen strawberries
- 1 vanilla bean, seeded
- 28 ounces coconut cream
- 1/2 cup maple syrup

Method:
1. Place cream in a food processor and pulse for 1 minute until soft peaks come together.
2. Then tip the cream in a bowl, add remaining ingredients in the blender and blend until thick mixture comes together.

3. Add the mixture into the cream, fold until combined, and then transfer ice cream into a freezer-safe bowl and freeze for 4 hours until firm, whisking every 20 minutes after 1 hour.
4. Serve straight away.

Nutrition Value:
Calories: 100 Cal; Fat: 100 g; Carbs: 100 g; Protein: 100 g; Fiber: 100 g

Salted Caramel Chocolate Cups

Preparation time: 5 minutes; Cooking time: 2 minutes; Servings: 12
Ingredients:
- ¼ teaspoon sea salt granules
- 1 cup dark chocolate chips, unsweetened
- 2 teaspoons coconut oil
- 6 tablespoons caramel sauce

Method:
1. Take a heatproof bowl, add chocolate chips and oil, stir until mixed, then microwave for 1 minute until melted, stir chocolate and continue heating in the microwave for 30 seconds.
2. Take twelve mini muffin tins, line them with muffin liners, spoon a little bit of chocolate mixture into the tins, spread the chocolate in the bottom and along the sides, and freeze for 10 minutes until set.
3. Then fill each cup with ½ tablespoon of caramel sauce, cover with remaining chocolate and freeze for another 2salt0 minutes until set.
4. When ready to eat, peel off liner from the cup, sprinkle with sauce, and serve.

Nutrition Value:
Calories: 80 Cal; Fat: 5 g; Carbs: 10 g; Protein: 1 g; Fiber: 0.5 g

Chocolate Peanut Butter Energy Bites

Preparation time: 1 hour and 5 minutes; Cooking time: 0 minute; Servings: 4
Ingredients:
- 1/2 cup oats, old-fashioned
- 1/3 cup cocoa powder, unsweetened
- 1 cup dates, chopped
- 1/2 cup shredded coconut flakes, unsweetened
- 1/2 cup peanut butter

Method:
1. Place oats in a food processor along with dates and pulse for 1 minute until the paste starts to come together.
2. Then add remaining ingredients, and blend until incorporated and very thick mixture comes together.
3. Shape the mixture into balls, refrigerate for 1 hour until set and then serve.

Nutrition Value:
Calories: 88.6 Cal; Fat: 5 g; Carbs: 10 g; Protein: 2.3 g; Fiber: 1.6 g

Mango Coconut Cheesecake

Preparation time: 4 hours and 10 minutes; Cooking time: 0 minute; Servings: 4
Ingredients:
For the Crust:
- 1 cup macadamia nuts
- 1 cup dates, pitted, soaked in hot water for 10 minutes

For the Filling:
- 2 cups cashews, soaked in warm water for 10 minutes
- 1/2 cup and 1 tablespoon maple syrup
- 1/3 cup and 2 tablespoons coconut oil
- 1/4 cup lemon juice

- 1/2 cup and 2 tablespoons coconut milk, unsweetened, chilled

For the Topping:
- 1 cup fresh mango slices

Method:
1. Prepare the crust, and for this, place nuts in a food processor and process until mixture resembles crumbs.
2. Drain the dates, add them to the food processor and blend for 2 minutes until thick mixture comes together.
3. Take a 4-inch cheesecake pan, place date mixture in it, spread and press evenly, and set aside.
4. Prepare the filling and for this, place all its ingredients in a food processor and blend for 3 minutes until smooth.
5. Pour the filling into the crust, spread evenly, and then freeze for 4 hours until set.
6. Top the cake with mango slices and then serve.

Nutrition Value:
Calories: 200 Cal; Fat: 11 g; Carbs: 22.5 g; Protein: 2 g; Fiber: 1 g

Rainbow Fruit Salad

Preparation time: 10 minutes; Cooking time: 0 minute; Servings: 4
Ingredients:
For the Fruit Salad:
- 1 pound strawberries, hulled, sliced
- 1 cup kiwis, halved, cubed
- 1 1/4 cups blueberries
- 1 1/3 cups blackberries
- 1 cup pineapple chunks

For the Maple Lime Dressing:
- 2 teaspoons lime zest
- 1/4 cup maple syrup
- 1 tablespoon lime juice

Method:
1. Prepare the salad, and for this, take a bowl, place all its ingredients and toss until mixed.
2. Prepare the dressing, and for this, take a small bowl, place all its ingredients and whisk well.
3. Drizzle the dressing over salad, toss until coated and serve.

Nutrition Value:
Calories: 88.1 Cal; Fat: 0.4 g; Carbs: 22.6 g; Protein: 1.1 g; Fiber: 2.8 g

Cookie Dough Bites

Preparation time: 4 hours and 10 minutes; Cooking time: 0 minute; Servings: 18
Ingredients:
- 15 ounces cooked chickpeas
- 1/3 cup vegan chocolate chips
- 1/3 cup and 2 tablespoons peanut butter
- 8 Medjool dates pitted
- 1 teaspoon vanilla extract, unsweetened
- 2 tablespoons maple syrup
- 1 1/2 tablespoons almond milk, unsweetened

Method:
1. Place chickpeas in a food processor along with dates, butter, and vanilla and then process for 2 minutes until smooth.
2. Add remaining ingredients, except for chocolate chips, and then pulse for 1 minute until blends and dough comes together.
3. Add chocolate chips, stir until just mixed, then shape the mixture into 18 balls and refrigerate for 4 hours until firm.

4. Serve straight away
Nutrition Value:
Calories: 200 Cal; Fat: 9 g; Carbs: 26 g; Protein: 1 g; Fiber: 0 g

Dark Chocolate Bars

Preparation time: 1 hour and 10 minutes; Cooking time: 2 minutes; Servings: 12
Ingredients:

- 1 cup cocoa powder, unsweetened
- 3 Tablespoons cacao nibs
- 1/8 teaspoon sea salt
- 2 Tablespoons maple syrup
- 1 1/4 cup chopped cocoa butter
- 1/2 teaspoons vanilla extract, unsweetened
- 2 Tablespoons coconut oil

Method:
1. Take a heatproof bowl, add butter, oil, stir, and microwave for 90 to 120 seconds until melts, stirring every 30 seconds.
2. Sift cocoa powder over melted butter mixture, whisk well until combined, and then stir in maple syrup, vanilla, and salt until mixed.
3. Distribute the mixture evenly between twelve mini cupcake liners, top with cacao nibs, and freeze for 1 hour until set.
4. Serve straight away
Nutrition Value:
Calories: 100 Cal; Fat: 9 g; Carbs: 8 g; Protein: 2 g; Fiber: 2 g

Almond Butter, Oat and Protein Energy Balls

Preparation time: 1 hour and 10 minutes; Cooking time: 3 minutes; Servings: 4
Ingredients:

- 1 cup rolled oats
- ½ cup honey
- 2 ½ scoops of vanilla protein powder
- 1 cup almond butter
- Chia seeds for rolling

Method:
1. Take a skillet pan, place it over medium heat, add butter and honey, stir and cook for 2 minutes until warm.
2. Transfer the mixture into a bowl, stir in protein powder until mixed, and then stir in oatmeal until combined.
3. Shape the mixture into balls, roll them into chia seeds, then arrange them on a cookie sheet and refrigerate for 1 hour until firm.
4. Serve straight away
Nutrition Value:
Calories: 200 Cal; Fat: 10 g; Carbs: 21 g; Protein: 7 g; Fiber: 4 g

Chocolate and Avocado Truffles

Preparation time: 1 hour and 10 minutes; Cooking time: 1 minute; Servings: 18
Ingredients:

- 1 medium avocado, ripe
- 2 tablespoons cocoa powder
- 10 ounces of dark chocolate chips

Method:
1. Scoop out the flesh from avocado, place it in a bowl, then mash with a fork until smooth, and stir in 1/2 cup chocolate chips.
2. Place remaining chocolate chips in a heatproof bowl and microwave for 1 minute until chocolate has melted, stirring halfway.

3. Add melted chocolate into avocado mixture, stir well until blended, and then refrigerate for 1 hour.
4. Then shape the mixture into balls, 1 tablespoon of mixture per ball, and roll in cocoa powder until covered.
5. Serve straight away.

Nutrition Value:
Calories: 59 Cal; Fat: 4 g; Carbs: 7 g; Protein: 0 g; Fiber: 1 g

Coconut Oil Cookies

Preparation time: 10 minutes; Cooking time: 10 minutes; Servings: 15
Ingredients:
- 3 1/4 cup oats
- 1/2 teaspoons salt
- 2 cups coconut Sugar
- 1 teaspoons vanilla extract, unsweetened
- 1/4 cup cocoa powder
- 1/2 cup liquid Coconut Oil
- 1/2 cup peanut butter
- 1/2 cup cashew milk

Method:
1. Take a saucepan, place it over medium heat, add all the ingredients except for oats and vanilla, stir until mixed, and then bring the mixture to boil.
2. Simmer the mixture for 4 minutes, mixing frequently, then remove the pan from heat and stir in vanilla.
3. Add oats, stir until well mixed and then scoop the mixture on a plate lined with wax paper.
4. Serve straight away.

Nutrition Value:
Calories: 112 Cal; Fat: 6.5 g; Carbs: 13 g; Protein: 1.4 g; Fiber: 0.1 g

Dark Chocolate Raspberry Ice Cream

Preparation time: 5 minutes; Cooking time: 0 minute; Servings: 2
Ingredients:
- 2 frouncesen bananas, sliced
- ¼ cup fresh raspberries
- 2 tablespoons cocoa powder, unsweetened
- 2 tablespoons raspberry jelly

Method:
1. Place all the ingredients in a food processor, except for berries and pulse for 2 minutes until smooth.
2. Distribute the ice cream mixture between two bowls, stir in berries until combined, and then serve immediately.

Nutrition Value:
Calories: 104 Cal; Fat: 0 g; Carbs: 25 g; Protein: 0 g; Fiber: 5 g

Mango Ice Cream

Preparation time: 5 minutes; Cooking time: 0 minute; Servings: 1
Ingredients:
- 2 frouncesen bananas, sliced
- 1 cup diced frouncesen mango

Method:
1. Place all the ingredients in a food processor and pulse for 2 minutes until smooth.
2. Distribute the ice cream mixture between two bowls and then serve immediately.

Nutrition Value:
Calories: 74 Cal; Fat: 0 g; Carbs: 17 g; Protein: 0 g; Fiber: 4 g

Peanut Butter and Honey Ice Cream

Preparation time: 5 minutes; Cooking time: 0 minute; Servings: 2
Ingredients:
- 2½ tablespoons peanut butter
- 2 bananas frouncesen, sliced
- 1½ tablespoons honey

Method:
1. Place all the ingredients in a food processor and pulse for 2 minutes until smooth.
2. Distribute the ice cream mixture between two bowls and then serve immediately.

Nutrition Value:
Calories: 190 Cal; Fat: 11 g; Carbs: 20 g; Protein: 4 g; Fiber: 0 g

Blueberry Ice Cream

Preparation time: 5 minutes; Cooking time: 0 minute; Servings: 2
Ingredients:
- 2 frouncesen bananas, sliced
- ½ cup blueberries

Method:
1. Place all the ingredients in a food processor and pulse for 2 minutes until smooth.
2. Distribute the ice cream mixture between two bowls and then serve immediately.

Nutrition Value:
Calories: 68 Cal; Fat: 0 g; Carbs: 17 g; Protein: 0 g; Fiber: 2 g

Chocolate Pudding

Preparation time: 5 minutes; Cooking time: 0 minute; Servings: 4
Ingredients:
- 3/4 cup cocoa powder
- 12 ounces tofu, silken
- 1/3 cup almond milk, unsweetened
- 1/2 cup sugar
- Whipped cream for topping

Method:
1. Place all the ingredients in a food processor and pulse for 2 minutes until smooth.
2. Distribute the pudding between four bowls, refrigerate for 15 minutes, then top with whipped topping and serve immediately.

Nutrition Value:
Calories: 109.5 Cal; Fat: 4.3 g; Carbs: 4.8 g; Protein: 12.1 g; Fiber: 1.8 g

Whipped Cream

Preparation time: 5 minutes; Cooking time: 0 minute; Servings: 2
Ingredients:
- ¼ cup powdered sugar
- 1 teaspoon vanilla extract, unsweetened
- 14 ounces coconut milk, unsweetened, chilled

Method:
1. Take a bowl, chill it overnight in the freezer, then separate coconut milk and solid and add solid from coconut milk into the chilled bowl.
2. Add remaining ingredients and beat for 3 minutes until smooth and well combined.
3. Serve straight away.

Nutrition Value:
Calories: 40.4 Cal; Fat: 1 g; Carbs: 8 g; Protein: 0 g; Fiber: 0 g

Almond Butter Cookies

Preparation time: 35 minutes; Cooking time: 5 minutes; Servings: 13

Ingredients:
- 1/4 cup sesame seeds
- 1 cup rolled oats
- 3 Tablespoons sunflower seeds, roasted, unsalted
- 1/8 teaspoon sea salt
- 1 1/2 Tablespoons coconut flour
- 1/2 cup coconut sugar
- 1/2 teaspoons vanilla extract, unsweetened
- 3 Tablespoons coconut oil
- 2 Tablespoons almond milk, unsweetened
- 1/3 cup almond butter, salted

Method:
1. Take a saucepan, place it over medium heat, pour in milk, stir in sugar and oil and bring the mixture to a low boil.
2. Boil the mixture for 1 minute, then remove the pan from heat, and stir in remaining ingredients until incorporated and well combined.
3. Drop the prepared mixture onto a baking sheet lined with wax paper, about 13 cookies, and let the cookies stand for 25 minutes until firm and set.
4. Serve straight away.

Nutrition Value:
Calories: 158 Cal; Fat: 10 g; Carbs: 15 g; Protein: 3.4 g; Fiber: 1.8 g

Peanut Butter Fudge

Preparation time: 50 minutes; Cooking time: 1 minute; Servings: 8
Ingredients:
- 1/2 cup peanut butter
- 2 tablespoons maple syrup
- 1/4 teaspoon salt
- 2 tablespoons coconut oil, melted
- 1/4 teaspoon vanilla extract, unsweetened

Method:
1. Take a heatproof bowl, place all the ingredients in it, microwave for 15 seconds, and then stir until well combined.
2. Take a freezer-proof container, line it with parchment paper, pour in fudge mixture, spread evenly and freeze for 40 minutes until set and harden.
3. When ready to eat, let fudge set for 5 minutes, then cut it into squares and serve.

Nutrition Value:
Calories: 96 Cal; Fat: 3.6 g; Carbs: 14.6 g; Protein: 1.5 g; Fiber: 0.3 g

Coconut Cacao Bites

Preparation time: 1 hour and 10 minutes; Cooking time: 0 minute; Servings: 20
Ingredients:
- 1 1/2 cups almond flour
- 3 dates, pitted
- 1 1/2 cups shredded coconut, unsweetened
- 1/4 teaspoons ground cinnamon
- 2 Tablespoons flaxseed meal
- 1/16 teaspoon sea salt
- 2 Tablespoons vanilla protein powder
- 1/4 cup cacao powder
- 3 Tablespoons hemp seeds
- 1/3 cup tahini
- 4 Tablespoons coconut butter, melted

Method:
1. Place all the ingredients in a food processor and pulse for 5 minutes until the thick paste comes together.
2. Drop the mixture in the form of balls on a baking sheet lined with parchment sheet, 2 tablespoons per ball and then freeze for 1 hour until firm to touch.
3. Serve straight away.

Nutrition Value:

Calories: 120 Cal; Fat: 4.5 g; Carbs: 15 g; Protein: 4 g; Fiber: 2 g

Gingerbread Energy Bites

Preparation time: 40 minutes; Cooking time: 5 minutes; Servings: 14
Ingredients:

- 12 dates, pitted, chopped
- 1 cup toasted pecans
- 2 ounces dark chocolate
- ¼ teaspoon cloves
- 1 teaspoon ground ginger
- 1 tablespoon molasses
- 1 teaspoon cinnamon
- ¼ teaspoon salt
- ¼ teaspoon ground nutmeg

Method:

1. Place all the ingredients in a food processor, except for chocolate, pulse for 2 minutes until combined.
2. Shape the mixture into 1-inch balls and place the balls on a cookie sheet lined with wax paper.
3. Place chocolate in a heatproof bowl, microwave for 2 minutes until it has melted, stirring every 30 seconds.
4. Pour the melted chocolate in a piping bag, drizzle it over prepared balls, refrigerate for 30 minutes until chocolate has hardened, and then serve.

Nutrition Value:
Calories: 111 Cal; Fat: 2 g; Carbs: 23 g; Protein: 1 g; Fiber: 2 g

Chocolate Cookies

Preparation time: 40 minutes; Cooking time: 5 minutes; Servings: 4
Ingredients:

- 1/2 cup coconut oil
- 1 cup agave syrup
- 1/2 cup cocoa powder
- 1/2 teaspoon salt
- 2 cups peanuts, chopped
- 1 cup peanut butter
- 2 cups sunflower seeds

Method:

1. Take a small saucepan, place it over medium heat, add the first three ingredients, and cook for 3 minutes until melted.
2. Boil the mixture for 1 minute, then remove the pan from heat and stir in salt and butter until smooth.
3. Fold in nuts and seeds until combined, then drop the mixture in the form of molds onto the baking sheet lined with wax paper and refrigerate for 30 minutes.
4. Serve straight away.

Nutrition Value:
Calories: 148 Cal; Fat: 7.4 g; Carbs: 20 g; Protein: 1.5 g; Fiber: 0.6 g

Peanut Butter Mousse

Preparation time: 50 minutes; Cooking time: 0 minute; Servings: 5
Ingredients:

- 3 Tablespoons agave nectar
- 14 ounces coconut milk, unsweetened, chilled
- 4 Tablespoons creamy peanut butter, salted

Method:

1. Separate coconut milk and its solid, then add solid from coconut milk into the bowl and beat for 45 seconds until fluffy.
2. Then beat in remaining ingredients until smooth, refrigerate for 45 minutes and serve.

Nutrition Value:
Calories: 270 Cal; Fat: 20 g; Carbs: 19 g; Protein: 5 g; Fiber: 1 g

Chocolate Peanut Butter Bars

Preparation time: 1 hour and 15 minutes; Cooking time: 5 minutes; Servings: 4
Ingredients:
For the Bars:
- 2½ cups puffed brown rice cereal
- ¼ teaspoon salt
- 1/3 cup maple syrup
- 2 tablespoons coconut oil
- ½ cup peanut butter

For the Chocolate Topping:
- 6 ounces dark chocolate, chopped
- 2 tablespoons peanut butter

For Garnish:
- 1 teaspoon flaky sea salt
- ¼ cup chopped roasted peanuts

Method:
1. Take a saucepan, place it over medium-low heat, add salt, butter, coconut oil, and maple syrup, whisk well and bring the mixture to a boil.
2. Then simmer the mixture for 3 minutes, whisking continuously, and remove the pan from heat.
3. Place cereal in a bowl, pour prepared butter syrup over it, and stir until combined and completely coated.
4. Take an 8 by 8 inched baking pan, line it with parchment paper, grease with oil, pour cereal mixture in it and spread and press the mixture evenly and then let the mixture stand for 30 minutes.
5. Prepare the chocolate topping, and for this, place its ingredients in a heatproof bowl and microwave for 2 minutes until chocolate has melted, stirring every 30 seconds.
6. Drizzle chocolate over firmed bars, sprinkle with salt, garnish with peanuts, refrigerate for 30 minutes, then cut it into sixteen bars and serve.

Nutrition Value:
Calories: 210 Cal; Fat: 8 g; Carbs: 26 g; Protein: 11 g; Fiber: 3 g

Mint Chocolate Chip Cheesecake

Preparation time: 5 hours and 15 minutes; Cooking time: 0 minute; Servings: 6
Ingredients:
For the Crust:
- 7.5 ounces hazelnuts
- 2 tablespoons cocoa powder
- 3.5 ounces dates, pitted
- 1.5 ounces dark chocolate, melted
- 1/8 teaspoon salt
- 1 tablespoon coconut oil, melted

For the Mint Layer:
- ½ cup spinach leaves
- 7 ounces cashew nuts, soaked in warm water for 10 minutes
- 1/3 cup coconut oil, melted
- 1 teaspoon vanilla extract, unsweetened
- 1/4 cup maple syrup
- 3 teaspoons mint extract, unsweetened

Method:
1. Prepare the crust, and for this, place all its ingredients in a food processor and pulse for 3 to 5 minutes until the thick paste comes together.
2. Take a cake tin, line it with baking paper, pour crust mixture in it and spread and press the mixture evenly in the bottom, and freeze until required.
3. Prepare mint layer and for this, drain cashews, transfer them into a food processor, add remaining ingredients, and pulse for 8 minutes until smooth.

4. Pour the creamy mint mixture into prepared crust, smooth the top and freeze for 4 hours until set.
5. Decorate the cake with mint leaves, cut it into slices, and then serve.

Nutrition Value:
Calories: 274.2 Cal; Fat: 12.5 g; Carbs: 32.1 g; Protein: 8.8 g; Fiber: 0.6 g

Chocolate Tart

Preparation time: 3 hours and 15 minutes; Cooking time: 0 minute; Servings: 8
Ingredients:
For the Crust:
- 1 cup almonds
- 2 tablespoons coconut oil
- ¼ teaspoon agave nectar
- 3 dates, pitted, soaked in warm water, drained
- 1 tablespoon cacao powder

For the Filling:
- 1 1/2 cups of soaked cashews
- 1/2 cup, plus 2 tablespoons water
- 1/2 cup, plus 2 tablespoons agave nectar
- 1/2 cup coconut oil
- 1/2 teaspoon vanilla
- 1/4 teaspoon Himalayan pink salt
- 1 cup raw cacao powder
- 2 tablespoons carob powder
- A handful of goji berries

Method:
1. Prepare the crust, and for this, place all its ingredients in a food processor and pulse for 3 to 5 minutes until the thick paste comes together.
2. Take a tart pan, pour crust mixture in it and spread and press the mixture evenly in the bottom and sides, and freeze until required.
3. Prepare the filling, and for this, place all its ingredients in a food processor and pulse for 3 minutes until smooth.
4. Pour the filling into the prepared tart, smooth the top and freeze for 3 hours until set.
5. Cut tart into slices and then serve.

Nutrition Value:
Calories: 485 Cal; Fat: 31 g; Carbs: 41 g; Protein: 9.7 g; Fiber: 8.1 g

Coconut Lemon Tart

Preparation time: 3 hours and 15 minutes; Cooking time: 10 minutes; Servings: 8
Ingredients:
For the Crust:
- 1/2 cup shredded coconut, unsweetened
- 1/2 cup almonds
- 1/2 cup pecans
- 1/2 cup dates

For the Filling:
- 1/2 tablespoon lemon zest
- 2 tablespoons cornstarch
- 1/2 cup agave nectar
- 1 1/2 cups and 2 tablespoons lemon juice
- 1/2 teaspoon agar powder
- 7.5 ounces coconut cream
- 1/4 cup water

Method:
1. Prepare the crust, and for this, place all its ingredients in a food processor and pulse for 3 to 5 minutes until the thick paste comes together.
2. Take a 10-inch pie pan, dust it lightly with coconut, pour crust mixture in it and spread and press the mixture evenly in the bottom and sides, and freeze until required.

3. Prepare the filling and for this, place a saucepan, place it over medium-low heat, add all the ingredients of filling, and whisk well and simmer for 10 minutes until the filling has thickened, whisking constantly.
4. Let filling cool for 5 minutes, pour the filling into the prepared tart, smooth the top and freeze for 3 hours until set.
5. Cut tart into slices and then serve.

Nutrition Value:
Calories: 249 Cal; Fat: 15 g; Carbs: 28 g; Protein: 2.8 g; Fiber: 1 g

Chocolate Espresso Pie

Preparation time: 3 hours and 20 minutes; Cooking time: 0 minute; Servings: 12
Ingredients:
For the Crust:
- 1/2 cup shredded coconut, unsweetened
- 1 1/2 cup dates, pitted
- 1/2 cup almonds
- 2 teaspoons cacao powder
- 1/4 cup maple syrup
- 3 tablespoons coconut oil

For the Filling:
- 3 dates, pitted
- 1 1/2 cup soaked cashews
- 1 tablespoon and 1 teaspoon espresso beans
- 3 tablespoons maple syrup
- 1 tablespoon and 1 teaspoon cacao powder
- 1/4 cup brewed coffee
- 1/2 cup cold water

Method:
1. Prepare the crust, and for this, place all its ingredients in a food processor and pulse for 3 to 5 minutes until the thick paste comes together.
2. Take an 8-inch cake pan, grease it with oil, pour crust mixture in it and spread and press the mixture evenly in the bottom and freeze until required.
3. Prepare the filling, and for this, place cashews in a food processor, pour in water, and pulse for 2 minutes until smooth.
4. Add dates, maple syrup, espresso beans, cocoa, and coffee, and blend until just mixed.
5. Pour the filling into prepared pan, smooth the top and freeze for 3 hours until set.
6. Cut pie into slices and then serve.

Nutrition Value:
Calories: 614 Cal; Fat: 31 g; Carbs: 77 g; Protein: 10 g; Fiber: 18 g

Chocolate Banana Cream Cake

Preparation time: 6 hours and 15 minutes; Cooking time: 0 minute; Servings: 4
Ingredients:
For the Crust:
- 2 tablespoons coconut cream
- 2 tablespoons coconut flour
- 1/8 teaspoon sea salt
- 1 1 tablespoon xylitol sweetener
- 1/8 teaspoon cinnamon
- 1 tablespoon almond butter

For the Banana Layer:
- 1 banana, sliced

For the Chocolate Cream Layer:
- 1 tablespoon cacao powder
- 1/8 teaspoon sea salt
- 1/8 teaspoon cinnamon
- 1 tablespoon xylitol sweetener
- 4 tablespoons melted coconut oil
- 2 tablespoons coconut milk
- For the Coconut Whipped Cream:
- 1 tablespoon xylitol sweetener

- 14 ounces coconut cream, chilled

For Toppings:
- Cacao nibs as needed
- Cinnamon powder as needed

Method:
1. Prepare the crust and for this, take a bowl, place all its ingredients in it and whisk until well combined.
2. Take a small tin, line it with parchment paper, place crust mixture in it, spread and press the mixture evenly in the bottom, then layer with banana and freeze until required.
3. Prepare the chocolate cream and for this, take a bowl, place all its ingredients in it and whisk until well combined.
4. Pour the chocolate cream over the banana layer in the prepared cake tin and return to the freezer until set.
5. Then prepare the coconut whipped cream and for this, take a bowl, place cream in it, beat at high speed until thickened, and then beat in sugar until mixed.
6. When cake has set, spread whipped cream on top, continue freezing until set and then slice to serve.

Nutrition Value:
Calories: 329 Cal; Fat: 29.5 g; Carbs: 15.3 g; Protein: 3.7 g; Fiber: 2 g

Peanut Butter Cheesecake

Preparation time: 5 minutes; Cooking time: 15 minutes; Servings: 8

Ingredients:

For the Crust:
- 1 cup dates, pitted, soaked in warm water for 10 minutes in water, drained
- 1/4 cup cocoa powder
- 3 Tablespoons melted coconut oil
- 1 cup rolled oats

For the Filling:
- 1 banana
- 1 1/2 cup cashews, soaked, drained
- 1/2 cup dates, pitted, soaked, drained
- 1/4 cup coconut oil
- 1 teaspoon vanilla extract, unsweetened
- 1/4 cup agave
- 1 cup peanut butter
- 1/2 cup coconut milk, chilled
- 1 tablespoon almond milk

For Garnish
- 2 tablespoons chocolate chips
- 2 tablespoons shredded coconut, unsweetened

Method:
1. Prepare the crust, and for this, place all its ingredients in a food processor and pulse for 3 to 5 minutes until the thick paste comes together.
2. Take a pie pan, grease it with oil, pour crust mixture in it and spread and press the mixture evenly in the bottom and along the sides, and freeze until required.
3. Prepare the filling and for this, place all its ingredients in a food processor, and pulse for 2 minutes until smooth.
4. Pour the filling into prepared pan, smooth the top, sprinkle chocolate chips and coconut on top and freeze for 4 hours until set.
5. Cut cake into slices and then serve.

Nutrition Value:
Calories: 509 Cal; Fat: 32.2 g; Carbs: 47.6 g; Protein: 11 g; Fiber: 3.7 g

Key Lime Pie

Preparation time: 3 hours and 15 minutes; Cooking time: 0 minute; Servings: 12
Ingredients:
For the Crust:
- ¾ cup coconut flakes, unsweetened
- 1 cup dates, soaked in warm water for 10 minutes in water, drained

For the Filling:
- ¾ cup of coconut meat
- 1 ½ avocado, peeled, pitted
- 2 tablespoons key lime juice
- ¼ cup agave

Method:
1. Prepare the crust, and for this, place all its ingredients in a food processor and pulse for 3 to 5 minutes until the thick paste comes together.
2. Take an 8-inch pie pan, grease it with oil, pour crust mixture in it and spread and press the mixture evenly in the bottom and along the sides, and freeze until required.
3. Prepare the filling and for this, place all its ingredients in a food processor, and pulse for 2 minutes until smooth.
4. Pour the filling into prepared pan, smooth the top, and freeze for 3 hours until set.
5. Cut pie into slices and then serve.

Nutrition Value:
Calories: 213 Cal; Fat: 10 g; Carbs: 29 g; Protein: 1200 g; Fiber: 6 g

Chocolate Mint Grasshopper Pie

Preparation time: 4 hours and 15 minutes; Cooking time: 0 minute; Servings: 4
Ingredients:
For the Crust:
- 1 cup dates, soaked in warm water for 10 minutes in water, drained
- 1/8 teaspoons salt
- 1/2 cup pecans
- 1 teaspoons cinnamon
- 1/2 cup walnuts

For the Filling:
- ½ cup mint leaves
- 2 cups of cashews, soaked in warm water for 10 minutes in water, drained
- 2 tablespoons coconut oil
- 1/4 cup and 2 tablespoons of agave
- 1/4 teaspoons spirulina
- 1/4 cup water

Method:
1. Prepare the crust, and for this, place all its ingredients in a food processor and pulse for 3 to 5 minutes until the thick paste comes together.
2. Take a 6-inch springform pan, grease it with oil, place crust mixture in it and spread and press the mixture evenly in the bottom and along the sides, and freeze until required.
3. Prepare the filling and for this, place all its ingredients in a food processor, and pulse for 2 minutes until smooth.
4. Pour the filling into prepared pan, smooth the top, and freeze for 4 hours until set.
5. Cut pie into slices and then serve.

Nutrition Value:
Calories: 223.7 Cal; Fat: 7.5 g; Carbs: 36 g; Protein: 2.5 g; Fiber: 1 g

Peanut Butter Energy Bars

Preparation time: 5 hours and 15 minutes; Cooking time: 5 minutes; Servings: 16
Ingredients:
- 1/2 cup cranberries
- 12 Medjool dates, pitted
- 1 cup roasted almond
- 1 tablespoon chia seeds

- 1 1/2 cups oats
- 1/8 teaspoon salt
- 1/4 cup and 1 tablespoon agave nectar
- 1/2 teaspoon vanilla extract, unsweetened
- 1/3 cup and 1 tablespoon peanut butter, unsalted
- 2 tablespoons water

Method:
1. Place an almond in a food processor, pulse until chopped, and then transfer into a large bowl.
2. Add dates into the food processor along with oats, pour in water, and pulse for dates are chopped.
3. Add dates mixture into the almond mixture, add chia seeds and berries and stir until mixed.
4. Take a saucepan, place it over medium heat, add remaining butter and remaining ingredients, stir and cook for 5 minutes until mixture reaches to a liquid consistency.
5. Pour the butter mixture over date mixture, and then stir until well combined.
6. Take an 8 by 8 inches baking tray, line it with parchment sheet, add date mixture in it, spread and press it evenly and refrigerate for 5 hours.
7. Cut it into sixteen bars and serve.

Nutrition Value:
Calories: 187 Cal; Fat: 7.5 g; Carbs: 27.2 g; Protein: 4.7 g; Fiber: 2 g

Black Bean Brownie Pops

Preparation time: 45 minutes; Cooking time: 2 minutes; Servings: 12
Ingredients:
- 3/4 cup chocolate chips
- 15 ounce cooked black beans
- 1 tablespoon maple syrup
- 5 tablespoons cacao powder
- 1/8 teaspoon sea salt
- 2 tablespoons sunflower seed butter

Method:
1. Place black beans in a food processor, add remaining ingredients, except for chocolate, and pulse for 2 minutes until combined and the dough starts to come together.
2. Shape the dough into twelve balls, arrange them on a baking sheet lined with parchment paper, then insert a toothpick into each ball and refrigerate for 20 minutes.
3. Then meat chocolate in the microwave for 2 minutes, and dip brownie pops in it until covered.
4. Return the pops into the refrigerator for 10 minutes until set and then serve.

Nutrition Value:
Calories: 130 Cal; Fat: 6 g; Carbs: 17 g; Protein: 4 g; Fiber: 1 g

Lemon Cashew Tart

Preparation time: 3 hours and 15 minutes; Cooking time: 0 minute; Servings: 12
Ingredients:
For the Crust:
- 1 cup almonds
- 4 dates, pitted, soaked in warm water for 10 minutes in water, drained
- 1/8 teaspoon crystal salt
- 1 teaspoon vanilla extract, unsweetened

For the Cream:
- 1 cup cashews, soaked in warm water for 10 minutes in water, drained
- 1/4 cup water
- 1/4 cup coconut nectar
- 1 teaspoon coconut oil
- 1 teaspoon vanilla extract, unsweetened
- 1 lemon, Juiced

- 1/8 teaspoon crystal salt

For the Topping:
- Shredded coconut as needed

Method:
1. Prepare the cream and for this, place all its ingredients in a food processor, pulse for 2 minutes until smooth, and then refrigerate for 1 hour.
2. Then prepare the crust, and for this, place all its ingredients in a food processor and pulse for 3 to 5 minutes until the thick paste comes together.
3. Take a tart pan, grease it with oil, place crust mixture in it and spread and press the mixture evenly in the bottom and along the sides, and freeze until required.
4. Pour the filling into the prepared tart, smooth the top, and refrigerate for 2 hours until set.
5. Cut tart into slices and then serve.

Nutrition Value:
Calories: 166 Cal; Fat: 10 g; Carbs: 15 g; Protein: 5 g; Fiber: 1 g

Peppermint Oreos

Preparation time: 2 hours; Cooking time: 0 minute; Servings: 12
Ingredients:
For the Cookies:
- 1 cup dates
- 2/3 cup brazil nuts
- 3 tablespoons carob powder
- 2/3 cup almonds
- 1/8 teaspoon sea salt
- 3 tablespoons water

For the Crème:
- 2 tablespoons almond butter
- 1 cup coconut chips
- 2 tablespoons melted coconut oil
- 1 cup coconut shreds
- 3 drops of peppermint oil
- 1/2 teaspoon vanilla powder

For the Dark Chocolate:
- 3/4 cup cacao powder
- 1/2 cup date paste
- 1/3 cup coconut oil, melted

Method:
1. Prepare the cookies, and for this, place all its ingredients in a food processor and pulse for 3 to 5 minutes until the dough comes together.
2. Then place the dough between two parchment sheets, roll the dough, then cut out twenty-four cookies of the desired shape and freeze until solid.
3. Prepare the crème, and for this, place all its ingredients in a food processor and pulse for 2 minutes until smooth.
4. When cookies have harden, sandwich crème in between the cookies by placing dollops on top of a cookie and then pressing it with another cookie.
5. Freeze the cookies for 30 minutes and in the meantime, prepare chocolate and for this, place all its ingredients in a bowl and whisk until combined.
6. Dip frouncesen cookie sandwich into chocolate, at least two times, and then freeze for another 30 minutes until chocolate has hardened.
7. Serve straight away.

Nutrition Value:
Calories: 470 Cal; Fat: 32 g; Carbs: 51 g; Protein: 7 g; Fiber: 12 g

Caramel Brownie Slice

Preparation time: 4 hours; Cooking time: 0 minute; Servings: 16
Ingredients:

For the Base:
- ¼ cup dried figs
- 1 cup dried dates
- ½ cup cacao powder
- ½ cup pecans
- ½ cup walnuts

For the Caramel Layer:
- ¼ teaspoons sea salt
- 2 cups dried dates, soaked in water for 1 hour
- 3 Tablespoons coconut oil
- 5 Tablespoons water

For the Chocolate Topping:
- 1/3 cup agave nectar
- ½ cup cacao powder
- ¼ cup of coconut oil

Method:
1. Prepare the base, and for this, place all its ingredients in a food processor and pulse for 3 to 5 minutes until the thick paste comes together.
2. Take an 8 by 8 inches baking dish, grease it with oil, place base mixture in it and spread and press the mixture evenly in the bottom, and freeze until required.
3. Prepare the caramel layer, and for this, place all its ingredients in a food processor and pulse for 2 minutes until smooth.
4. Pour the caramel into the prepared baking dish, smooth the top and freeze for 20 minutes.
5. Then prepare the topping and for this, place all its ingredients in a food processor, and pulse for 1 minute until combined.
6. Gently spread the chocolate mixture over the caramel layer and then freeze for 3 hours until set.
7. Serve straight away.

Nutrition Value:
Calories: 128 Cal; Fat: 12 g; Carbs: 16 g; Protein: 2 g; Fiber: 3 g

Snickers Pie

Preparation time: 4 hours; Cooking time: 0 minute; Servings: 16
Ingredients:
For the Crust:
- 12 Medjool dates, pitted
- 1 cup dried coconut, unsweetened
- 5 tablespoons cocoa powder
- 1/2 teaspoon sea salt
- 1 teaspoon vanilla extract, unsweetened
- 1 cup almonds

For the Caramel Layer:
- 10 Medjool dates, pitted, soaked for 10 minutes in warm water, drained
- 2 teaspoons vanilla extract, unsweetened
- 3 teaspoons coconut oil
- 3 tablespoons almond butter, unsalted

For the Peanut Butter Mousse:
- 3/4 cup peanut butter
- 2 tablespoons maple syrup
- 1/2 teaspoon vanilla extract, unsweetened
- 1/8 teaspoon sea salt
- 28 ounces coconut milk, chilled

Method:
1. Prepare the crust, and for this, place all its ingredients in a food processor and pulse for 3 to 5 minutes until the thick paste comes together.
2. Take a baking pan, line it with parchment paper, place crust mixture in it and spread and press the mixture evenly in the bottom, and freeze until required.

3. Prepare the caramel layer, and for this, place all its ingredients in a food processor and pulse for 2 minutes until smooth.
4. Pour the caramel on top of the prepared crust, smooth the top and freeze for 30 minutes until set.
5. Prepare the mousse and for this, separate coconut milk and its solid, then add solid from coconut milk into a food processor, add remaining ingredients and then pulse for 1 minute until smooth.
6. Top prepared mousse over caramel layer, and then freeze for 3 hours until set.
7. Serve straight away.

Nutrition Value:
Calories: 456 Cal; Fat: 33 g; Carbs: 37 g; Protein: 8.3 g; Fiber: 5 g

Double Chocolate Orange Cheesecake

Preparation time: 4 hours; Cooking time: 0 minute; Servings: 12
Ingredients:
For the Base:
- 9 Medjool dates, pitted
- 1/3 cup Brazil nuts
- 2 tablespoons maple syrup
- 1/3 cup walnuts
- 2 tablespoons water
- 3 tablespoons cacao powder

For the Chocolate Cheesecake:
- 1/2 cup cacao powder
- 1 1/2 cups cashews, soaked for 10 minutes in warm water, drained
- 1/3 cup liquid coconut oil
- 1 teaspoon vanilla extract, unsweetened
- 1/3 cup maple syrup
- 1/3 cup water

For the Orange Cheesecake:
- 2 oranges, juiced
- 1/4 cup maple syrup
- 1 cup cashews, soaked for 10 minutes in warm water, drained
- 1 teaspoon vanilla extract, unsweetened
- 2 tablespoons coconut butter
- 1/2 cup liquid coconut oil
- 2 oranges, zested
- 4 drops of orange essential oil

For the Chocolate Topping:
- 3 tablespoons cacao powder
- 3 drops of orange essential oil
- 2 tablespoons liquid coconut oil
- 3 tablespoons maple syrup

Method:
1. Prepare the base, and for this, place all its ingredients in a food processor and pulse for 3 to 5 minutes until the thick paste comes together.
2. Take a cake tin, place crust mixture in it and spread and press the mixture evenly in the bottom, and freeze until required.
3. Prepare the chocolate cheesecake, and for this, place all its ingredients in a food processor and pulse for 2 minutes until smooth.
4. Pour the chocolate cheesecake mixture on top of the prepared base, smooth the top and freeze for 20 minutes until set.
5. Then prepare the orange cheesecake and for this, place all its ingredients in a food processor, and pulse for 2 minutes until smooth
6. Top orange cheesecake mixture over chocolate cheesecake, and then freeze for 3 hours until hardened.
7. Then prepare the chocolate topping and for this, take a bowl, add all the ingredients in it and stir until well combined.

8. Spread chocolate topping over the top, freeze the cake for 10 minutes until the topping has hardened and then slice to serve.

Nutrition Value:

Calories: 508 Cal; Fat: 34.4 g; Carbs: 44 g; Protein: 8 g; Fiber: 3 g

Coconut Ice Cream Cheesecake

Preparation time: 3 hours; Cooking time: 0 minute; Servings: 4

Ingredients:

For the First Layer:

- 1 cup mixed nuts
- 3/4 cup dates, soaked for 10 minutes in warm water
- 2 tablespoons almond milk

For the Second Layer:

- 1 medium avocado, diced
- 1 cup cashew nuts, soaked for 10 minutes in warm water
- 3 cups strawberries, sliced
- 1 tablespoon chia seeds, soaked in 3 tablespoons soy milk
- 1/2 cup agave
- 1 cup melted coconut oil
- 1/2 cup shredded coconut
- 1 lime, juiced

Method:

1. Prepare the first layer, and for this, place all its ingredients in a food processor and pulse for 3 to 5 minutes until the thick paste comes together.
2. Take a springform pan, place crust mixture in it and spread and press the mixture evenly in the bottom, and freeze until required.
3. Prepare the second layer, and for this, place all its ingredients in a food processor and pulse for 2 minutes until smooth.
4. Pour the second layer on top of the first layer, smooth the top, and freeze for 4 hours until hard.
5. Serve straight away.

Nutrition Value:

Calories: 411.3 Cal; Fat: 30.8 g; Carbs: 28.7 g; Protein: 4.7 g; Fiber: 1.3 g

Matcha Coconut Cream Pie

Preparation time: 5 minutes; Cooking time: 0 minute; Servings: 4

Ingredients:

For the Crust:

- 1/2 cup ground flaxseed
- 3/4 cup shredded dried coconut
- 1 cup Medjool dates, pitted
- 3/4 cup dehydrated buckwheat groats
- 1/4 teaspoons sea salt

For the Filling:

- 1 cup dried coconut flakes
- 4 cups of coconut meat
- 1/4 cup and 2 Tablespoons coconut nectar
- 1/2 Tablespoons vanilla extract, unsweetened
- 1/4 teaspoons sea salt
- 2/3 cup and 2 Tablespoons coconut butter
- 1 Tablespoons matcha powder
- 1/2 cup coconut water

Method:

1. Prepare the crust, and for this, place all its ingredients in a food processor and pulse for 3 to 5 minutes until the thick paste comes together.

2. Take a 6-inch springform pan, grease it with oil, place crust mixture in it and spread and press the mixture evenly in the bottom and along the sides, and freeze until required.
3. Prepare the filling and for this, place all its ingredients in a food processor, and pulse for 2 minutes until smooth.
4. Pour the filling into prepared pan, smooth the top, and freeze for 4 hours until set.
5. Cut pie into slices and then serve.

Nutrition Value:
Calories: 209 Cal; Fat: 18 g; Carbs: 10 g; Protein: 1 g; Fiber: 2 g

Chocolate Peanut Butter Cake

Preparation time: 5 minutes; Cooking time: 0 minute; Servings: 8
Ingredients:
For the Base:
- 1 tablespoon ground flaxseeds
- 1/8 cup millet
- 3/4 cup peanuts

- 1/4 cup and 2 tablespoons shredded coconut unsweetened
- 1 teaspoon hemp oil
- 1/2 cup flake oats

For the Date Layer:
- 1 tablespoon ground flaxseed
- 1 cup dates
- 1 tablespoon hemp hearts

- 2 tablespoons coconut
- 3 tablespoons cacao

For the Chocolate Layer:
- 3/4 cup coconut flour
- 2 tablespoons and 2 teaspoons cacao
- 1 tablespoon maple syrup
- 8 tablespoons warm water

- 2 tablespoons coconut oil
- 1/2 cup coconut milk
- 2 tablespoons ground flaxseed

For the Chocolate Topping:
- 7 ounces coconut cream
- 2 1/2 tablespoons cacao

- 1 teaspoon agave

For Assembly:
- 1/2 cup almond butter

Method:
1. Prepare the crust, and for this, place all its ingredients in a food processor and pulse for 3 to 5 minutes until the thick paste comes together.
2. Take a loaf tin, grease it with oil, place crust mixture in it and spread and press the mixture evenly in the bottom and along the sides, and freeze until required.
3. Prepare the date layer, and for this, place all its ingredients in a food processor and pulse for 2 minutes until smooth.
4. Prepare the chocolate layer, and for this, place flour and flax in a bowl and stir until combined.
5. Take a saucepan, add remaining ingredients, stir until mixed and cook for 5 minutes until melted and smooth.
6. Add it into the flour mixture, stir until dough comes together, and set aside.
7. Prepare the chocolate topping, place all its ingredients in a food processor and pulse for 3 to 5 minutes until smooth.
8. Press date layer into the base layer, refrigerate for 1 hour, then press chocolate layer on its top, finish with chocolate topping, refrigerate for 3 hours and serve.

Nutrition Value:
Calories: 390 Cal; Fat: 24.3 g; Carbs: 35 g; Protein: 10.3 g; Fiber: 2 g

Chocolate Raspberry Brownies

Preparation time: 4 hours; Cooking time: 0 minute; Servings: 4
Ingredients:
For the Chocolate Brownie Base:
- 12 Medjool Dates, pitted
- 3/4 cup oat flour
- 3/4 cup almond meal
- 3 tablespoons cacao
- 1 teaspoon vanilla extract, unsweetened
- 1/8 teaspoon sea salt
- 3 tablespoons water
- 1/2 cup pecans, chopped

For the Raspberry Cheesecake:
- 3/4 cup cashews, soaked, drained
- 6 tablespoons agave nectar
- 1/2 cup raspberries
- 1 teaspoon vanilla extract, unsweetened
- 1 lemon, juiced
- 6 tablespoons liquid coconut oil

For the Chocolate Coating:
- 2 1/2 tablespoons cacao powder
- 3 3/4 tablespoons coconut Oil
- 2 tablespoons maple syrup
- 1/8 teaspoon sea salt

Method:
1. Prepare the crust, and for this, place all its ingredients in a food processor and pulse for 3 to 5 minutes until the thick paste comes together.
2. Take a 6-inch springform pan, grease it with oil, place crust mixture in it and spread and press the mixture evenly in the bottom and along the sides, and freeze until required.
3. Prepare the cheesecake topping, and for this, place all its ingredients in a food processor and pulse for 2 minutes until smooth.
4. Pour the filling into prepared pan, smooth the top, and freeze for 8 hours until solid.
5. Prepare the chocolate coating and for this, whisk together all its ingredients until smooth, drizzle on top of the cake and then serve.

Nutrition Value:
Calories: 371 Cal; Fat: 42.4 g; Carbs: 42 g; Protein: 5.5 g; Fiber: 2 g

Brownie Batter

Preparation time: 5 minutes; Cooking time: 0 minute; Servings: 4
Ingredients:
- 4 Medjool dates, pitted, soaked in warm water
- 1.5 ounces chocolate, unsweetened, melted
- 2 tablespoons maple syrup
- 4 tablespoons tahini
- ½ teaspoon vanilla extract, unsweetened
- 1 tablespoon cocoa powder, unsweetened
- 1/8 teaspoon sea salt
- 1/8 teaspoon espresso powder
- 2 to 4 tablespoons almond milk, unsweetened

Method:
1. Place all the ingredients in a food processor and process for 2 minutes until combined.
2. Set aside until required.

Nutrition Value:
Calories: 44 Cal; Fat: 1 g; Carbs: 6 g; Protein: 2 g; Fiber: 0 g

Strawberry Mousse

Preparation time: 5 minutes; Cooking time: 15 minutes; Servings: 4
Ingredients:

- 8 ounces coconut milk, unsweetened
- 2 tablespoons honey
- 5 strawberries

Method:
1. Place berries in a blender and pulse until the smooth mixture comes together.
2. Place milk in a bowl, whisk until whipped, and then add remaining ingredients and stir until combined.
3. Refrigerate the mousse for 10 minutes and then serve.

Nutrition Value:
Calories: 145 Cal; Fat: 23 g; Carbs: 15 g; Protein: 5 g; Fiber: 1 g

Blueberry Mousse

Preparation time: 20 minutes; Cooking time: 0 minute; Servings: 2
Ingredients:
- 1 cup wild blueberries
- 1 cup cashews, soaked for 10 minutes, drained
- 1/2 teaspoon berry powder
- 2 tablespoons coconut oil, melted
- 1 tablespoon lemon juice
- 1 teaspoon vanilla extract, unsweetened
- 1/4 cup hot water

Method:
1. Place all the ingredients in a food processor and process for 2 minutes until smooth.
2. Set aside until required.

Nutrition Value:
Calories: 433 Cal; Fat: 32.3 g; Carbs: 44 g; Protein: 5.1 g; Fiber: 0 g

Chapter 9: Homemade Basics, Sauces, and Condiments

Green Goddess Hummus

Preparation time: 5 minutes; Cooking time: 0 minute; Servings: 6
Ingredients:

- ¼ cup tahini
- ¼ cup lemon juice
- 2 tablespoons olive oil
- ½ cup chopped parsley
- ¼ cup chopped basil
- 3 tablespoons chopped chives
- 1 large clove of garlic, peeled, chopped
- ½ teaspoon salt
- 15-ounce cooked chickpeas
- 2 tablespoons water

Method:
1. Place all the ingredients in the order in a food processor or blender and then pulse for 3 to 5 minutes at high speed until the thick mixture comes together.
2. Tip the hummus in a bowl and then serve.

Nutrition Value:
Calories: 110.4 Cal; Fat: 6 g; Carbs: 11.5 g; Protein: 4.8 g; Fiber: 2.6 g

Garlic, Parmesan and White Bean Hummus

Preparation time: 5 minutes; Cooking time: 0 minute; Servings: 6
Ingredients:

- 4 cloves of garlic, peeled
- 12 ounces cooked white beans
- 1/8 teaspoon salt
- ½ lemon, zested
- 1 tablespoon lemon juice
- 1 tablespoon olive oil
- 3 tablespoon water
- 1/4 cup grated Parmesan cheese

Method:
1. Place all the ingredients in the order in a food processor or blender and then pulse for 3 to 5 minutes at high speed until the thick mixture comes together.
2. Tip the hummus in a bowl and then serve.

Nutrition Value:
Calories: 90 Cal; Fat: 7 g; Carbs: 5 g; Protein: 2 g; Fiber: 1 g

Tomato Jam

Preparation time: 10 minutes; Cooking time: 20 minutes; Servings: 16
Ingredients:

- 2 pounds tomatoes
- ¼ teaspoon. ground black pepper
- ½ teaspoon. salt
- ¼ cup coconut sugar
- ½ teaspoon. white wine vinegar
- ¼ teaspoon. smoked paprika

Method:
1. Place a large pot filled with water over medium heat, bring it to boil, then add tomatoes and boil for 1 minute.
2. Transfer tomatoes to a bowl containing chilled water, let them stand for 2 minutes, and then peel them by hand.
3. Cut the tomatoes, remove and discard seeds, then chop tomatoes and place them in a large pot.
4. Sprinkle sugar over coconut, stir until mixed and let it stand for 10 minutes.
5. Then place the pot over medium-high heat, cook for 15 minutes, then add remaining ingredients except for vinegar and cook for 10 minutes until thickened.
6. Remove pot from heat, stir in vinegar and serve.

Nutrition Value:
Calories: 17.6 Cal; Fat: 1.3 g; Carbs: 1.5 g; Protein: 0.2 g; Fiber: 0.3 g

Kale and Walnut Pesto

Preparation time: 5 minutes; Cooking time: 10 minutes; Servings: 4

Ingredients:

- 1/2 bunch kale, leaves chop
- 1/2 cup chopped walnuts
- 2 cloves of garlic, peeled
- 1/4 cup nutritional yeast
- ½ of lemon, juiced
- 1/4 cup olive oil
- ¼ teaspoon. ground black pepper
- 1/3 teaspoon. salt

Method:

1. Place a large pot filled with water over medium heat, bring it to boil, then add kale and boil for 5 minutes until tender.
2. Drain kale, then transfer it in a blender, add remaining ingredients and then pulse for 5 minutes until smooth.
3. Serve straight away.

Nutrition Value:
Calories: 344 Cal; Fat: 29 g; Carbs: 16 g; Protein: 9 g; Fiber: 6 g

Buffalo Chicken Dip

Preparation time: 5 minutes; Cooking time: 15 minutes; Servings: 4

Ingredients:

- 2 cups cashews
- 2 teaspoons garlic powder
- 1 1/2 teaspoons salt
- 2 teaspoons onion powder
- 3 tablespoons lemon juice
- 1 cup buffalo sauce
- 1 cup of water
- 14-ounce artichoke hearts, packed in water, drained

Method:

1. Switch on the oven, then set it to 375 degrees F and let it preheat.
2. Meanwhile, pour 3 cups of boiling water in a bowl, add cashews and let soak for 5 minutes.
3. Then drain the cashew, transfer them into the blender, pour in water, add lemon juice and all the seasoning and blend until smooth.
4. Add artichokes and buffalo sauce, process until chunky mixture comes together, and then transfer the dip to an ovenproof dish.
5. Bake for 20 minutes and then serve.

Nutrition Value:
Calories: 100 Cal; Fat: 100 g; Carbs: 100 g; Protein: 100 g; Fiber: 100 g

Barbecue Tahini Sauce

Preparation time: 5 minutes; Cooking time: 0 minute; Servings: 8

Ingredients:

- 6 tablespoons tahini
- 3/4 teaspoon garlic powder
- 1/8 teaspoon red chili powder
- 2 teaspoons maple syrup
- 1/4 teaspoon salt
- 3 teaspoons molasses
- 3 teaspoons apple cider vinegar
- 1/4 teaspoon liquid smoke
- 10 teaspoons tomato paste
- 1/2 cup water

Method:

1. Place all the ingredients in the order in a food processor or blender and then pulse for 3 to 5 minutes at high speed until smooth.

2. Tip the sauce in a bowl and then serve.

Nutrition Value:

Calories: 86 Cal; Fat: 5 g; Carbs: 7 g; Protein: 2 g; Fiber: 0 g

Vegan Ranch Dressing

Preparation time: 5 minutes; Cooking time: 0 minute; Servings: 16

Ingredients:

- 1/4 teaspoon. ground black pepper
- 2 teaspoon. chopped parsley
- 1/2 teaspoon. garlic powder
- 1 tablespoon chopped dill
- 1/2 teaspoon. onion powder
- 1 cup vegan mayonnaise
- 1/2 cup soy milk, unsweetened

Method:

1. Take a medium bowl, add all the ingredients in it and then whisk until combined.
2. Serve straight away

Nutrition Value:

Calories: 16 Cal; Fat: 9 g; Carbs: 0 g; Protein: 0 g; Fiber: 0 g

Cashew Yogurt

Preparation time: 12 hours and 5 minutes; Cooking time: 0 minute; Servings: 8

Ingredients:

- 3 probiotic supplements
- 2 2/3 cups cashews, unsalted , soaked in warm water for 15 minutes
- 1/4 teaspoon sea salt
- 4 tablespoon lemon juice
- 1 1/2 cup water

Method:

1. Drain the cashews, add them into the food processor, then add remaining ingredients, except for probiotic supplements, and pulse for 2 minutes until smooth.
2. Tip the mixture in a bowl, add probiotic supplements, stir until mixed, then cover the bowl with a cheesecloth and let it stand for 12 hours in a dark and cool room.
3. Serve straight away.

Nutrition Value:

Calories: 252 Cal; Fat: 19.8 g; Carbs: 14.1 g; Protein: 8.3 g; Fiber: 1.5 g

Nacho Cheese Sauce

Preparation time: 15 minutes; Cooking time: 5 minutes; Servings: 12

Ingredients:

- 2 cups cashews, unsalted , soaked in warm water for 15 minutes
- 2 teaspoons salt
- 1/2 cup nutritional yeast
- 1 teaspoon garlic powder
- 1/2 teaspoon smoked paprika
- 1/2 teaspoon red chili powder
- 1 teaspoon onion powder
- 2 teaspoons Sriracha
- 3 tablespoons lemon juice
- 4 cups water, divided

Method:

1. Drain the cashews, transfer them to a food processor, then add remaining ingredients, reserving 3 cups water, and, and pulse for 3 minutes until smooth.
2. Tip the mixture in a saucepan, place it over medium heat and cook for 3 to 5 minutes until the sauce has thickened and bubbling, whisking constantly.
3. When done, taste the sauce to adjust seasoning and then serve.

Nutrition Value:

Calories: 128 Cal; Fat: 10 g; Carbs: 8 g; Protein: 5 g; Fiber: 1 g

Thai Peanut Sauce

Preparation time: 10 minutes; Cooking time: 10 minutes; Servings: 4

Ingredients:

- 2 tablespoons ground peanut, and more for topping
- 2 tablespoons Thai red curry paste
- ½ teaspoon salt
- 1 tablespoon sugar
- 1/2 cup creamy peanut butter
- 2 tablespoons apple cider vinegar
- 3/4 cup coconut milk, unsweetened

Method:

1. Take a saucepan, place it over low heat, add all the ingredients, whisk well until combined, and then bring the sauce to simmer.
2. Then remove the pan from heat, top with ground peanuts, and serve.

Nutrition Value:

Calories: 397 Cal; Fat: 50 g; Carbs: 16 g; Protein: 26 g; Fiber: 4 g

Garlic Alfredo Sauce

Preparation time: 10 minutes; Cooking time: 5 minutes; Servings: 4

Ingredients:

- 1 1/2 cups cashews, unsalted , soaked in warm water for 15 minutes
- 6 cloves of garlic, peeled, minced
- 1/2 medium sweet onion, peeled, chopped
- 1 teaspoon salt
- 1/4 cup nutritional yeast
- 1 tablespoon lemon juice
- 2 tablespoons olive oil
- 2 cups almond milk, unsweetened
- 12 ounces fettuccine pasta, cooked, for serving

Method:

1. Take a small saucepan, place it over medium heat, add oil and when hot, add onion and garlic, and cook for 5 minutes until sauté.
2. Meanwhile, drain the cashews, transfer them into a food processor, add remaining ingredients including onion mixture, except for pasta, and pulse for 3 minutes until very smooth.
3. Pour the prepared sauce over pasta, toss until coated and serve.

Nutrition Value:

Calories: 439 Cal; Fat: 20 g; Carbs: 52 g; Protein: 15 g; Fiber: 4 g

Spicy Red Wine Tomato Sauce

Preparation time: 5 minutes; Cooking time: 1 hour; Servings: 4

Ingredients:

- 28 ounces puree of whole tomatoes, peeled
- 4 cloves of garlic, peeled
- 1 tablespoon dried basil
- ¼ teaspoon ground black pepper
- 1 tablespoon dried oregano
- ¼ teaspoon red pepper flakes
- 1 tablespoon dried sage
- 1 tablespoon dried thyme
- 3 teaspoon coconut sugar
- 1/2 of lemon, juice
- 1/4 cup red wine

Method:

1. Take a large saucepan, place it over medium heat, add tomatoes and remaining ingredients, stir and simmer for 1 hour or more until thickened and cooked.
2. Serve sauce over pasta.

Nutrition Value:

Calories: 110 Cal; Fat: 2.5 g; Carbs: 9 g; Protein: 2 g; Fiber: 2 g

Vodka Cream Sauce

Preparation time: 5 minutes; Cooking time: 5 minutes; Servings: 1

Ingredients:

- 1/4 cup cashews, unsalted , soaked in warm water for 15 minutes
- 24-ounce marinara sauce
- 2 tablespoons vodka
- 1/4 cup water

Method:

1. Drain the cashews, transfer them in a food processor, pour in water, and blend for 2 minutes until smooth.
2. Tip the mixture in a pot, stir in pasta sauce and vodka and simmer for 3 minutes over medium heat until done, stirring constantly.
3. Serve sauce over pasta.

Nutrition Value:

Calories: 207 Cal; Fat: 16 g; Carbs: 9.2 g; Protein: 2.4 g; Fiber: 4.3 g

Hot Sauce

Preparation time: 10 minutes; Cooking time: 15 minutes; Servings: 6

Ingredients:

- 4 Serrano peppers, destemmed
- 1/2 of medium white onion, chopped
- 1 medium carrot, chopped
- 10 habanero chilies, destemmed
- 6 cloves of garlic, unpeeled
- 2 teaspoons sea salt
- 1 cup apple cider vinegar
- 1/2 teaspoon brown rice syrup
- 1 cup of water

Method:

1. Take a skillet pan, place it medium heat, add garlic, and cook for 15 minutes until roasted, frequently turning garlic, set aside to cool.
2. Meanwhile, take a saucepan, place it over medium-low heat, add remaining ingredients in it, except for salt and syrup, stir and cook for 12 minutes until vegetables are tender.
3. When the garlic has roasted and cooled, peel them and add them to a food processor.
4. Then add cooked saucepan along with remaining ingredients, and pulse for 3 minutes until smooth.
5. Let sauce cool and then serve straight away

Nutrition Value:

Calories: 137 Cal; Fat: 0 g; Carbs: 30 g; Protein: 4 g; Fiber: 10 g

Hot Sauce

Preparation time: 5 minutes; Cooking time: 0 minute; Servings: 16

Ingredients:

- 4 cloves of garlic, peeled
- 15 Hot peppers, de-stemmed, chopped
- 1/2 teaspoon. coriander
- 1/2 teaspoon. sea salt
- 1/2 teaspoon. red chili powder
- 1/2 of lime, zested
- 1/4 teaspoon. cumin
- 1/2 lime, juiced
- 1 cup apple cider vinegar

Method:

1. Place all the ingredients in the order in a food processor or blender and then pulse for 3 to 5 minutes at high speed until smooth.
2. Tip the sauce in a bowl and then serve.

Nutrition Value:

Calories: 5 Cal; Fat: 0 g; Carbs: 1 g; Protein: 0 g; Fiber: 0.3 g

Barbecue Sauce

Preparation time: 5 minutes; Cooking time: 0 minute; Servings: 16
Ingredients:

- 8 ounces tomato sauce
- 1 teaspoon garlic powder
- ¼ teaspoon ground black pepper
- 1/2 teaspoon. sea salt
- 2 Tablespoons Dijon mustard
- 3 packets stevia
- 1 teaspoon molasses
- 1 Tablespoon apple cider vinegar
- 2 Tablespoons tamari
- 1 teaspoon liquid aminos

Method:
1. Take a medium bowl, place all the ingredients in it, and stir until combined.
2. Serve straight away

Nutrition Value:
Calories: 29 Cal; Fat: 0.1 g; Carbs: 7 g; Protein: 0.1 g; Fiber: 0.1 g

Bolognese Sauce

Preparation time: 10 minutes; Cooking time: 45 minutes; Servings: 8
Ingredients:

- ½ of small green bell pepper, chopped
- 1 stalk of celery, chopped
- 1 small carrot, chopped
- 1 medium white onion, peeled, chopped
- 2 teaspoons minced garlic
- 1/2 teaspoon crushed red pepper flakes
- 3 tablespoons olive oil
- 8-ounce tempeh, crumbled
- 8 ounces white mushrooms, chopped
- 1/2 cup dried red lentils
- 28-ounce crushed tomatoes
- 28-ounce whole tomatoes, chopped
- 1 teaspoon dried oregano
- 1/2 teaspoon fennel seed
- 1/2 teaspoon ground black pepper
- 1/2 teaspoon salt
- 1 teaspoon dried basil
- 1/4 cup chopped parsley
- 1 bay leaf
- 6-ounce tomato paste
- 1 cup dry red wine

Method:
1. Take a Dutch oven, place it over medium heat, add oil, and when hot, add the first six ingredients, stir and cook for 5 minutes until sauté.
2. Then switch heat to medium-high level, add two ingredients after olive oil, stir and cook for 3 minutes.
3. Switch heat to medium-low level, stir in tomato paste, and continue cooking for 2 minutes.
4. Add remaining ingredients except for lentils, stir and bring the mixture to boil.
5. Switch heat to the low level, simmer sauce for 10 minutes, covering the pan partially, then add lentils and continue cooking for 20 minutes until tender.
6. Serve sauce with cooked pasta.

Nutrition Value:
Calories: 208.8 Cal; Fat: 12 g; Carbs: 17.8 g; Protein: 10.6 g; Fiber: 3.8 g

Alfredo Sauce

Preparation time: 5 minutes; Cooking time: 0 minute; Servings: 4
Ingredients:

- 1 cup cashews, unsalted, soaked in warm water for 15 minutes
- 1 teaspoon minced garlic
- 1/4 teaspoon ground black pepper
- 1/3 teaspoon salt
- 1/4 cup nutritional yeast
- 2 tablespoons tamari
- 2 tablespoons olive oil

- 4 tablespoons water

Method:
1. Drain the cashews, transfer them into a food processor, add remaining ingredients in it, and pulse for 3 minutes until thick sauce comes together.
2. Serve straight away.

Nutrition Value:
Calories: 105.7 Cal; Fat: 5.3 g; Carbs: 11 g; Protein: 4.7 g; Fiber: 2 g

Garden Pesto

Preparation time: 5 minutes; Cooking time: 0 minute; Servings: 10
Ingredients:
- 1/4 cup pistachios, shelled
- 3/4 cup parsley leaves
- 1 cup cilantro leaves
- ½ teaspoon minced garlic
- 1/4 cup mint leaves
- 1 cup basil leaves
- ¼ teaspoon ground black pepper
- 1/3 teaspoon salt
- 1/2 cup olive oil
- 1 1/2 teaspoons miso
- 2 teaspoons lemon juice

Method:
1. Place all the ingredients in the order in a food processor or blender and then pulse for 3 to 5 minutes at high speed until smooth.
2. Tip the pesto in a bowl and then serve.

Nutrition Value:
Calories: 111.5 Cal; Fat: 11.5 g; Carbs: 2.8 g; Protein: 1.2 g; Fiber: 1.4 g

Cilantro and Parsley Hot Sauce

Preparation time: 5 minutes; Cooking time: 0 minute; Servings: 4
Ingredients:
- 2 cups of parsley and cilantro leaves with stems
- 4 Thai bird chilies, destemmed, deseeded, torn
- 2 teaspoons minced garlic
- 1 teaspoon salt
- 1/4 teaspoon coriander seed, ground
- 1/4 teaspoon ground black pepper
- 1/2 teaspoon cumin seeds, ground
- 3 green cardamom pods, toasted, ground
- 1/2 cup olive oil

Method:
1. Take a spice blender or a food processor, place all the ingredients in it, and process for 5 minutes until the smooth paste comes together.
2. Serve straight away.

Nutrition Value:
Calories: 130 Cal; Fat: 14 g; Carbs: 2 g; Protein: 1 g; Fiber: 1 g

Chapter 10: Drinks

Spiced Buttermilk

Preparation time: 5 minutes; Cooking time: 0 minute; Servings: 2

Ingredients:

- 3/4 teaspoon ground cumin
- 1/4 teaspoon sea salt
- 1/8 teaspoon ground black pepper
- 2 mint leaves
- 1/8 teaspoon lemon juice
- ¼ cup cilantro leaves
- 1 cup of chilled water
- 1 cup vegan yogurt, unsweetened
- Ice as needed

Method:

1. Place all the ingredients in the order in a food processor or blender, except for cilantro and ¼ teaspoon cumin, and then pulse for 2 to 3 minutes at high speed until smooth.
2. Pour the milk into glasses, top with cilantro and cumin, and then serve.

Nutrition Value:

Calories: 92 Cal; Fat: 2 g; Carbs: 5 g; Protein: 11 g; Fiber: 0.5 g

Turmeric Lassi

Preparation time: 5 minutes; Cooking time: 0 minute; Servings: 2

Ingredients:

- 1 teaspoon grated ginger
- 1/8 teaspoon ground black pepper
- 1 teaspoon turmeric powder
- 1/8 teaspoon cayenne
- 1 tablespoon coconut sugar
- 1/8 teaspoon salt
- 1 cup vegan yogurt
- 1 cup almond milk

Method:

1. Place all the ingredients in the order in a food processor or blender and then pulse for 2 to 3 minutes at high speed until smooth.
2. Pour the lassi into two glasses and then serve.

Nutrition Value:

Calories: 128 Cal; Fat: 3 g; Carbs: 20 g; Protein: 3 g; Fiber: 1 g

Brownie Batter Orange Chia Shake

Preparation time: 5 minutes; Cooking time: 0 minute; Servings: 2

Ingredients:

- 2 tablespoons cocoa powder
- 3 tablespoons chia seeds
- ¼ teaspoon salt
- 4 tablespoons chocolate chips
- 4 teaspoons coconut sugar
- ½ teaspoon orange zest
- ½ teaspoon vanilla extract, unsweetened
- 2 cup almond milk

Method:

1. Place all the ingredients in the order in a food processor or blender and then pulse for 2 to 3 minutes at high speed until smooth.
2. Pour the smoothie into two glasses and then serve.

Nutrition Value:

Calories: 487 Cal; Fat: 31 g; Carbs: 57 g; Protein: 9 g; Fiber: 11 g

Saffron Pistachio Beverage

Preparation time: 5 minutes; Cooking time: 0 minute; Servings: 2

Ingredients:
- 8 strands of saffron
- 1 tablespoon cashews
- 1/4 teaspoon ground ginger
- 2 tablespoons pistachio
- 1/8 teaspoon cloves
- 1/4 teaspoon ground black pepper
- 1/4 teaspoon cardamom powder
- 3 tablespoons coconut sugar
- 1/4 teaspoon cinnamon
- 1/8 teaspoon fennel seeds
- 1/4 teaspoon poppy seeds

Method:
1. Place all the ingredients in the order in a food processor or blender and then pulse for 2 to 3 minutes at high speed until smooth.
2. Pour the smoothie into two glasses and then serve.

Nutrition Value:
Calories: 96 Cal; Fat: 3 g; Carbs: 15 g; Protein: 1 g; Fiber: 3 g

Mexican Hot Chocolate Mix

Preparation time: 5 minutes; Cooking time: 0 minute; Servings: 2
Ingredients:
For the Hot Chocolate Mix:
- 1/3 cup chopped dark chocolate
- 1/8 teaspoon cayenne
- 1/8 teaspoon salt
- 1/2 teaspoon cinnamon
- 1/4 cup coconut sugar
- 1 teaspoon cornstarch
- 3 tablespoons cocoa powder
- 1/2 teaspoon vanilla extract, unsweetened

For Serving:
- 2 cups milk, warmed

Method:
1. Place all the ingredients of hot chocolate mix in the order in a food processor or blender and then pulse for 2 to 3 minutes at high speed until ground.
2. Stir 2 tablespoons of the chocolate mix into a glass of milk until combined and then serve.

Nutrition Value:
Calories: 127 Cal; Fat: 5 g; Carbs: 20 g; Protein: 1 g; Fiber: 2 g

Pumpkin Spice Frappuccino

Preparation time: 5 minutes; Cooking time: 0 minute; Servings: 2
Ingredients:
- ½ teaspoon ground ginger
- 1/8 teaspoon allspice
- ½ teaspoon ground cinnamon
- 2 tablespoons coconut sugar
- 1/8 teaspoon nutmeg
- ¼ teaspoon ground cloves
- 1 teaspoon vanilla extract, unsweetened
- 2 teaspoons instant coffee
- 2 cups almond milk, unsweetened
- 1 cup of ice cubes

Method:
1. Place all the ingredients in the order in a food processor or blender and then pulse for 2 to 3 minutes at high speed until smooth.
2. Pour the Frappuccino into two glasses and then serve.

Nutrition Value:
Calories: 90 Cal; Fat: 6 g; Carbs: 5 g; Protein: 2 g; Fiber: 1 g

Cookie Dough Milkshake

Preparation time: 5 minutes; Cooking time: 0 minute; Servings: 2

Ingredients:

- 2 tablespoons cookie dough
- 5 dates, pitted
- 2 teaspoons chocolate chips
- 1/2 teaspoon vanilla extract, unsweetened
- 1/2 cup almond milk, unsweetened
- 1 ½ cup almond milk ice cubes

Method:

1. Place all the ingredients in the order in a food processor or blender and then pulse for 2 to 3 minutes at high speed until smooth.
2. Pour the milkshake into two glasses and then serve with some cookie dough balls.

Nutrition Value:

Calories: 208 Cal; Fat: 9 g; Carbs: 30 g; Protein: 2 g; Fiber: 2 g

Strawberry and Hemp Smoothie

Preparation time: 5 minutes; Cooking time: 0 minute; Servings: 2

Ingredients:

- 3 cups fresh strawberries
- 2 tablespoons hemp seeds
- 1/2 teaspoon vanilla extract, unsweetened
- 1/8 teaspoon sea salt
- 2 tablespoons maple syrup
- 1 cup vegan yogurt
- 1 cup almond milk, unsweetened
- 1 cup of ice cubes
- 2 tablespoons hemp protein

Method:

1. Place all the ingredients in the order in a food processor or blender, except for protein powder, and then pulse for 2 to 3 minutes at high speed until smooth.
2. Pour the smoothie into two glasses and then serve.

Nutrition Value:

Calories: 258 Cal; Fat: 17 g; Carbs: 12 g; Protein: 14 g; Fiber: 2 g

Blueberry, Hazelnut and Hemp Smoothie

Preparation time: 5 minutes; Cooking time: 0 minute; Servings: 2

Ingredients:

- 2 tablespoons hemp seeds
- 1 ½ cups frozen blueberries
- 2 tablespoons chocolate protein powder
- 1/2 teaspoon vanilla extract, unsweetened
- 2 tablespoons chocolate hazelnut butter
- 1 small frozen banana
- 3/4 cup almond milk

Method:

1. Place all the ingredients in the order in a food processor or blender and then pulse for 2 to 3 minutes at high speed until smooth.
2. Pour the smoothie into two glasses and then serve.

Nutrition Value:

Calories: 376 Cal; Fat: 25 g; Carbs: 26 g; Protein: 14 g; Fiber: 4 g

Mango Lassi

Preparation time: 5 minutes; Cooking time: 0 minute; Servings: 2

Ingredients:

- 1 ¼ cup mango pulp
- 1 tablespoon coconut sugar
- 1/8 teaspoon salt
- 1/2 teaspoon lemon juice
- 1/4 cup almond milk, unsweetened
- 1/4 cup chilled water
- 1 cup cashew yogurt

Method:
1. Place all the ingredients in the order in a food processor or blender and then pulse for 2 to 3 minutes at high speed until smooth.
2. Pour the lassi into two glasses and then serve.

Nutrition Value:
Calories: 218 Cal; Fat: 2 g; Carbs: 44 g; Protein: 3 g; Fiber: 1 g

Mocha Chocolate Shake

Preparation time: 5 minutes; Cooking time: 0 minute; Servings: 2
Ingredients:
- 1/4 cup hemp seeds
- 2 teaspoons cocoa powder, unsweetened
- 1/2 cup dates, pitted
- 1 tablespoon instant coffee powder
- 2 tablespoons flax seeds
- 2 1/2 cups almond milk, unsweetened
- 1/2 cup crushed ice

Method:
1. Place all the ingredients in the order in a food processor or blender and then pulse for 2 to 3 minutes at high speed until smooth.
2. Pour the smoothie into two glasses and then serve.

Nutrition Value:
Calories: 357 Cal; Fat: 21 g; Carbs: 31 g; Protein: 12 g; Fiber: 5 g

Chard, Lettuce and Ginger Smoothie

Preparation time: 5 minutes; Cooking time: 0 minute; Servings: 2
Ingredients:
- 10 Chard leaves, chopped
- 1-inch piece of ginger, chopped
- 10 lettuce leaves, chopped
- ½ teaspoon black salt
- 2 pear, chopped
- 2 teaspoons coconut sugar
- ¼ teaspoon ground black pepper
- ¼ teaspoon salt
- 2 tablespoons lemon juice
- 2 cups of water

Method:
1. Place all the ingredients in the order in a food processor or blender and then pulse for 2 to 3 minutes at high speed until smooth.
2. Pour the smoothie into two glasses and then serve.

Nutrition Value:
Calories: 514 Cal; Fat: 0 g; Carbs: 15 g; Protein: 4 g; Fiber: 4 g

Red Beet, Pear and Apple Smoothie

Preparation time: 5 minutes; Cooking time: 0 minute; Servings: 2
Ingredients:
- 1/2 of medium beet, peeled, chopped
- 1 tablespoon chopped cilantro
- 1 orange, juiced
- 1 medium pear, chopped
- 1 medium apple, cored, chopped
- 1/4 teaspoon ground black pepper
- 1/8 teaspoon rock salt
- 1 teaspoon coconut sugar
- 1/4 teaspoons salt
- 1 cup of water

Method:
1. Place all the ingredients in the order in a food processor or blender and then pulse for 2 to 3 minutes at high speed until smooth.
2. Pour the smoothie into two glasses and then serve.

Nutrition Value:
Calories: 132 Cal; Fat: 0 g; Carbs: 34 g; Protein: 1 g; Fiber: 5 g

Berry and Yogurt Smoothie

Preparation time: 5 minutes; Cooking time: 0 minute; Servings: 2

Ingredients:
- 2 small bananas
- 3 cups frozen mixed berries
- 1 ½ cup cashew yogurt
- 1/2 teaspoon vanilla extract, unsweetened
- 1/2 cup almond milk, unsweetened

Method:
1. Place all the ingredients in the order in a food processor or blender and then pulse for 2 to 3 minutes at high speed until smooth.
2. Pour the smoothie into two glasses and then serve.

Nutrition Value:
Calories: 326 Cal; Fat: 6.5 g; Carbs: 65.6 g; Protein: 8 g; Fiber: 8.4 g

Chocolate and Cherry Smoothie

Preparation time: 5 minutes; Cooking time: 0 minute; Servings: 2

Ingredients:
- 4 cups frozen cherries
- 2 tablespoons cocoa powder
- 1 scoop of protein powder
- 1 teaspoon maple syrup
- 2 cups almond milk, unsweetened

Method:
1. Place all the ingredients in the order in a food processor or blender and then pulse for 2 to 3 minutes at high speed until smooth.
2. Pour the smoothie into two glasses and then serve.

Nutrition Value:
Calories: 324 Cal; Fat: 5 g; Carbs: 75.1 g; Protein: 7.2 g; Fiber: 11.3 g

Strawberry and Chocolate Milkshake

Preparation time: 5 minutes; Cooking time: 0 minute; Servings: 2

Ingredients:
- 2 cups frozen strawberries
- 3 tablespoons cocoa powder
- 1 scoop protein powder
- 2 tablespoons maple syrup
- 1 teaspoon vanilla extract, unsweetened
- 2 cups almond milk, unsweetened

Method:
1. Place all the ingredients in the order in a food processor or blender and then pulse for 2 to 3 minutes at high speed until smooth.
2. Pour the smoothie into two glasses and then serve.

Nutrition Value:
Calories: 199 Cal; Fat: 4.1 g; Carbs: 40.5 g; Protein: 3.7 g; Fiber: 5.5 g

Banana and Protein Smoothie

Preparation time: 5 minutes; Cooking time: 0 minute; Servings: 2

Ingredients:
- 2/3 cup frozen pineapple chunk
- 10 frozen strawberries
- 2 frozen bananas
- 2 scoops protein powder
- 2 teaspoons cocoa powder
- 2 tablespoons maple syrup
- 2 teaspoons vanilla extract, unsweetened
- 2 cups almond milk, unsweetened

Method:

1. Place all the ingredients in the order in a food processor or blender and then pulse for 2 to 3 minutes at high speed until smooth.
2. Pour the smoothie into two glasses and then serve.

Nutrition Value:
Calories: 272 Cal; Fat: 3.8 g; Carbs: 59.4 g; Protein: 4.3 g; Fiber: 7.1 g

Mango, Pineapple and Banana Smoothie

Preparation time: 5 minutes; Cooking time: 0 minute; Servings: 2
Ingredients:
- 2 cups pineapple chunks
- 2 frozen bananas
- 2 medium mangoes, destoned, cut into chunks
- 1 cup almond milk, unsweetened
- Chia seeds as needed for garnishing

Method:
1. Place all the ingredients in the order in a food processor or blender and then pulse for 2 to 3 minutes at high speed until smooth.
2. Pour the smoothie into two glasses and then serve.

Nutrition Value:
Calories: 287 Cal; Fat: 1.2 g; Carbs: 73.3 g; Protein: 3.5 g; Fiber: 8 g

Blueberry and Banana Smoothie

Preparation time: 5 minutes; Cooking time: 0 minute; Servings: 2
Ingredients:
- 2 frozen bananas
- 2 cups frozen blueberries
- 2 cups almond milk, unsweetened
- 1/2 teaspoon or so cinnamon
- dash of vanilla extract

Method:
1. Place all the ingredients in the order in a food processor or blender and then pulse for 2 to 3 minutes at high speed until smooth.
2. Pour the smoothie into two glasses and then serve.

Nutrition Value:
Calories: 244 Cal; Fat: 3.8 g; Carbs: 51.5 g; Protein: 4 g; Fiber: 7.3 g

'Sweet Tang' and Chia Smoothie

Preparation time: 5 minutes; Cooking time: 0 minute; Servings: 2
Ingredients:
- 4 large plums
- 2 tablespoon chia seeds
- 1/2 cup pineapple chunks
- 1/2 cup ice cubes
- 3/4 cup coconut water

Method:
1. Place all the ingredients in the order in a food processor or blender and then pulse for 2 to 3 minutes at high speed until smooth.
2. Pour the smoothie into two glasses and then serve.

Nutrition Value:
Calories: 406 Cal; Fat: 9.3 g; Carbs: 77.4 g; Protein: 6.3 g; Fiber: 13 g

Strawberry, Mango and Banana Smoothie

Preparation time: 5 minutes; Cooking time: 0 minute; Servings: 2
Ingredients:
- 1 medium frozen banana
- 1 cup of frozen strawberries

- 2 tablespoons ground chia seeds
- 1 cup chopped mango
- 2 tablespoons cashew butter
- 1 cup coconut milk, unsweetened

Method:
1. Place all the ingredients in the order in a food processor or blender and then pulse for 2 to 3 minutes at high speed until smooth.
2. Pour the smoothie into two glasses and then serve.

Nutrition Value:
Calories: 299 Cal; Fat: 15 g; Carbs: 42 g; Protein: 5 g; Fiber: 8 g

Strawberry and Pineapple Smoothie

Preparation time: 5 minutes; Cooking time: 0 minute; Servings: 2

Ingredients:
- 2 cups frozen strawberries
- 2 tablespoons almond butter
- 2 cups chopped pineapple
- 1 ½ cup chilled almond milk, unsweetened

Method:
1. Place all the ingredients in the order in a food processor or blender and then pulse for 2 to 3 minutes at high speed until smooth.
2. Pour the smoothie into two glasses and then serve.

Nutrition Value:
Calories: 255 Cal; Fat: 11 g; Carbs: 39 g; Protein: 6 g; Fiber: 8 g

Strawberry, Blueberry and Banana Smoothie

Preparation time: 5 minutes; Cooking time: 0 minute; Servings: 2

Ingredients:
- 1 tablespoon hulled hemp seeds
- ½ cup of frozen strawberries
- 1 small frozen banana
- ½ cup frozen blueberries
- 2 tablespoons cashew butter
- ¾ cup cashew milk, unsweetened

Method:
1. Place all the ingredients in the order in a food processor or blender and then pulse for 2 to 3 minutes at high speed until smooth.
2. Pour the smoothie into two glasses and then serve.

Nutrition Value:
Calories: 334 Cal; Fat: 17 g; Carbs: 46 g; Protein: 7 g; Fiber: 7 g

Pineapple and Spinach Juice

Preparation time: 5 minutes; Cooking time: 0 minute; Servings: 2

Ingredients:
- 2 medium red apples, cored, peeled, chopped
- 3 cups spinach
- ½ of a medium pineapple, peeled
- 2 lemons, peeled

Method:
1. Process all the ingredients in the order in a juicer or blender and then strain it into two glasses.
2. Serve straight away.

Nutrition Value:
Calories: 131 Cal; Fat: 0.5 g; Carbs: 34.5 g; Protein: 1.7 g; Fiber: 5 g

Green Lemonade

Preparation time: 5 minutes; Cooking time: 0 minute; Servings: 2

Ingredients:
- 10 large stalks of celery, chopped
- 2 medium green apples, cored, peeled, chopped
- 2 medium cucumbers, peeled, chopped
- 2 inches piece of ginger
- 10 stalks of kale, chopped
- 2 cups parsley

Method:
1. Process all the ingredients in the order in a juicer or blender and then strain it into two glasses.
2. Serve straight away.

Nutrition Value:
Calories: 102.3 Cal; Fat: 1.1 g; Carbs: 26.2 g; Protein: 4.7 g; Fiber: 8.5 g

Sweet and Sour Juice

Preparation time: 5 minutes; Cooking time: 0 minute; Servings: 2
Ingredients:
- 2 medium apples, cored, peeled, chopped
- 2 large cucumbers, peeled
- 4 cups chopped grapefruit
- 1 cup mint

Method:
1. Process all the ingredients in the order in a juicer or blender and then strain it into two glasses.
2. Serve straight away.

Nutrition Value:
Calories: 90 Cal; Fat: 0 g; Carbs: 23 g; Protein: 0 g; Fiber: 9 g

Apple, Carrot, Celery and Kale Juice

Preparation time: 5 minutes; Cooking time: 0 minute; Servings: 2
Ingredients:
- 5 curly kale
- 2 green apples, cored, peeled, chopped
- 2 large stalks celery
- 4 large carrots, cored, peeled, chopped

Method:
1. Process all the ingredients in the order in a juicer or blender and then strain it into two glasses.
2. Serve straight away.

Nutrition Value:
Calories: 183 Cal; Fat: 2.5 g; Carbs: 46 g; Protein: 13 g; Fiber: 3 g

Banana Milk

Preparation time: 5 minutes; Cooking time: 0 minute; Servings: 2
Ingredients:
- 2 dates
- 2 medium bananas, peeled
- 1 teaspoon vanilla extract, unsweetened
- 1/2 cup ice
- 2 cups of water

Method:
1. Place all the ingredients in the order in a food processor or blender and then pulse for 2 to 3 minutes at high speed until smooth.
2. Pour the smoothie into two glasses and then serve.

Nutrition Value:

Calories: 79 Cal; Fat: 0 g; Carbs: 19.8 g; Protein: 0.8 g; Fiber: 6 g

Hazelnut and Chocolate Milk

Preparation time: 5 minutes; Cooking time: 0 minute; Servings: 2

Ingredients:

- 2 tablespoons cocoa powder
- 4 dates, pitted
- 1 cup hazelnuts
- 3 cups of water

Method:

1. Place all the ingredients in the order in a food processor or blender and then pulse for 2 to 3 minutes at high speed until smooth.
2. Pour the smoothie into two glasses and then serve.

Nutrition Value:

Calories: 120 Cal; Fat: 5 g; Carbs: 19 g; Protein: 2 g; Fiber: 1 g

Fruit Infused Water

Preparation time: 5 minutes; Cooking time: 0 minute; Servings: 2

Ingredients:

- 3 strawberries, sliced
- 5 mint leaves
- ½ of orange, sliced
- 2 cups of water

Method:

1. Divide fruits and mint between two glasses, pour in water, stir until just mixed, and then refrigerate for 2 hours.
2. Serve straight away.

Nutrition Value:

Calories: 5.4 Cal; Fat: 0.1 g; Carbs: 1.3 g; Protein: 0.1 g; Fiber: 0.4 g

Chapter 11: 21-Day Meal Plan

DAY	BREAKFAST	LUNCH	DINNER	DESSERT
1	Peanut Butter and Pumpkin Smoothie	Farro, Cannellini Bean, and Pesto Salad	Spiced Carrot and Lentil Soup	Blueberry Mousse
2	Scrambled Tofu Breakfast Tacos	Pasta with Kidney Bean Sauce	Pilaf with Garbanzos and Dried Apricots	Chocolate Avocado Ice Cream
3	Chocolate, Avocado, and Banana Smoothie	Chickpea Shakshuka	Pasta with Creamy Greens and Lemon	Mango Coconut Chia Pudding
4	Chickpea Flour Omelet	Szechuan Tofu and Veggies	Kung Pao Brussels Sprouts	Salted Caramel Chocolate Cups
5	Peanut Butter Vanilla Green Shake	Butternut Squash Linguine	Chickpea Noodle Soup	Mango Coconut Cheesecake
6	Chickpea and Zucchini Scramble	Vegetarian fajitas	Split Pea Pesto Stuffed Shells	Almond Butter, Oat and Protein Energy Balls
7	Chocolate Oat Smoothie	Burrito-Stuffed Sweet Potatoes	Wonton Soup	Coconut Oil Cookies
8	Enchilada Breakfast Casserole	Grilled Corn Salad Bowl	Thai Peanut and Sweet Potato Buddha Bowl	Mango Ice Cream
9	Wild Ginger Green Smoothie	Sweetcorn and Zucchini Fritters	Potato and Kale Soup	Chocolate Pudding
10	Vegan Breakfast Sandwich	Sweet Potato, Kale and Chickpea Soup	Vegetarian Biryani	Almond Butter Cookies
11	Spiced Strawberry Smoothie	Curried Apple and Sweet Potato Soup	Pomegranate and Walnut Stew	Coconut Cacao Bites
12	Vegan Fried Egg	Pesto with Squash Ribbons and Fettuccine	Ramen with Miso Shiitake	Blueberry Ice Cream
13	Double Chocolate Hazelnut Espresso Shake	Potato and Corn Chowder	Spinach and Cannellini Bean Stew	Chocolate Cookies
14	Spinach Artichoke Quiche	Thai Red Curry with Vegetables	Tofu with Bok Choy	Chocolate Banana Cream Cake
15	Strawberry, Banana and Coconut Shake	Cabbage Stew	Spicy Bean Stew	Key Lime Pie
16	Pumpkin Muffins	Thai Green Curry with Spring Vegetables	Lentil Meatballs with Coconut Curry Sauce	Lemon Cashew Tart
17	Ginger and Greens Smoothie	Eggplant, Onion and Tomato Stew	Brussel Sprouts Stew	Caramel Brownie Slice
18	Chickpeas On Toast	Grilled Asparagus and Shiitake Tacos	Tikka Masala with Cauliflower	Double Chocolate Orange Cheesecake

19	Chocolate Cherry Smoothie	Vegetarian Gumbo	Black Bean and Quinoa Stew	Matcha Coconut Cream Pie
20	Waffles with Fruits	BBQ Chickpea and Cauliflower Flatbreads	Portobello Mushroom Stew	Chocolate Raspberry Brownies
21	Mixed Berry Smoothie	Sweet Potato and Cauliflower Salad	Summer Pesto Pasta	Strawberry Mousse

Conclusion

There are a lot of benefits of a plant-based diet if people hold themselves accountable and do not lose motivation as the days pass by. The true objective should always be to live as a healthier person throughout the entire life.

At the end of this cookbook, here are quick tips for you that will help you get most out of the plant-based diet. Increase the use of whole foods in your diet. It is stable already at breakfast for most people but also utilize them whenever possible as they provide much-needed carbs and energy. Eating oatmeal for breakfast is a good start in following this diet.

Bon Appetite!

Manufactured by Amazon.ca
Bolton, ON